Young People
Inequality
and Youth Work

Young People, Inequality and Youth Work is the final book in a series of three dealing with youth issues. The first book, *Youth Work*, was published in conjunction with the British Association of Social Workers. The second book was *Welfare and Youth Work Practice*. All three books are edited by Tony Jeffs and Mark Smith.

Young People, Inequality and Youth Work

Edited by

Tony Jeffs and **Mark Smith**

MACMILLAN

Selection and editorial matter, Chapters 2 and 7 © Tony Jeffs
and Mark Smith 1990
Individual chapters © Don Blackburn, Annie Franklin and
Bob Franklin, Peter Kent-Baguley, Keith Popple,
Jean Spence 1990

First published 1990 by
THE MACMILLAN PRESS LTD
Houndmills, Basingstoke, Hampshire RG21 2XS
and London
Companies and representatives
throughout the world

ISBN 0–333–40979–5 hardcover
ISBN 0–333–40980–9 paperback

A catalogue record for this book is available
from the British Library.

12   11   10   9   8   7   6   5   4
03   02   01   00   99   98   97   96   95

Printed in Hong Kong

Contents

List of Tables

List of Figures

List of Abbreviations

ACE	Advisory Centre for Education
ALTARF	All London Teachers Against Racism and Fascism
CDP	Community Development Project
CP	Community Programme
CRC	Community Relations Commission
CRE	Commission for Racial Equality
CSO	Central Statistical Office
DES	Department of Education and Science
DHSS	Department of Health and Social Security
FPSC	Family Policy Studies Centre
GLC	Greater London Council
ILEA	Inner London Education Authority
JCGT	National Joint Council For Gay Teenagers
L & GYM	Lesbian and Gay Youth Movement
Mencap	National Society for Mentally Handicapped Children
MSC	Manpower Services Commission
NACYS	National Advisory Council for the Youth Service
NAME	National Anti-Racist Movement in Education
NAYC	National Association of Youth Clubs
NYB	National Youth Bureau
OPCS	Office of Population Censuses and Surveys
PHAB	Physically Handicapped and Able Bodied (Clubs)
PSI	Policy Studies Institute
RAT	Racism Awareness Training

TES	*Times Educational Supplement*
UCCA	Universities Central Council on Admissions
YMCA	Young Men's Christian Association
YOP	Youth Opportunities Programme
YTS	Youth Training Scheme
YSIC	Youth Service Information Centre
YWCA	Young Women's Christian Association

Introduction

TONY JEFFS and MARK SMITH

This is the last of three books that have taken as their themes youth work practice, organisation and the social and economic position of young people. In this book we try to avoid revisiting issues and topics dealt with in the other two, concentrating on the social and economic inequalities experienced by young people.

Many of the inequalities that are discussed in this book are reproduced with the help of youth workers and youth organisations. At the same time, with the growth of black political organisation, the re-emergence of the women's movement, the development of lesbian and gay groups, and enhancement of politics around disability, alternative forms of practice have entered the arena. They demonstrate that it is still possible to address questions of inequality and exploitation in day-to-day practice, and that it is still possible to be optimistic about elements of practice, even though successive governments have sought to constrain and marginalise such work. As we have argued elsewhere (Jeffs & Smith, 1988), the front-line nature of youth work organisation and contradictions in policy-makers' expectations of this area of welfare allow a degree of freedom to practitioners. Even within quite constrained situations, there remains the chance of enabling young people to see something of the forces that influence and restrict their lives. Crucially, there is usually some opportunity, however limited, to work with young people so that they may act upon their understandings. One of our central concerns in this and other books has been to throw some light on the reasons why such chances have not always been taken, and why certain sites of inequality and oppression, such as those relating to class, still lack sustained critical practice.

The way in which so-called 'progressive' youth work practice has evolved, along specific lines of division, has determined the structure of this book. But approaching the area in this way is fraught with dangers. By examining the discrete, we can easily overlook the interconnections and commonalities. Further, this separation can lead to the trivialising of fundamental ills into 'issues' and, as a consequence, piecemeal responses which add to the process of marginalisation. This is a danger of much so-called 'issue-based' work (see Smith, 1988, pp. 79–81; Jeffs & Smith, 1989b). Partly for this reason we have brought class division and experience into the centre of the debate, although it has not been represented in a distinctive or major way in practice. This is not to deny in any way that people by virtue of their gender, race, sexuality, age or disabilities suffer major deprivations and discrimination. Capitalism emerged into a situation already stratified, not just by class, but also by these other social divisions. Class relations are shot through with other modes of social differentiation. 'In reproducing capitalism, the state is obliged to reproduce those relationships also' (Coates, 1984, p. 156). Further, the situation is far from static. The very means that are used as the basis of differentiation are also a foundation for powerful collective identities acquired 'by means of their roots in tradition' (Gilroy, 1987, p. 247). Not only are race, gender and other divisions articulated within class, but class relations are also articulated within, say, race. Hence we do not want to enter sterile arguments about what form of division is more important or fundamental. Rather we wish to place the cards on the table in such a way as to open up practice which addresses the causes, rather than the symptoms, of injustice and inequality.

In a similar vein, the function of the book is not to attempt to rework debates regarding the nature of equality and inequality. This is done elsewhere (see, for example, Green, 1981; Giddens & Held, 1982; Turner 1986; Hindness, 1987). Rather, our aim has been to concentrate on an examination

of the differences in life chances and experiences encountered by young people in Great Britain. This is largely
undertaken in relation to youth work.

At this stage we would like to take the opportunity to
thank the contributors. Equally our gratitude needs to be
recorded in respect of a number of individuals whose names
are absent from the contents page. As always, any enterprise
such as this, which consumes so much time and energy,
results in the acquisition of debts. Most importantly, we
would like to thank friends and families. The order changes
but the names remain predominantly the same. To begin,
because they complained so much about not coming first in
the last dedication, thanks go to Andrew and Alistair Jeffs,
in the case of the latter notably for the loan of his library
ticket on a number of occasions. To Chris Gibbs who
changed her name but not her cheerful tolerance and
willingness to offer encouragement. To Christopher Rogers
and Alex Rogers for happily operating around us and
generously sacrificing both space and time. To Marion Leigh
for her comments on the manuscript. Finally to Jackie
Apperley who has scant patience with dedications and the
like but who, nevertheless, deserves a great deal of thanks.
Despite a heavy work-load she found time to act as an
unpaid researcher. We will break with an often followed
precedent in these matters and avoid gushing thanks to those
who might further our careers or lend us money. Instead we
will dedicate the book to Sidney G. Hedges, a writer from a
different tradition and era, but one who certainly delivered
the goods. As avid collectors of his work we would appreciate hearing from others who share this interest or who wish
to dispose of duplicates.

TONY JEFFS
MARK SMITH

1

Age and Power

ANNIE FRANKLIN and BOB FRANKLIN

Ageism involves a cruel irony. White racists never become black and male chauvinists do not become women, but those who hold ageist views must necessarily grow old and, by so doing, fall victim of their own prejudices (Comfort, 1976, p. 4). Ageism, unlike racism and sexism is universal in its discriminations. Young people are also victims of ageism but their experience of the injustices of childhood and adolescence do not necessarily mitigate against later adult prejudicial attitudes towards young people.

In this chapter we attempt some preliminary theorising of a concept of ageism which explores the cultural, political and socio-economic bases of discrimination against people on the basis of age, in much the same way that racism and sexism express power relationships determined by race and gender. Both ends of the age spectrum are examined in order to establish similarities, as well as to enable comparison, in the treatment of young and old people. This is an ambitious brief given limited space and the end-product may well resemble a proposal for further work rather than a completed enterprise.

The term 'ageism' frequently appears in discussions of the direction and experience of youth work practice. However, as with the other forms of social division discussed in this book, there has been little rigour in usage. 'Ageism' was first used in 1969 (Butler, p. 243) and signals a 'pejorative image of someone' (Hendricks and Hendricks, 1977, p. 14). It involves 'discrimination against people on the basis of . . . age' and 'deprives people of power and influence' (Kuhn,

1978, p. 7). The victims of this system of prejudice and power are 'the young as well as the old' (ibid., p. 7) and, like racism and sexism, the myths it seeks to promote are based upon 'fear and folklore' (Comfort, 1977, p. 35). This brief definition requires two points of clarification.

First, it is important to acknowledge that ageing involves two processes which have been described as physiological and sociogenic (Comfort, 1976, p. 11); the former is only incidentally relevant, the latter crucial to a discussion of ageism. Physiological ageing is a biological process which manifests itself in physical growth, deterioration and decline. Human beings can only marginally affect this process as developments in medical science merely offer means to slow its pace. Sociogenic ageing consists of the 'role which our folklore, prejudices and misconceptions about age impose upon "the old"' (Comfort, 1976, p. 11), but since such ageing, in Townsend's phrase, is 'socially manufactured' (1981, p. 5), it is capable of being radically modified by human intervention. Historians (Ariès, 1962, p. 329; Laslett, 1965, p. 105; Plumb, 1972, p. 105) have offered similar arguments suggesting that childhood is not simply an age state but a social construct informed by contemporary, but shifting, attitudes and conceptions. While the physiological process of ageing is undeniable and may contain implications for the position of both young and old in society, it is clearly sociogenic ageing, the various ways in which society structures particular stages of the life cycle, which in this context is of central interest.

Second, ageism exacerbates other forms of powerlessness deriving from class, gender and race; three lengthy but important digressions are necessary here. In terms of their social class the elderly are heterogeneous. The majority are working-class and relatively poor although, paradoxically, some of the most wealthy and powerful in society are old. The very phrase 'Old Age Pensioner' with its implications of low income and status indicates a condition of powerlessness rather than an age state and is almost synonymous with the working-class elderly. 'Would anyone for instance dare to apply the designation "O.A.P." to a retired judge living on a pension?'; the phrase has 'wholly working-class connotations' (Elder, 1977, pp. 18–19). By comparison, the middle-class elderly continue to enjoy higher incomes, better pensions, more savings, superior housing and better health and life expectancy than their working-class peers (Taylor and Ford, 1983, p. 184). However the status of members of all social classes is diminished by age itself. Retirement deprives middle-class professionals of occupational status, their incomes are substantially reduced and they become the butt of jokes expressing negative stereotypes about the elderly; like their working-class age peers, if to a lesser degree, they are 'old fogies'.

Young people similarly reflect the inequalities doled out by the class system, with the children of the poor more likely to occupy poor housing and less likely to receive higher education. However, without regard to social class, the young are more likely to be unemployed and, if in work, to earn low wages, simply because of their youth (CSO, 1986, p. 132; see also Chapter 7). Young people will also be subject to prejudicial and discriminatory judgements which typically view them as threatening, delinquent, irresponsible and troublesome.

Ageism reinforces sexism in at least two ways. First, women substantially outnumber men amongst the elderly. Eighty per cent of the 3·2 million people aged seventy and above are women and, therefore, 'statistically the majority of those who suffer from loneliness, poverty and ill health in old age are women' (Lockwood, 1978, p. 6). Second, the ageing process is unequal in its treatment of the sexes. Society tends to value men for their intellectual abilities, their experience, but especially for occupational and career achievements which tend to develop with age. Even their physical appearance can be considered enhanced by age, with greying hair and wrinkles perceived as conveying 'maturity'. Women however are valued more for their physical beauty (often measured directly by youth), their sexuality and their capacity to reproduce, which are each undermined by age. One stereotype of women defines them as carers, nurturers, wives and mothers and when old women are unable to contribute to society through any of these assigned roles they are deemed obsolete (Harrison,

1983, p. 217). Ageing may flatter men but nearly always threatens women. Advertisements, especially those for cosmetics, play on women's desire for youth by offering them wish-fulfilment fantasies in which they are mistaken for their daughters; it is doubtful whether fathers would be happy to be mistaken for their sons (Nilsen, 1978, p. 177). However the status of 'girl' is not a desirable one. Young women suffer prejudice in education, training and employment opportunities, but these gender discriminations are reinforced by age. Girls under eighteen receive the lowest wages of any social group and, because of their youth, girls are denied the possibility of achieving their traditionally allocated roles of housewife and mother with the attendant, if limited, status and rights they bestow.

Afro-Caribbean and Asian people must confront racism in important spheres of education and employment and therefore income and occupational status, but again these problems vary with age. Elderly black people suffer at least a passive rascism within Health and Social Service institutions, are more likely to depend on supplementary benefit for their primary source of income and those who came to Britain as dependents may be considered ineligible for benefits and become totally reliant on relatives (Coombe, 1978, p. 10; Fennell *et al.*, 1988, p. 123). These problems are compounded by ignorance of benefit entitlement, coupled with poorer housing than their white peers. For young black people, unemployment is the highest for any social category, and there are increased reports of racism within Youth Training Schemes. Moreover it is young black people who form a disproportionately high percentage of police stop-and-search targets, are more likely to be treated severely by the juvenile justice system and are more readily perceived as hostile by the police when arrested (Popple and Popple, 1986, pp. 195–200).

In these various ways age, as a structure of powerlessness, reinforces the inequalities consequent upon class, gender and race. Ageism is, of course, different in its implications for the young and old, but in some instances it is remarkably similar. Undoubtedly the most telling expression of the powerlessness of both groups is their subjection to physical abuse. 'Granny battering', as social work professionals have dubbed the practice, appears to be increasingly commonplace but estimates are unreliable and may well be exaggerated by media sensationalism. Current research is limited and the causes of such abuse are uncertain (Cornell and Gelles, 1982, p. 457). Nevertheless quiescence by the victim in such violence expresses their perceived as well as actual subordination. One explanation of the relationship between age and power interprets the latter as a consequence of an individual's access to resources and, in turn, sees such access varying with age.

Age, power and resources

Power is a complex concept whose meaning is uncertain. It is what philosophers delight in describing as an essentially contested concept. Since a precise definition is not critical for present purposes, Bertrand Russell's claim that, 'power is the production of intended effects' (Russell, 1983, p. 35) will serve as a starting-point.

Two observations are necessary at the outset. First, power is not an attribute of individuals but an expression of a relationship between them. Everyone possesses some power, but it is power relative to others which is important and Russell acknowledges that A is more powerful than B where 'A achieves many intended effects and B only a few' (ibid.). More important is the observation that A is more powerful than B if A achieves objectives at the expense of B or if B is obliged to alter objectives in order that A's objectives can be achieved.

Second, discussions of power can evoke inappropriate and misleading imagery. Power is not always, although it can be, expressed in dramatic confrontations or battles between powerful individuals, classes, races or nations. It is more commonplace for power relations to become routinised within the life of a society so that overt opposition between dominant and subordinate groups is rare. The most effective exercise of power is a quiet affair in which individuals and groups may be ignorant of their subordination.

Analyses of power, like many other aspects of social theorising, have been influenced by Marx's suggestion that social classes are decisive to an understanding of the distribution of power within society and polity. Writing in the mid-nineteenth century, Marx identified three social classes distinguished by their ownership and control of a particular factor of production and the differing forms of income which these productive resources generated. The aristocracy owned land which earned income in the form of rents, the capitalists or bourgeoisie possessed capital which generated profits and the working-class or proletariat was propertyless, owning merely its labour power which it was obliged to sell in return for wages. The landowners would become increasingly insignificant as society polarised into two hostile classes; owners and non-owners of the means of production.

Marx's basic assumption, derived from the economist Ricardo, was that labour was the ultimate and unique source of value. He reasoned that the working class was exploited by the bourgeoisie who paid the former only subsistence wages, which were considerably less than the full values of the goods the workers produced. The bourgeoisie retained for themselves (in Marx's word 'expropriated') the additional value (surplus value) in the form of profits. For Marx, this 'contradiction' at the very heart of the capitalist system of production held the key to understanding power relations between the two classes:

> The specific economic form in which unpaid surplus labour is pumped out of direct producers, determines the relationship of rulers and ruled . . . It is always the direct relationship of the owners of the conditions of production to the direct producers . . . which reveals the innermost secret, the hidden basis of the entire social structure and with it the political form . . . the corresponding specific form of the state. (Marx, 1974, p. 791)

On this account the economically dominant class was necessarily politically powerful and the capitalist state became simply 'a committee for managing the common affairs of the whole bourgeoisie' (Marx and Engels, 1969, p. 82). The different agencies of the state, controlled by the capitalists, deploy a combination of physical repression and ideological manipulation to create a stable political climate in which their economic interests can flourish.

Marx's analysis has been criticised on a number of grounds. The division of society into owners and non-owners of capital seems to ignore important and relevant distinctions between different occupational groups in the latter category, with regard to levels of income and wealth, patterns of expenditure and attitudes, as well as the division between manual and non-manual work and the related problem of the 'boundary question' (Meiksins, 1986, p. 102). Most important, for present purposes, is the suggestion that Marx's analysis is reductionist, seeking to understand all social conflict and inequality through the category of social class. However, the argument runs, other forms of inequality deriving from race, gender or age are not class-based and require a different theoretical analysis. Parkin's remarks typify such criticism:

> Now that racial, ethnic and religious conflicts have moved towards the centre of the political stage in many industrial societies, any general model of class or stratification that does not fully incorporate this fact, must forfeit all credibility. (Parkin, 1979, p. 9)

Parkin's argument is reminiscent of Weber's distinction between social classes and status groups; the former being distinguished by their economic position, the latter by the differing degrees of prestige or 'social honour' which society invests in their members. In brief every power relationship is not reducible to an economic root. Gender, race and age are status attributes leading to the social subordination of these groups quite independently of class such that they might 'cut across' class relations, creating a complex pattern of relationships of power and subordination. The difficulty with the Weberian position is that, in a society where wealth and its acquisition is a major component of social prestige, the divorce between class and status is not clear. However it does point to a problem for Marx. If it is conceded that class determines the broad parameters or range within which individuals or groups gain access to power, it does not explain why an individual's capacity to exercise power varies across that range as a consequence of changes in age without any preceding causal shift in social position.

Some clues to a different theoretical framework can be found in Rowntree's classic study of poverty and his observation that poverty was a function of the relationship between the labour market and different stages of the life cycle characterised by events such as marriage, childbirth and retirement. He concluded that the 'life of the labourer is marked by five alternative periods of want and comparative plenty . . .' During childhood he will probably be in poverty, and is likely to 'sink back into poverty when . . . he is too old to work' (Rowntree, 1901, p. 136). Rowntree graphically describes the direct correlation between age and access to resources (see Figure 1.1). A similar pattern of poverty continues to characterise youth and old age today.

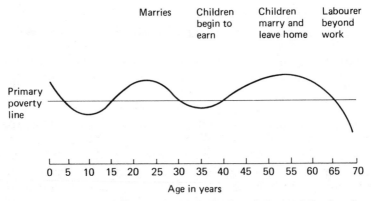

Source: Rowntree B.S., *Poverty: A Study of Town Life*, London: Macmillan, 1901, p. 136.

Figure 1.1 *Poverty and the life cycle*

Subsequent social theorists have attempted to develop Rowntree's insight by relating age to resources and power, but their approach has often been flawed by a commitment to individualism. Hesse-Biber and Williamson (1984) use resource theory to investigate power relations within the family. Their primary assumption is that 'the balance of power in decision making is on the side of the individual who can offer the greatest resources' (p. 262). The definition of resources is more wide-ranging than Rowntree's and includes income, education and occupation, as well as physical attractiveness and strength. The authors' rather banal conclusion is that the most well-resourced family member, who is best able to meet the needs and aspirations of others in the family, is the most powerful. The article does however contain points of interest. Most important is the suggestion that different stages of the life cycle are associated with different resources. 'There tends to be a curvilinear relationship', the authors claim, 'between power resources and age; the possession of resources is limited during the younger years; increases during the middle years and declines with advancing years. This relationship remains even for individuals at the upper socio-economic levels except in cases of extreme wealth' (ibid., p. 263). This analysis is ultimately unsatisfactory because of its individualism. It smacks of a crudely restated utilitarianism which understands even intimate familial relationships as a consequence of a calculating self-interest.

Leftwich (1983) offers the most theoretically rigorous attempt to relate power to resources and age. He accepts a broad definition of the term 'resources' but understands them as the property or assets of groups, as well as individuals, and his analysis is consequently more holistic. He makes two basic assumptions. First, he believes that the political life of a society is intimately related to its economic, social, cultural and moral affairs and cannot be analysed in isolation from them; society must be understood as a totality or 'whole'. 'The central point to emphasise', he claims, 'is that the politics of society . . . is . . . inextricably involved with how resources are used, produced, organised, distributed and redistributed, and by whom and with what consequences' (p. 12). Resources here include capital, land, labour, education, knowledge, health, physical strength and physical attractiveness.

Second, all societies, despite their apparent diversity, possess five fundamental structural features: a system of production which uses and produces resources through the labour process; a system of distribution which allocates the rewards and products of labour; a system of power and decision making which determines how decisions are made and by whom; a system of social organisation which prescribes the structure of families and organises communities into clans or lineages or age sets; a system of culture and ideology (or perhaps a plurality of such systems) which includes the society's customs involving a range of religious beliefs, ethical values and superstitions (ibid., pp. 14–16).

These five features of society interact, overlap and are mutually reinforcing. The productive activities of a community will in part form but also express the character of its political life and, in turn, the culture and ideology of that society. It follows that a society characterised by inequalities of ownership and control of the major productive resources would exhibit other inequalities, perhaps in its political and social structures. These may entail unequal participation in decision making or perhaps the emergence of status groups or social classes based upon wealth, gender or age. The culture and ideology of such a society would also reflect and justify or oppose these material inequalities rooted in production. The justifications might range in sophistication and type from elaborate political theorising such as Rousseau's *Discourse* (1963), 'On The Origins of Inequality', to 'commonsense' views or beliefs which hold that 'inequality is inevitable' or that it is 'part of human nature'. It might also be expected that, in such a society, competition, individualism and hierarchy would not only flourish but be highly valued. By contrast a society characterised by greater equality in the system of production, for example the hunting and gathering community of the Mbuti so sensitively portrayed in Turnbull's (1976) classic study, might be expected to exhibit an equivalent egalitarianism in its political and cultural structures. There is equal participation in political life and an absence of any social division or rank and a cultural system which stresses the values of co-operation and communitarianism.

This theoretical framework has a major implication for the analysis of ageism. It requires that the relative powerlessness of younger and older people must be explored not only through the political, but also the related economic and cultural dimensions. To understand ageism it is necessary to examine the negative stereotypes and images of young and old people which are current in society and try to establish how those images reflect the participation (or more accurately the exclusion) of these age groups, in the political and productive spheres. In doing this we might also want to consider how such images and stereotypes affect participation in other spheres such as education and leisure. Youth workers can all too easily make use of, and reinforce, negative views of young people. Ideas in this scheme are not passive, but active, forces which in turn help to create and condition the possibilities for participation by both groups in the political and productive life of the community.

Ageism: cultural dimensions

Prejudice against young and old people is evident in everyday language and colloquial expression, in the portrayal of both groups in the media and in the stereotypes, myths and fallacies about young and old people current in society. This section explores some of the cultural or ideological aspects of ageism by examining the images of younger and older people which are presented in different media of mass communication. The subsequent two sections look at the access of young and old people to economic and political resources and attempt to interpret or decode the cultural images of these two age groups by reference to their evident powerlessness.

As with racist and sexist perceptions of black people and women, the prevalent ageist images of younger and older people are less than flattering. Both age groups are perceived as dependent, vulnerable and in need of protection; the dominant attitude towards both tends in the direction of paternalism. In the case of younger people the paternalism is justified on the twin grounds (both presumed rather than proved) of their lack of experience and their inability to make considered and informed decisions which inevitably, it is claimed, lead them into error; in brief, the young are

considered largely 'pre-rational'. Paternalism at the other
extreme of the age spectrum is justified because older people
are less rational and able to make decisions than they were
previously. Stereotypes of the elderly routinely insist that
older age is accompanied by a decline in intellectual capacity, loss of memory and a tendency towards senility despite
evidence to the contrary (Comfort, 1977, pp. 90–93). Given
this similarity of attitude towards the young and the old, it is
not surprising that old age is often characterised in everyday
language as a return to a 'second childhood'; in Philip
Larkin's more literate, but no less bigoted formulation, old
age is a 'hideous inverted childhood' (Larkin, 1974, p. 20).
'That's how you know you are old', confided one old man, it
isn't how you feel, 'it's the way other people avoid you,
ignore you, or talk to you as if you didn't know a pig's arse
was pork' (Seabrook, 1980, p. 27).

Stereotypes of young and old people have other points of
contact. Both groups are considered to enjoy something of a
privileged existence, unconstrained by the strictures of a
working routine and spared the economic worries of 'adult'
life, which for the young are to come, and for the elderly are
behind them; the emphasis is again upon protection and
paternalism. Old people 'potter' and busy themselves with
their hobbies. Retirement is a time for relaxation after a
working life; a chance to 'live out your days in peace'. In
reality, leisure activities cost money which neither the
majority of the young nor of the old can afford, which is why
'the telly and forty winks are the mainstay of leisure in
British old age' (Midwinter, 1983, p. 11). Childhood is
similarly considered a period of learning, personal development and unlimited freedom. However the hallmark of
freedom is the capacity for autonomy in decision making,
which both young and old people are denied. There is a
difference between free time for leisure activities and enforced demeaning idleness which creates dependency. Retirement and childhood impose the latter by excluding old
and young people from the labour market. 'The young',
according to Blythe, 'are thought not to have politically,
sexually and economically arrived, the old are assumed to be
politically, sexually and economically finished' (Blythe,

1979, p. 93). These negative images of young and old people are reinforced by the mass media which display a substantial ageist bias. Such bias is functional and 'negative media stereotyping of socially disadvantaged groups . . . facilitates control over them by rationalising their subordination, economic exploitation and devalued status in the larger society' (Powell and Williamson, 1985, p. 38).

Three points are especially noteworthy concerning media presentations of older people. First, television misrepresents the percentage of older people in the population. In an American study of 'prime time' television drama which monitored 1365 programmes over a ten-year period, only 2·3 per cent of characters cast were aged over 65 compared to 11 per cent in the actual population (Gerbner *et al.*, 1980, p. 38). Media exclusion of the elderly is more apparent when advertisements are examined. A survey of advertisements appearing in seven magazines during a twelve-month period revealed that, of the 17 830 people appearing in them, only 3·1 per cent were elderly (Gantz *et al.*, 1980, pp. 55–60).

Second, when the existence of older people is conceded by television, they tend to be associated with 'evil, failure and unhappiness' (Aronoff, 1974, p. 87). Older men are likely to play 'bad guys' (drunks or petty criminals or the homeless who are frequently portrayed as 'dirty tramps') while women tend to be cast in the role of victim (Gerbner *et al.*, 1977, p. 177). It should not cause surprise that working-class, black, old women suffer the worst television image, with one study concluding that they 'are only cast to be killed. They rarely have any other role' (ibid.). This presentation of old women as victims is important in its social consequences, nurturing fears about mugging and leaving the house at night.

Third, old people are more likely to be portrayed as figures of fun or characters to be treated with disrespect (Gerbner *et al.*, 1980, p. 45). A study asked magazine readers to select three words from a list of twelve which best described how persons over 65 were depicted on television; the most popular were 'ridiculous, decrepit and childish' (Hemmings and Ellis, 1976, p. 24). In a society whose members seem increasingly obsessed with retaining the physical features of youth, older people are presented as decrepit victims to be patronised or pitied. Occasionally there can be youthful exceptions, to be admired: 'well you don't look your age'.

The research quoted above is American in origin (to our knowledge no equivalent British research exists) but even brief reflection on images of older people on British television confirms the findings. Three examples will serve to illustrate the point. In 'Steptoe and Son', Albert is the archetypal dirty old man who leers at Harold's girlfriends. He is a selfish and clinging parent, conservative and inflexible in his attitudes and, at times, overtly racist. Dependent and parasitic upon Harold, he occasionally steals from him. 'EastEnders' explores the range of stereotypes of old women; interestingly there are no old men in the series. Dot is a hypocrite whose obsession with religion and love of quoting from the Bible does little to curtail her vicious gossiping. Lou was the classic matriarch, who brooks no opposition and dominates the Fowler extended family. Ethel, by comparison, is a tragic, timid, old woman with failing health; helpless and alone, her only companion is an old dog. 'Last of the Summer Wine' offers more stereotypes. It is a classic portrayal of three retired men blissfully (childishly?) happy, unconcerned by financial worries, spending their 'twilight' years in the pursuit of foolish, cranky and idiotic activities. Compo is another 'dirty old man' cast in no more sophisticated mould than those portrayed by Benny Hill or Les Dawson, who constantly pursues the domineering and apparently physically undesirable Nora Batty (see Midwinter, 1983, p. 19).

The stereotyped images of young people in the media similarly tend to 'legitimise existing patterns of domination within the socio-political order' (Powell and Williamson, 1985, p. 38). The young, like the old, are substantially under-represented on television compared to their numbers in the population. The under-18 age group constitutes 30 per cent of the American population but only 8 per cent of its fictional population (Gerbner *et al.*, 1980, p. 35). On British television there is no programme intended for an adult audience which features children as central characters; children can be prominent only in programmes aimed at young

people. The majority of characters presented on television
are between 25 and 50 years of age, which closely reflects the
distribution of age groups with disposable consumer income.
The message is clear: young and old people have few
resources and a limited role as consumers; their existence is,
quite literally, hardly worth acknowledging.

Images of young people in newspapers typically reflect
two antithetical types. First, there are 'the model adolescents who have knuckled down and achieved something
worthwhile – the prize winners, award winners and channel
swimmers', and second, but less acceptable, 'the anti-social
hooligan elements – the delinquent hooligans and sexually
precocious' (Murdock, 1976, p. 16). Murdock's study of
newspaper stories in local papers suggests that headlines like
'Boy 16 Swims The Channel' typifies the former stereotype
while 'Youth Threatened With Knife While Gang Go On
Rampage' characterises the less desirable second image.
Both stereotypes, according to Murdock, are typical of the
routeing news coverage of young people which tends to
explain the differences between the two groups in terms of
individual ability and motivation, ignoring complex relationships between '"success" and "failure" and the advantages and disadvantages inherent in the British class structure' (ibid., p. 16).

The use of language in newspaper reports about young
people is significant but not neutral. Reports of exceptional
achievers nearly always use the expression 'young people'
whereas coverage of 'bad' behaviour invariably uses the
pejorative 'youth'. It is always 'youths' and never 'young
people' who 'go on the rampage' while 'young people' are
more likely to 'organise sponsored runs for charity'. The
appearance of one or the other of these designations in a
headline therefore signals much of the general flavour of the
subsequent report (Smith, D., 1984, p. 41).

A different image of young people, particularly young
women, presents them as sexually desirable and, as noted in
the earlier discussion of women and ageism, attempts to
make 'youth' synonymous with 'beauty'. In television drama, but especially advertisements, there are barely con-
cealed messages about childhood sexuality. One advertise-

ment offers the visual image of a group of 'cute' young girls, aged between seven and ten years, holding a piece of fruit, and carries the message, 'small ones are more juicy'. Little wonder that Ives claims 'children are frequently displayed as sex objects in art, literature and advertising', but complains that, 'their own self-directed sexuality is denied and punished by adults' (Ives, 1986, p. 143). This contradiction is played out in much youth work. The posters that appear on club walls, and the representations in videos and in records give one message, the workers' policing interventions another.

The overwhelming majority of reports concerning young people are negative. Young people, like the mods and rockers in Stan Cohen's classic study (1972), are easily converted by the media into 'folk devils', scapegoats for the wider society's concern or 'moral panic' that its traditions, values and institutions are under attack. Young people are too frequently perceived and presented as a threat (Murdock, 1984, p. 81). Occasionally, of course, young people may present a genuine threat to social order. The rapid growth of youth organisations between 1880 and 1914 can be interpreted as an attempt to organise the leisure and recreation activities of working-class adolescents to divert their attention from the revolutionary politics of the day; a 'way of patching up social divisions' (Murdock, 1976, p. 19). However the political postures of young people in the 1980s are different and many resent the stigmatising imagery which presents all young people as if they were a social problem (Coffield *et al.*, 1986, p. 210). Academic research is not without blame here and can, by concentrating on unusual and esoteric behaviour, '. . . underwrite popular notions about the uniqueness and . . . abnormality of youth' (Parker, 1974, p. 27).

Black young people get a particularly bad press. They are seldom reported as the disproportionate sufferers of unemployment and disadvantage, bearing the brunt of the recession (not to mention racism) but usually as 'muggers', 'drug abusers' and, in Troyna's phrase, 'the outsiders within; a problem to, and essentially different from, the mainstream of the society' (Troyna, 1981, p. 80). The classic portrayal of black youth is that of 'rioter'. Black young people by virtue of age and race are presented as doubly alien and therefore especially threatening to the mainstream values of society. The existence of black young people, 'adds a significant extra dimension to the established imagery of street crime and crowd disorders' (Murdock, 1984, p. 81).

These negative images of young and old people which are presented by the media have two important effects. First, they influence attitudes towards young and old people and therefore the ways in which they are treated by the general public as well as social and welfare professionals. Second, and more significantly, these images influence young and old people's self-perceptions. Stereotyping can lead to a self-fulfilling prophecy in which the experience of youth and old age is increasingly shaped and influenced by the ways in which young and old people see themselves. Ageist attitudes portray old people and 'expect them to be impotent, asexual, senile, confused, forgetful, frail, useless, unproductive, helpless, childlike, unattractive, smelly, unhappy, inactive, unemployable, uncreative, unable, perverted, unathletic, stooped and slow . . . In a society with such attitudes it is . . . nearly impossible to completely circumvent compliance with the expectation' (Jensen and Oakley, 1982, p. 20). This negative social estimation constantly undermines the self-images of both groups, enhancing feelings of powerlessness and dependency. Moreover, if television is influential in nurturing and sustaining these myths, it is important to note that young and old people are the two largest audiences for its output (Rubin, 1982, p. 540) and therefore highly vulnerable to its messages. Such stereotyping and its impact upon self-perception would appear to be an important site for youth work intervention.

Ageism: political dimensions

The negative images of young and old people prevalent in the media express and reinforce the powerlessness of these groups and, in turn, reflect the control of resources by the middle-aged. The result is political alienation for the young and old who are, 'effectively deprived of actual power in society' (Agnello, 1973, p. 256). For Maggie Kuhn, founder of the Gray Panthers, this powerlessness implies a coalition of both age groups in order to redress this political imbalance. 'Young people' she claims, 'are abused, no one takes them seriously and I believe it is we the grannies and the old folks who have to be the advocates of the young . . . the old and the young need to get together' (Kuhn, 1978, p. 8).

Young people's lack of power can be discussed very briefly since it is so complete. People under eighteen effectively possess no political rights as a consequence of both legal and attitudinal factors. Laws prohibit young people from voting, joining a political party and, at least until they are twenty-one, from being a candidate in a local or national election. For adults each of these activities is fundamental to a democratic way of life and the denial of any would constitute a breach of basic human rights. It is adult attitudes towards young people's competences, as well as the legal barriers, which exclude the latter from political life. Here the exclusion results from the adult judgement that young people lack experience and knowledge of political affairs and the rationality born of maturity necessary to exercise meaningful political choice. This judgement not only endorses the legal exclusion of young people from formal political institutions and procedures such as political parties and elections, but ridicules and systematically devalues and discourages their involvement in pressure group politics, demonstrations or political discussion. Young people's political opinions and political activities based upon them are dismissed as absurd; they are considered 'pre-political' (Franklin, 1986, p. 28).

Some young people can vote, of course. (Division of the electorate into age groups usually places the youngest voters between 18 and 22.) However in the 1987 general election this age group had the lowest turn-out rate among the electorate with less than half voting (Crewe, 1987, p. 9). This may confirm Agnello's (1973) view of young people as the most alienated from the political system or it may simply express a belief among young voters that none of the existing major political parties has effective youth policies or will represent their interests.

There are two other causal factors involved in the powerlessness of young people which, in part, explain older people's lack of political leverage. First, young and old people, as social groupings, are both highly heterogeneous and, although distinguished by their members' ages, express a diversity of other characteristics centring upon class, gender, race, disability, wealth, income and education which typifies other age groups. While common age is a possible basis for organising and uniting a group, these other characteristics generate interests which are potentially divisive. Even the groupings 'young' and 'old' cover a considerable range of ages from nought to twenty-one and sixty to ninety-five and above. Moreover many people are reluctant to label themselves 'young' or 'old' because of the negative connotations of these terms.

The potential electoral impact of both age groups is further limited because their members are relatively evenly dispersed geographically. This is especially important in its effects on older voters who constitute 20 per cent of the electorate and whose votes could, if organised in support of a particular party, be crucial to the outcome of a general election. Incidentally, the case of older voters illustrates well the limits to political change which even large minority groups can achieve through the ballot.

There is a need for caution in assessing the impact of age upon electoral choice. Stereotypes of older voters as more conservative and younger voters as wildly radical, if not revolutionary, are not supported by evidence. In the 1987 General Election the Conservatives attracted a majority of electors' support among all age groups. The proportion of votes given to the three major parties (Conservatives 45 per cent, Labour 34 per cent, SDP/Liberal Alliance 21 per cent) by the youngest voters, aged 18–22, was almost identical to the electoral preferences of all voters, which tends to support the judgement of a previous study that, 'the electoral effect of age is virtually nil' (Rose and McAlister, 1986, p. 67).

Legal and attitudinal constraints, as well as those which derive from the social and geographical heterogeneity of younger and older people, combine to limit severely the political participation and power of these groups. However, none of these factors is as important as their exclusion from the world of work. Three especially significant consequences flow from this exclusion.

First, work provides common interests around which a group can organise. It is relationships at work which generate a sense of solidarity and feelings of living a shared and common way of life. Exclusion from work tends to atomise, isolate and, in a curious way, privatise individuals and their aspirations and interests, rendering them politically ineffectual. This is true not only for young and old people, but others excluded from paid, collective work such as unemployed people and housewives.

Second, exclusion from the world of work means that people are not producers and therefore are only in a limited way consumers. They are consequently denied two of the most effective sanctions which people, working collectively, can apply to exercise power in an industrial society: withdrawal of labour and withdrawal of consumer power.

Third, the law excludes anyone under 16 years of age from full-time work and thereby effective trades union membership; only two per cent of people aged 65 and above are members (Abrams and O'Brien, 1981, p. 10). But it is trades unions which have traditionally served as the effective vehicles for conveying and securing the economic and political demands of working people. This exclusion is significant since it denies young and old people access to a trades union's educational and informational resources; its political and organisational experience and skills; and participation in the political power which derives from collective action which can unite and mobilise support and resources at a national and international level. Trades unions are important institutions connecting the structures of production and distribution in a social system with the structure of politics and decision making. They illustrate well how the exclusion of groups from one sphere has direct implications for their involvement in the other.

Ageism: economic dimensions

An examination of the role of younger and older people in the economic system is central to an understanding of their subordinate status in society. Young and old people are numerically the largest groups suffering poverty which is, at least informally, conceded by the existence of, for example, concessionary charges for buses trains, the cinema and hairdressers. These 'cheap rates' are patronising and unfair since young and old people do not require charity but sufficient income to make autonomous choices (Midwinter, 1983, p. 6). Their poverty reflects their largely dependent status as people who derive income from the state or other individuals. Between 1979 and 1981 the number of children living below the poverty line increased by 90 per cent and, according to Department of Health and Social Security (DHSS) statistics, in 1981 3·7 million (25 per cent) children were living on low income, with 1·7 million living on or below the poverty line (Sharron, 1985, p. 22). For the majority of older people the state retirement pension is their economic mainstay, although it is insufficient. However not everyone qualifies for even this entitlement, and in 1983, 809 000 did not receive the full rate and 39 000 people aged 80-plus received only the non-contributory rate of £20·20p (Black, 1986, p. 21); this latter group is growing approximately 15 times faster than the population as a whole (OPCS, 1985, p. 26).

Part of the explanation for the poverty of both groups is their forced exclusion from the labour market. The young below school-leaving age are prohibited from full-time work and the provisions of The Children and Young Persons Act 1933 set the conditions under which they may engage in part-time work (MacLennan 1985, p. 7). Retirement forces older people to leave their work and is an obvious example of age-based discrimination. Retirement has become a kind of 'mass redundancy' (Comfort, 1977, p. 16) and early retirement an increasingly convenient policy option for governments confronted by high levels of unemployment. Young and old people also suffer more subtle forms of age discrimination, such as the failure to hire or promote because of age. Too many job descriptions still prejudicially specify that, 'only candidates between 25 and 45 need apply'.

Such discrimination causes loss of income and occupational status, which are the major sources of class-based inequality, but also results in loss of self-respect and morale. 'The real curse of being old', as Comfort acknowledges, 'is the ejection from a citizenship traditionally based on work . . . it is demeaning idleness, non-use, not being called on any longer to contribute and hence being put down as a spent person of no public account, instructed to run away and play until death comes out to call us to bed' (1977, p. 16). Comfort's remarks apply with equal force to young people and anyone who is unemployed.

Moreover age-based discrimination results in a waste of goods and services which young and old people could produce; instead of being considered an economic burden, young and old people should be viewed as a phenomenal economic resource which is currently wasted. The economic circumstances of young people differ according to whether they are above or below minimum school-leaving age. Nearly all children and young people below school-leaving age will be wholly or in part dependent for income upon their parent(s). As many as 80 per cent of boys and 87 per cent of girls receive pocket money and those who do not tend to have part-time employment (Finn, 1984, p. 47). Finn claims that assessing a figure for pocket money is difficult since the total sometimes includes a sum for school meals or clothes, but the majority of young people in his survey received less than three pounds a week and 22 per cent less than a pound (ibid., p. 49). Such monies were nearly always given in return for work in the house, although 84 per cent of girls compared with only 35 per cent of boys were involved in domestic labour (ibid., p. 49).

Many young people under school-leaving age have jobs. A recent study claimed that 75 per cent of young people were involved in the juvenile labour market (ibid., p. 36) while another claimed that 40 per cent of young people were working in jobs other than babysitting or running errands (MacLennan, 1985, p. 23). One-tenth of the two and a half

million working children identified in one survey had two
jobs in addition to their school work (Belfield and Carroll,
1985, p. 8), with 80 per cent of these working illegally either
because the job requires them to work long or unsocial hours
or because they are below the legal working age of 13
(Moorehead, 1987, p. 41). The wages for such work are low
and conditions are predictably poor. Most young people
earn £1 an hour or less and even in London 15 per cent are
earning less than 50p an hour (MacLennan, p. 26). Finn
found that more than half of those leaving part-time work
cited low pay as a reason and one informant claimed, in a
remark which must be a contender for understatement of the
year, 'it was not well paid – 10p an hour and I had to lift
heavy weights' (Finn, 1984, p. 40). An incoherent
framework of law controlling child labour, and the absence
of any effective enforcement agency, guarantee poor working conditions. Young workers have no job security, enjoy
no entitlement to sick pay, have no right to claim unfair
dismissal, have no claim to compensation for industrial
injury (even though a third of young workers reported their
involvement in an accident or injury) and no right to be a
member of a trades union and therefore to the protection
which adult workers enjoy.

In brief, young people who wish to supplement their
pocket money are exploited in a Dickensian labour market
characterised by insecurity, low pay and poor conditions. In
later years when they leave school young people have few
opportunities to strengthen their economic position. They
confront either unemployment with an income derived from
supplementary benefit, a place on a Youth Training Scheme
(YTS) or a job which is likely to be poorly paid.

The recession in the British economy since the mid-1970s
has been especially severe in its impact on employment for
young people with levels of unemployment far outstripping
those of other age groups; there is not so much a crisis of
surplus labour as of 'surplus youth labour' (Bates *et al.*,
1984, p. 8). Firms seeking to cut labour costs tend to reduce
recruitment and/or cut training programmes; measures
which both restrict job opportunities for young people. In
January 1988 a third of people unemployed were under 25

years of age (Department of Employment, Section 26).
Given this concentration of unemployment, it is hardly
surprising that more than three-quarters of young people
reported feelings of depression about being unemployed or
that three out of five unemployed young people said they
could not manage on the limited sums of money allowed
(DES, 1983b, p. 29).

However youth unemployment, as Willis observed, deprives people of more than an income. They are denied the
transition into a 'general political, social and cultural adulthood' which work has traditionally allowed them to achieve.
They are in 'a new social state' of 'suspended animation'
characterised by dependence on parent(s) or the state and
deprived of 'real power in the market place' (1984(a), p.
476). For young women, it is alleged, an increasingly
common escape route from this social state is to become
pregnant, get off the register and establish a single-parent
home (Willis, 1984(b), p. 13). Just how marked this trend is,
however, is open to debate.

An alternative to unemployment is a place on YTS. The
advent of YTS and its predecessor, Youth Opportunities
Programme (YOP), have restructured the process of work
entry to such a degree that completion of a YTS scheme may
now be an expectation for both employers and young
people, with the normal sequence being school to YTS
to job or unemployment (Roberts, 1984, p. 84). Criticisms of
such schemes abound but usually focus on the poor quality
of training, low levels of remuneration and the poor job
prospects upon completion.

Some young people will find full-time employment but
jobs are usually unskilled, carry low status and offer little
security. Young people have tended to be peripheral workers employed in periods of labour shortages and denied jobs
during recessions. They are expected to perform tasks and
accept conditions which few adults would tolerate. This is
not a new feature of the labour market and Roberts notes
that, as recently as the inter-war years, young people were 'a
constant stream of cheap expendable labour . . . hired as
errand boys, floor sweepers and such like, paid juvenile
wages and dismissed once they ceased to be juveniles'

(Roberts, 1984, pp. 2–3). Earnings for young people retain their longstanding position at the bottom of the wage ladder (CSO, 1986, p. 132).

The economic powerlessness of the elderly, like that of the young reflects their exclusion from the labour market. Their exclusion is a consequence of a relatively new phenomenon called retirement which assumes that all men (at 65) and all women at 60 (although this latter is changing) without regard to competence, skills, health or disposition should, and would wish to withdraw from employment. There is a discernible irony in the fact that Otto von Bismarck, who introduced the first legislation legally defining 'old age' in 1889, The Old Age And Survivors Pension Act, was 74 years old but Chancellor of the German Empire.

Economic recession has lowered the age of *de facto* retirement; 'early retirement' is now commonplace. This tendency makes accurate estimates of unemployment in higher age ranges notoriously difficult. However it is clear that older people who are unemployed remain without work for longer. As many as 50 per cent of unemployed women aged 50 to 55 had been unemployed for over a year and the proportion rises to two-thirds for those in the 55 to 59 range; almost identical figures apply for men in the same age groups (Department of Employment, 1986(a)).

Many people over retirement age continue to work; 62 per cent of respondents to one survey stayed at work for financial reasons (Parker, 1980, p. 28), while others simply refuse to accept the enforced idleness which society tries to impose on them. Approximately one-third of economically active men and women remain in employment after the official retirement age (ibid., pp. 27–8). Men aged 65–73 work on average 25 hours a week and women aged 60–73 average 22 hours a week, but 10 per cent of men and 9 per cent of women work in excess of 38 hours (Department of Employment, 1985, table 151). Their jobs tend to be preponderantly unskilled manual or junior non-manual.

The majority of older people thus derive their income from state benefit but, 'if you only have a state pension to live on, then you are officially a pauper' (Midwinter, 1983, p. 6). Pensions have only risen between 5 and 10 per cent in relative worth in the last twenty years (Thomson, 1986, p. 409). Two million old people, 20 per cent of pensioners, claim supplementary pension (CSO, 1986, p. 61) to make ends meet.

Young and old people share quite similar economic circumstances. Both are excluded from the labour market although many of them are obliged by financial necessity to work on a part- or full-time basis and constitute a reserve army of labour in a secondary labour market characterised by low pay, poor conditions, limited rights and little job security. If they do not work, both groups are dependent for income upon relatives or state benefits; for many this means poverty. But the implications of these circumstances extend beyond the economic sphere. In a society besotted with material well-being, those without income and wealth are guaranteed low status and political powerlessness. As in many other areas of discrimination, there is a tendency to blame the victim. The resulting negative stereotypes of young and old people reinforce their economic condition and justify society's maltreatment of both groups.

Prospects

Ageism, like racism and sexism, expresses a power relationship between a dominant and subordinate group. The complex package of patronising and prejudicial views about young and old people which ageism embodies, justifies and sustains many of the injustices which these age groups suffer. Power relationships, however, are not immutable and age-ism must be confronted at the personal and political levels to generate change.

At the personal level it is important that if individuals make ageist remarks they are confronted. Anyone who argues that 'old workers should retire to make way for the young' or jokes that, 'you can't put an old head on young shoulders' or accuses Tom, Dick or Harry of being 'a dirty old man', should be challenged and asked to explain their remarks. Similarly, job descriptions which specify that, 'no one under 25 or over 45 need apply', would be less commonplace if everyone telephoned employers to ask why they discriminated in this way.

However, it is collective action which offers greater possibilities for effective change. Young and old people must organise themselves politically around those deprivations they share as a consequence of age. In America the Gray Panthers, an umbrella grouping of young and old people, seeks to promote legislation to outlaw discrimination on the basis of age and to modify the many existing laws which do so discriminate. As a consequence of such pressure, laws exist in many American states which prohibit age discrimination in much the same way that British law forbids racist and sexist discrimination.

In the British context it is vital that trades unions, the labour movement and pressure groups, as well as the more progressive parties, adopt policies directed against ageism. It is important that they inform their members and the wider society of ageism's damaging effects and raise awareness of the issue in much the same way that trades unions have, in recent years, confronted racism and sexism in the workplace.

However political action is unlikely to end the discriminations of ageism. Indeed we have argued throughout that the political, economic and cultural spheres are closely interconnected and mutually influential. If this analysis is correct, the abolition of cultural prejudices and discriminatory practices against young and old people will require a fundamental revision of the economic as well as political involvement of these groups in their community. Simone de Beauvior acknowledged as much in her claim that 'society cares about the individual only in so far as he is profitable. The young know this. Their anxiety as they enter in upon social life matches the anguish of the old as they are excluded from it . . . Between youth and old age there turns the machine . . . the crusher . . . It is the whole system that is at issue and our claim cannot be otherwise than radical – change life itself' (1985, p. 604).

2

Demography, Location and Young People

TONY JEFFS and MARK SMITH

As an age-specific agency the Youth Service is particularly vulnerable to shifts in the size and location of its client group. Despite a key relationship between supply and demand, questions of demography have aroused little interest amongst Youth Service administrators, practitioners or academics. Virtually nothing has been written on the topic and, surprisingly, the Service has paid scant attention to the policy implications of, for example, the sharp decline in the numbers of young people in Great Britain and Northern Ireland observable between the late 1980s and the end of the century (Figure 2.1). This chapter will certainly not fill the gap but it will, it is hoped, go some way towards encouraging a heightened awareness of the centrality of demography to discussions regarding youth policy.

The possibility that the viability of sections of the Youth Service might in some way be affected by a falling away in the numbers of young people who would have been difficult to envisage until fairly recently. The Service has for identifiable periods encountered pressure as a consequence of peaks in the birth rate. These were predominantly viewed as temporary phenomena of excessive demand. Since accurate records have been available with the inauguration of the decennial census in 1801, fluctuations have commonly occurred in the size of age groups. These have resulted from the impact of peaks in the birth-rate which periodically take place as a consequence of specific influences. The most

recent of these was the so-called 'baby-boom' which bridged
the ending of the Second World War. The consequences of
that peak, as with its predecessors, are still felt, for it continues to break like a wave on the shore, rippling forward
until it eventually fades or is in turn overtaken by a subsequent wave. The impact of a particular peak in the birth rate
is twofold. Firstly, it means that the individuals born during
that period move forward through time as a phalanx,
disrupting the balance between generations, at one point
creating pressure on primary schools; next on the secondary
sector; then on the labour market as they spill forth; and
eventually stretching the resources available for the elderly.
In less obvious ways the size of the cohort may, for example,
influence the balance between political parties in elections,
the cultural climate or patterns of consumption regarding
products and services.

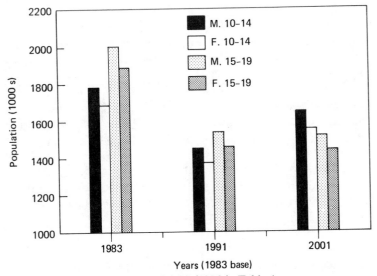

Source: Based on figures in OPCS (1986c), Table 1.

Figure 2.1 *1983-based population projections, 1983–2001: sex and
age-groups (England)*

Secondly, the presence of that bulge will reverberate as
their children, grandchildren and great-grandchildren pro-

duce future peaks, albeit smaller, in the birth rate and, at the other end, the death rate. The postwar baby-boom will certainly continue to have an impact, unless nuclear war or some other unforeseen catastrophe intervenes, well into the coming century. As well as these peaks there occur marked troughs in the birth rate. For example, in the inter-war years economic slump, gathering war clouds and finally the onset of hostilities all combined to subdue it. Consequently, the baby-boom was preceded by a dip in the birth rate. This has meant that the numbers leaving the labour market during the 1980s have been lower than the numbers entering. However, this certainly cannot be citied as the pre-eminent cause of the mass youth unemployment which has been a feature of the 1970s and 1980s, not least because those years witnessed rates of unemployment amongst older, pre-retirement workers that rose with almost equal ferocity. Nevertheless it has been a contributing factor.

These more dramatic, but short-term, movements have to be placed in the context of demographic changes that continue over substantially longer periods. In particular, the impact of these peaks and troughs on the demographic structure needs to be linked to a long-term decline in the birth rate, to the extent that this now stands at about 15 per cent below the long-term replacement level. During the next two decades, given the age balance of the population, it may return to a closer approximation of that earlier level (Thompson, 1987; Werner, 1988a). The fertility rate has been declining for over a century now and is contributing to the rapid decrease in the numbers of young people in Great Britain and Northern Ireland that will take place over the next two decades.

Disappearing youth?

For a number of reasons, such as better health, leading to greater longevity; smaller family size; and the shift from children being a source of income to being a drain on it, the proportion of the overall population under 20 has steadily declined for more than a 150 years. In 1821 this age group accounted for 50 per cent of the population; by 1911 the figure was just under 33 per cent and today it is below 16 per cent. When the data for the numbers of teenagers in the population during the 1980s and 1990s are examined then the scale of the decline can be seen to be gathering pace. In 1980 they made up 11·6 per cent of the population; by 1985 10·9. In 1994 the figure will be 8·3 per cent, the overall number with a largely static population during this period reducing from 6·3 to 4·6 million. It is hardly surprising that at the vox pop end of social policy, this trend has led to warnings that youth work is 'a declining industry' (Tutt, 1987, p. 7). In parallel to this, there has been taking place a gradual rise in the numbers of over-60s, so that by 1985, for the first time in the United Kingdom that age group outnumbered those aged under 16. It must be stressed that these trends are in no way a uniquely British phenomenon, but are to varying degrees replicated within all developed industrialised nations. Equally it 'has no historical precedent' (EEC, 1986, p. 4). For example, in the United States the birth rate has been falling since 1960 and by 1990 the number of people aged under 20 will dip below 30 per cent for the first time. In line with the British experience since 1983, the retired have also come to exceed the number of teenagers (Usdan, 1984). Within the EEC all the member states have recorded falling birth rates since 1964 and similar trends have been recorded in, amongst others, Australia and Japan (Davies *et al.*, 1987).

Decline in the number of young people can offer certain short-term advantages. Expenditure on child maintenance and schooling may be reduced, freeing resources either for additional investment on the residue or upon those at the upper end of the age structure. However, given the likelihood of the labour market demanding ever more highly-trained and technologically competent entrants, this scenario cannot be readily assumed. For a drop in numbers can equally incite, by way of compensation, increased educational expenditure at the more expensive upper end of higher and technical education, which would eradicate any savings at primary or secondary level. Superficially it may be assumed that a fall in the number of young people may also offer some respite regarding youth-related 'social problems', ones that had seemed impervious to earlier remedies. For example, the White Paper *Training For Employment* (Department of Employment, 1988a) views the drop in numbers of people aged 16 to 19 joining the labour market as likely to provide both an incentive for employers to invest more in training those available by way of compensation and an opportunity for the older unemployed to secure jobs that younger rivals might previously have taken. In similar vein it has been argued that diminishing numbers may even reduce levels of crime (Cunningham, 1985; Easterlin, 1980) as well as easing pressure on land and housing. Optimistic, not to say naive, views such as these are not universally shared (Steffensmeier, Streifel and Harper, 1987) and caution needs to be exercised.

It is perhaps not surprising that certain writers have been alarmed by the decline in the number of young people: 'the fate of the human species – or at least of certain national populations – is at stake in this process' (Bourgeois-Pichat, 1987, p. 25) is not an atypical expression of this stance. A similarly pessimistic response to the decline in the number of young people has emerged from the Economic and Social Consultative Assembly of the EEC. It argues that Europe is in danger of encountering a permanent shortage of young workers, whom it describes as 'the most mobile and adaptable, and the best trained in new technologies' (EEC, 1986, p. 18; see also Baker, 1986). What will happen it asks, 'to the spirit of initiative and innovativeness in an ageing and contracting population' (ibid.)? Noting with alarm that the age balance in the developing nations is at present comparable to that found in Europe during the period of the Industrial Revolution, it inquires 'whether societies where fifty and sixty year-olds are going to dominate, and where there will be more pensioners than children, can be genuinely forward-looking. It is more likely that they will devote themselves to contemplating their past grandeur' (ibid., p. 19).

Evidence to sustain such gloomy prognostications is not readily at hand. It is important to stress that they are based purely on conjecture. As Hall and Ogden note, the evidence

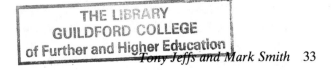
cited all too often takes as its reference point France during the 1930s, when an ageing population, it is argued, produced 'a decline in creativity and an increase in conservatism'. Yet, as they conclude, there is clearly 'nothing inevitable about this' (1985, p. 56). Reddaway (1977) certainly found nothing 'exciting' or overly worrying about zero population growth and scant evidence that an ageing population will affect productivity or labour mobility. Guilmot goes even further, pointing out that the productivity of employees aged below 30 is lower overall than of those aged 60 and above. Therefore, 'a reduction in the number of older working persons would . . . entail a more substantial fall in production than an equivalent reduction in the number of young active persons' (1978, p. 41). Jolly *et al.* conclude that 'when all the evidence has been considered, its contradictions and correlations noted, the relationship between age and performance remains extremely ambiguous . . . [it] indicated no consistent pattern of superiority in any age group' (1980, p. 62). Maillat, considering national as opposed to individual productivity, also argues for caution. In a survey of the evidence he stresses:

> Little is known about the relations between population trends and the pace of economic growth. The population is only one of the factors which explain economic growth rates, and certainly not the most important. Logically, therefore, it follows that a low rate of population increase is not in itself a determining element in the slowing-down of economic growth. (1978, p. 91)

Yet the EEC document takes no heed of the need for caution and operates from an assumption that relative, if not actual economic decline, will be the likely outcome of a reduction in the proportion of young people within a given society. Regarding solutions it appears to have little to offer, following an almost certainly correct assessment that 'it is unrealistic to claim that a democratic state can radically change birth rates' (EEC, 1986, p. 21). Therefore it concentrates upon arguing for a package of financial and social incentives designed to encourage individuals to have additional children and to secure the removal of all existing disincentives, this package being linked to substantially greater investment in the education and training of young people to maximise their potential, alongside increased allocation of resources for the re-training of older workers. Among the policy options emanating from other sources are 'naturalisation' policies which would lead to the acceptance of immigrants from over-populated countries; interventions to enable women to combine paid employment and child care more easily; and policies designed to encourage family formation and child birth, such as linking the size of the parents' pension to the number of children produced (see Mcintosh 1987; Demeny, 1987). What is striking is the similarity to a number of policy options considered in the sixteenth century to raise the birth rate. These included arguments to repeal the law of chastity in the Church, 'give those who marry a house and a portion of waste land at nominal rent, grant tax reliefs and privileges to those who had five children, and impose a swingeing tax on bachelors' (Hatcher, 1977, p. 67).

Considerable reservations must be expressed regarding the analysis that generates this concern over a decline in the number of young people. As already noted, the linking of social and economic decline to the demographic structure of a given society cannot be sustained on the basis of the available evidence. This is not to say that such a relationship may not exist, but that it would be dangerously simplistic in the absence of much more extensive research to seek to restructure social policy in general, and family policy in particular, on the basis of it. Historical linkages between military strength and population size have, certainly during the last two decades, been rent asunder by the development of new weapons, removing much of the need for mass mobilisation. The military imperative within social policy which was so influential in the past, not least as a justification for investment in youth facilities, has consequently ceased to figure in quite the same way in the policy equation. Technological changes now promise similarly to erode the tenuous relationship between national productivity and population size as they have fractured it in relation to military power. Ecological and environmental lobbyists also offer a cogent *raison d'être* for population control, even for an overall reduction. Moral panics relating to pollution, plus public consciousness of the finite supply of raw materials, have all eroded confidence in the economic case for population growth as a prerequisite of economic prosperity. Few, one suspects, would now confidently endorse the claim of Simon that with 'virtually every variant faster population growth shows better consumption results. The advantage is overwhelmingly with higher population growth' (1983, p. 21). Benefits of raising the birth rate are now rarely perceived as outweighing the costs within public discourse. It is essential, therefore, to come to terms with the changed, and changing, age structure of the population, not least because 'it is probably neither possible nor desirable to alter these trends' (Ermisch, 1983, p. 309).

Demographic change and the youth labour market

Concern regarding the impact of the declining number of young people entering the labour market seemed to come to the fore during 1988. In a matter of months there appeared the White Paper *Training For Employment* and a joint Department of Employment and MSC (Training Commission) study submitted to the National Economic Development Council (NEDC, 1988). Both forecast a highly optimistic future for young people in the labour market, predicting a rapid fall in youth unemployment with employers encountering considerable competition both in terms of the recruitment and retention of young staff. As a consequence of this they would be impelled dramatically to improve the quality of training for both new and existing members of the work-force. This optimism may prove to be excessive for, as already noted, it has not been numbers but an absence of 'aggregate demand in the economy' (Junankar, 1987, p. 11) which is the predominant cause of youth unemployment. Nevertheless it is probably the case that young people will benefit, in terms of access to the labour market, from the fall in overall numbers, given that it will coincide with a stabilisation in the size of the labour force. It is therefore possible that we are approaching an indeterminate period of scarcity that will turn the youth end of the labour market into a 'job-sellers'' one (Dixon, 1988).

Easterlin (1980), in particular, paints a rosy picture regarding the future life chances of young people as a consequence of demographic change, arguing that job openings will become more plentiful, pay rates for young workers superior relative to older workers and career advancement opportunities be transformed. Warming to the theme, he postulates that the more favourable economic climate for young people will mean that 'psychological stress will be reduced, and feelings of hopelessness or bitterness will be less prevalent' (Easterlin, 1980, p. 135). This may be an exaggeration, but, none the less, the reduction in numbers clearly is unlikely to exacerbate present levels of unemployment and the pressure on higher education places. Indeed with regard to the latter a government minister, for the first time in well over a decade, expressed the opinion that a buoyant youth labour market could entice young people away from further and higher education, putting at risk the 'supply of higher level skills' (*TES*, 1988). This may be premature but what is significant is that the concern has been given expression, especially as it follows a recognition by the government that the proportion of young people entering higher education would have to be raised from 13·9 to 18·5 per cent by the year 2000 in order to secure the requisite numbers of graduate and the equivalent level labour market entrants (DES, 1987b). Fears concerning the shortfall in the number of graduates are being increasingly articulated, especially in relation to a number of key areas of the labour market (Meadows & Cox, 1987).

Regarding two areas, both of which fall within its remit, the government has clearly anticipated serious problems arising before the end of the century and responded accordingly; these areas are teaching and nursing. In the case of the former the DES has removed need for entrants to possess a teaching qualification so that where future shortages occur older alternatively qualified applicants can be employed. As regards nursing, the shortage is predicted to be especially acute unless new routes of entry are adopted.

Consequently the government has accepted the *Nursing 2000* package for the reform of nurse education. In the absence of such a restructuring it is estimated that by the mid-1990s the NHS would be seeking to attract into nursing, on the basis of present training programmes and entry requirements, 50 per cent of all young women leaving school with between five GCSEs (grades A to C) and one A level to sustain staffing levels. Leaving aside the underlying sexism of such a calculation it nevertheless illustrates the potential for a significant alteration in the employment prospects of young people. It is in relation to nursing that the uneven impact of the decline in birth rate can perhaps initially be most graphically illustrated. For the predicted shortfall is expected to occur in its most severe form among those dubbed the 'better qualified entrants' to the youth labour market; those possessing five higher grade GCSEs or A levels. This segment is likely to be enticed in ever-growing numbers into higher education as the net is spread more widely to compensate for the overall fall in the potential client group. Employers will therefore have to compete more energetically for this group. As a consequence many gender and racial barriers within a number of sectors will be eroded, as has already been noted in relation to technician employment (*Employment Gazette*, 1988). The Trustee Savings Bank, realising that those from ethnic minorities will form a growing proportion of the youth work-force, is, according to Gapper (1988), 'recruiting intensely in schools with a large proportion of ethnic minority pupils; its intention is to have a reputation as an equal opportunity employer when other sources of young labour start to dry up'.

Similarly, this fall in the numbers of available young workers will encourage trends towards a more flexible work-force (Hakim, 1987) and the spread of job-splitting, home-working and job-sharing as a means of attracting or retaining in the labour market older workers and those with child-care responsibilities (Meager, 1988). The 17·5 per cent fall in the number of 18- to 24-year-olds in the United States between 1985 and 1995 has already led employers to export clerical work and data entry work to Eire, Barbados, Haiti and Singapore, using satellite communications (Barwick,

1988). Economic activity among students, already standing at 36 per cent for the 16–19 group (*Employment Gazette*, 1988) is also expected to be stimulated by the requirement of overcoming shortfalls in the youth labour market. In particular, there is already evidence that employers are displaying a preference for employing them for seasonal, casual, deskilled and poorly paid jobs, where they are pushing aside less well qualified applicants (Ball, 1988; Sweet, 1988). In this they are encouraged, perhaps not accidentally, by the introduction of loans, to supplement, for some, and to replace for others, student grants. Clearly limitations exist as to the size of this pool as a direct consequence of the class imbalance within the student population. For overwhelmingly it is those students from lower income backgrounds who are forced to work. This is in contrast to those whose background ensures that their desire for a loan flows more from a wish to maximise tax avoidance on the part of the parent(s) than from need on the part of the young person. Paradoxically, labour shortages in a number of employment sectors could encourage many to undertake higher education who were previously ambivalent towards it, firstly, as a consequence of the improvement in job prospects at the cessation of studies and, secondly, because opportunities for 'working your way through college' are likely to be more plentiful. What cannot be doubted is that higher education will decreasingly be associated with one age group: those in their upper teens and early twenties. The demands of the labour market and the need for institutions to retain viable numbers will combine to encourage the continuation of the trend towards a mixing of the generations within higher education.

Youth culture: under threat?

The shift taking place in the age profile of the population can be expected to have a profound impact upon other areas besides employment. A partial consequence of mass youth unemployment, accompanied by a lowering of the purchasing power of student grants, has been an overall decline in the importance of young people as consumers. Earnings of young people lagged behind those of older workers, and barely kept pace with inflation between 1979 and 1987 (Bryne, 1987). Attempts to further erode wage levels in order to make young people more attractive to employers are no more likely than earlier ones to have a positive impact upon the demand for their services. As Junanker and Neale (1987) note, the actual levels of young peoples' earnings have little measurable impact upon their attractiveness to employers. Those seeking explanations for youth unemployment are obliged to look further afield. As a rhetorical device, however, the lowering of youth earnings has played an important part in persuading young people that they are responsible, in some way, for their unemployment; that 'they have priced themselves out of the market'. The downward drift in their earnings may well now have bottomed out, but the fall has now merged into a deterioration in the composite spending power of young people consequent upon the relative and actual fall in their numbers. Inevitably the result will be further diminution of the youth consumer market. Consequently, as Matthews (1988) notes, the obsession amongst retailers and manufacturers with 'youth – understanding them, creating commercials for them, pleading with them to buy goods' is fast fading. New, enticing and reinvigorated growth markets lie elsewhere. There are, for example, two-income couples, of whom a growing number have no children, and, most significantly, those who in the argot of the advertisers are known as the 'empty-nesters': older couples, again often with two incomes or a healthy pension, low or non-existent mortgages and no dependent children, who in addition may have just inherited all or a share in a parental home for which they have no need. These are, in the words of one marketing agency, precisely the group 'who have the money and the leisure to try out new things' (ibid.).

Finance houses, travel firms and speculative builders have all been quick to cash in on this new market; others are now following post haste. In retailing fashion, traditionally seen as a youth-dominated market, Hepworths and Burtons are now concentrating their investment with an eye to the older market (Cunningham, 1985). Even the 'pop music' market, previously the most youth-orientated of all, is undergoing a change in the foci of its orientation. The teenage-dominated single now accounts for fewer than 3 per cent of sales. With producers and record companies 'faced with a declining teenage market, their ambitions turn increasingly to over-25 album buyers' (du Noyer, 1988, p. 45) to shore up the market. Similarly the commercial radio network is acknowledging that, as the number of teenagers dips, so does their spending power, therefore they are turning their attention to a bigger, older audience (Self, 1987). Reed (1987) notes that the film industry, which in the past tended unashamedly to pander to the adolescent, is increasingly 'focusing more on the elderly and issues of ageing' in a process he describes as the 'greying of Hollywood'.

All this reflects a pushing aside of young people from centre stage, indicating that they have lost much of the high ground that previously meant youth could so easily be translated into a key image: a metaphor for happiness, freedom, energy and appetite. One research report, produced as a marketing guide for industry, notes that a by-product of this change has been the erosion of what was so often glibly designated the generation gap. This suggests that we are witnessing the emergence of a generation who see themselves 'as responsible, sensible and caring, and intelligent and thoughtful – a far cry from the hedonism and rebellion once espoused by many of their parents' (Mintel, 1988, p. 7). Attitudinally closer to their parents, nevertheless, the survey found they still retain as their spending priorities clothes, records and tapes, and drinking outside the home. Yet economic and demographic changes mean that much of the old youth dominance of even these commercial arenas is fast evaporating. Generational differences in style, attitudes and tastes still exist but these are becoming less marked and, importantly, less differentiated, between young people of below 20 and those into their mid-twenties and beyond. This is perhaps inevitable, for as young people 'aspire to the material benefits of adult status' (Churchill, 1988, p. 7) so those aspirations become embodied and expressed not only in material forms but also in behavioural patterns. The youth market, if the term any longer has any meaning, becomes less identifiable as it achieves growing coterminosity with that catering for older consumers.

In a similar vein, Coleman and Husen argue that the characteristics and features that differentiate youth and adulthood are being eroded, with age corresponding 'less to life-style than in the past. There are certain ways of living, dressing and working that are characteristic of youth but that also continue among some people well into their 20s, 30s and 40s – and for a small fraction indefinitely' (1985, p. 11). This analysis inevitably poses the question of how long such a 'life-style' can continue to take unto itself the adjective 'youth'. For as the concept of youth is less and less age-related then it must possess diminishing relevance in this context. This is not to argue for some crude notion of 'mass society'. Fragmentation in life-styles will occur and remain significant. In parallel, consumption patterns will become increasingly differentiated and specialised. What is being argued is that youth of itself is less likely to be the point of reference for such fragmentations. Divisions will increasingly reflect deeper social fissures, such as class, race, gender, access to employment and regional location. All of which intersect in fundamental ways to produce highly variable life experiences and which have long made a mockery of attempts to construct undifferentiated notions of adolescence and youth transitions. This is a point well illustrated by Griffin, who concludes on the basis of her research that 'the experiences and prospects of young Asian and Afro-Caribbean women were no more equivalent to those of their white female peers than were the experiences of young women and young men, or of working class and middle-class school leavers' (1987, p. 31). Also the work of Willis (1984a) highlights the impact of long-term unemployment on the social and political attitudes of young people excluded from the labour market.

Care should be taken not to assume that youth sub-cultures and youth centrism have been arbitrarily swept aside by social and demographic change, consigned to irrelevance. But it is essential to remind ourselves that the sociology of youth cultures was always a flawed enterprise, a 'male-dominated tradition, as heavily reliant upon conceptions of boys' relations to the labour market and the market in consumer goods' (Dorn & South, 1983, p. 35). The sub-cultural categories were not totally mistaken, but they have subsequently been shown to be inapplicable to young women and as such parlously blind to gender (McRobbie, 1980; Griffin, 1985). Further, the concept of youth itself is highly problematic, being interpreted and understood in a variety of ways within and across different cultures. Abrams (1959), it should be noted in fairness, to a degree acknowledged this in his key study of the 'teenage consumer' over three decades ago, identifying the teenage market as one dominated by the white male working class. It is this sector that has subsequently suffered disproportionately from the rise in unemployment and the erosion of young people's earning capacity, and become demographically beleaguered.

The birth rate within the United Kingdom has not fallen uniformly in all classes. Both family size and the birth rate have dipped most markedly within working-class families. This has been a long-term trend, but it is one that has gathered pace since the Second World War. Indeed, to a considerable extent, it has been the growing uniformity in relation to preferred family size among the different social classes that has produced the current reduction in the national birth rate (Macfarlane and Mugford, 1984). Placed alongside the radical change in the ethnic composition of the working class since the 1950s, it is possible more clearly to understand how the old assumptions regarding the cohesion and dominance of this group within youth culture have been set aside. Working-class male youth still provide substance for moral panics such as arise from football hooliganism and crime, but less so. In the case of the former, in particular, the age range of those involved often makes it dishonest to designate this as any longer being a 'youth' problem. Certainly the violent and criminal behaviour of young males can still be a legitimate cause for concern, especially as it tends to be located in the public arena of shopping precincts, town centres and the like (Blagg, 1987). However such behaviour is certainly not any longer, if it ever was, the sole prerogative of the adolescent, any more than is football hooliganism. Correctly, violence is now being seen more as a 'male' problem rather than a youth problem.

For the Youth Service, in particular, much of this is bad news. Youth workers have, since the emergence of distinctive youth cultures, had a contradictory relationship with them. Many have condemned them as anti-social and divisive. Certainly the threat that respectable society felt these sub-cultures often posed has generated funds, and a measure of popular sympathy, for a service that in working alongside young people appeared to offer some possibility that the worst excesses might be contained. The 'youth saving' tradition has exploited youth cultures with all the skills of the merchandiser and huckster, although to differing ends. Equally the demonology of youth work has long been constructed upon the foundations of restraining threatening youth and capricious new sub-cultures. Linked to this has been the 'thin red line' self-image of the Youth Service, feeding upon the illusion of young people as an alien host which by sheer weight of numbers imperils social order and harmony. Both these have lost or are in the process of losing their negotiable value. Diminishing numbers coupled with the erosion of the boundaries that marked out distinctive youth sub-cultures must further denude the basis upon which the service resides. In addition, the Youth Service has been able in the past to exploit the apparent uniqueness of certain activities which were the preserve of the young people. The growing coterminosity of leisure pursuits that embrace a wider age range than that of the Youth Service will reduce further the attractiveness of 'youth provision'. As the age cohort shrinks, so commercial agencies will inevitably seek to broaden their appeal to sustain their market. This, alongside what the Mintel (1988) study described as the increasing sophistication of the young consumer, will again imperil the viability of much Youth Service provision. If, and admittedly it is a big if, the earning power of young people simultaneously enters a period of sustained upturn then the trend of the last thirty years of declining involvement and affiliation to distinct youth organisations (Evans, 1987) is likely to accelerate. Also likely to abet this trend will be the growth in the proportion of young people in both full- and part-time higher education during the next decade. Youth Service affiliation has always been negligible in this group. Proportionately the numbers of HE students are likely to increase substantially between now and the end of the century (DES, 1987b). This will occur for three reasons.

Firstly, the demand for graduates is predicted to rise sharply owing to the restructuring of the labour market. Secondly, the number of available places will remain roughly constant in spite of the diminished size of the cohort. Finally the changing class profile of school-leavers, 'will be operating to increase the average rate of participation in HE during the 1990s' (Ermisch, 1983, p. 268). As well as the class profile of the Youth Service age band, the ethnic balance is shifting. The proportion of Asian young people is growing, as a consequence of the age profile of that group and a fertility rate nearly three times that of both Whites and Afro-Caribbeans (CSO, 1988a, p. 30). While such global categories smooth over significant variations between their constituent groups, this is a segment of the community that has exhibited markedly low rates of affiliation to the Youth Service (DES, 1983b: see also Chapter 5). It can therefore be expected that the numbers of young people aged 14 to 20 affiliated to the Youth Service will fall, and not merely on a *pro rata* basis in line with demographic trends.

Artley argues that this process of generational merging is producing a state where 'the old try to look younger while the young prematurely age' (1988). The imagery may be seductive but some reservations need to be expressed as a reading of the previous chapter demonstrates. In the absence of much more substantive research it would be premature to write off youth sub-cultures as a potent social force or to assume that what may be occurring now represents a long-term trend. Demographic determinism is certainly as risky as its economic equivalent. Yet a strong suspicion is abroad that the old models of defining, categorising and delineating young people may no longer be, if they ever were, adequate. As Coleman and Husen note, 'there is a growing recognition that something fundamentally new is occurring in the transition to adulthood . . . a rather blurred borderline between youth and adulthood. This blurring arises because age corresponds less to life-style than in the past' (1985, p. 11). That analysis, while helpful, remains one-dimensional in that it ignores the reverse process by which so-called adult norms and life-styles intrude into the experiences of young people and 'children', blurring the distinction by making them older and more 'mature'.

This argument relates closely to that of Postman (1985) who posits that childhood itself is fast disappearing under the impact of new technology and a linked restructuring of the leisure and recreation patterns of both adults and young people, producing an increasing coterminosity between the two, whereby we are 'in the process of exorcising a two-hundred-year-old image of the young as child and replacing it with the imagery of the young as adult' (ibid., p. 125). Fast being eaten away are the old certainties regarding childhood and adolescence. Crude notions of transition from adolescence to maturity, dependence to independence, school to work begin to look frayed and outmoded. When the 'transition' stretches from years into decades, when career changes and re-training take place periodically throughout the working life; when separation, divorce and home-making are being undertaken or experienced by those of every age; when dependency becomes a lot more of the old than of the young: then much of the uniqueness of adolescence fades into insignificance and the question must invariably arise as to whether it is a unique stage or simply part of a seamless web? The evidence would suggest the latter.

Musgrove argued that adolescence was 'created along with the steam engine' (1964, p. 33), that it was a by-product of industrialisation and the forces it unleashed. It is a theory to which much research into the history of childhood and adolescence has lent credence (see for example, Walvin, 1982; Springhall, 1986). If, as Postman argues, 'childhood is solely a creation of culture' (1985, p. 144) and adolescence the epiphenomenon of a form of industrialisation, then it becomes a clear possibility that both are transitory. Not only may the cultural and social forms which adolescence takes be transformed, but new social relationships and industrial forces may so change the context and environment that the word loses its meaning and value, or becomes a synonym for puberty and physiological change. In this we should not lose sight of the fact that the terms 'youth' and 'adolescence' are not strictly interchangeable or that 'adolescence' really only came into general usage at the turn of the century (Springhall, 1986). Certainly it is not merely demographic change, falling numbers, that imperil the Youth Service in its present form. For those changes may be no more than a surface manifestation of much more fundamental shifts that are impairing the *raison d'être* upon which it is constructed, the very notions of adolescence, youth and, by implication, transition itself. It may be premature to announce the demise of adolescence but the omens most certainly encourage scepticism as to the wisdom of investing resources in institutions that are custom-built solely to service adolescence.

Political change and young people

The actual and relative decline in the numbers of young people will inevitably influence the political environment and impact upon the electoral system. The most obvious changes will flow from the shrinkage in the youth vote. The electoral significance of young and first-time voters must wane over time. It will be far less crucial for political parties to court their support as a constituent grouping, with the shifting balance in the composition of the electorate tilting the locus of power in favour of the older voter, with political debates coming to reflect this. To an extent this has already happened. Health, a service predominantly serving the needs of the elderly rather than the young, has during the last decade come to eclipse housing and education, both of which tend to be perceived in terms of catering for those in a lower age bracket. Similarly, the decline in the number of children has undoubtedly made the task of campaigners seeking to combat child poverty more difficult (Brown, 1988). Certainly the view that parents have children 'for reasons of personal pleasure rather than social obligation'

(Dilnot, *et al.*, 1984, p. 118) appears to have gathered momentum as the birth rate has fallen. Parenthood is becoming perceived by many as a 'good' opted for in 'preference' to a holiday, new car or second home and, *de facto*, no more deserving of subsidy.

According to those endorsing this view, responsibility for the care of the elderly is rarely seen as being comparable. For unlike the burden of child care, which it is argued is a choice, the task of caring for the elderly befalls individuals at random, consequent upon the lottery for survival or the misfortune of illness. It is also a response to an obligation, less a liability more a quasi-religious duty, undertaken by an individual, but which, by way of bonus, lifts a financial burden from the wider community. Investment in it therefore promises simultaneously to be both cost-effective and an endorsement of a moral commitment of the highest order; encouraging not mendacity but selfless sacrifice. How much more attractive, then, such expenditure on the elderly becomes, than lavishing money on ungrateful youth or 'irresponsible' parent(s) producing offspring they cannot adequately keep. Worryingly, child benefits are already among the least popular forms of welfare transfer and, therefore, can hardly be said to be in readiness to resist any onslaught from a position of strength (Jowell and Airey, 1984; Taylor-Gooby, 1985).

Pressure for generational reallocation of resources is likely to be cumulative. For not only will the number of elderly exceed those in their teens, but also within the wider population those with a caring responsibility for the former will outstrip those with adolescent offspring. *Pro rata* the potential size of the lobby advocating additional expenditure and support for the elderly therefore becomes both more substantive and vocal than that with a direct interest in seeking similar funding for young people. Thus, irrespective of the political climate in which social policy debates are located, those pleading for enhanced expenditure for services orientated towards young people can expect to encounter mounting resistance. Partially to counteract this permanent numerical disadvantage it has been suggested that parents should be given an additional vote for each of their children below the age of 18 (Demeny, 1987, p. 354) or that the voting age be substantially lowered to take account of the views, needs and aspirations of young people (Franklin, 1986). Without such a mechanism significant groups of young people will be disadvantaged. Further, schemes, such as that proffered in a throw-away fashion in the Griffiths Report, *Community Care: Agenda For Action*, for experimentation in the use of 'particularly school-leavers, YTS, etc.' as part of 'a multi-purpose auxiliary force' to provide home care services (HMSO, 1988b, p. ix) will attract attention. As the political voice of young people becomes easier to overlook, as the age of politicians rises in concert with that of the population, then the risk of further erosion of the young people's rights becomes more likely. It is, after all, a short step from compulsory YTS to compulsory community service and the crude and differentiating exploitation of young people on a basis which would be unacceptable if applied to the remainder of the population.

Almost axiomatically it has been assumed that an ageing electorate will have less and less sympathy towards radical and liberal parties. Of course a great deal depends upon how the terms radical and liberal are interpreted. Within the British context the simplistic assumption has been that the Labour Party represents the major embodiment of electoral radicalism, whilst the Conservatives, as their name implies, represent resistance to reform and change. Certainly voting patterns amongst the electorate have lent some credence to this view, with support for the Labour Party declining with age, although the degree of overall support has tended to fall away since 1945 (Elcock, 1983). However the evidence is contradictory. Far more significant than the presence of teenage radicalism has always been the reality of widespread indifference to politics among young people. The cumulative weight of the evidence indicates that 'political socialisation by families, schools and the media is simply continuing to produce disinterested school leavers' (Roberts, 1987, p. 21).

The diminishing proportion of young voters may work against the Left in the same way; it will probably reorientate the foci of political debate, but such assumptions must be treated with circumspection, firstly, because the high rates of abstention among young voters have always created a dis-juncture between beliefs and the expression of those beliefs in the ballot box. Research already indicates that as many as one-sixth of this group are absent from the electoral register, a figure that is likely to rise with the introduction of the Community Charge (Pinto-Duschinsky, 1987). Secondly, as the political opinions of young people appear to be more volatile and directly influenced by contemporary events and experiences than those of older voters (Cochran and Billig, 1983), it is more difficult to predict future voting behaviour among a sector of the electorate who have not yet in the main had the chance to vote. Thirdly, the falling away in numbers could be balanced by a reduction in youth centrism and affiliation to economic conservatism, as a consequence of greater exposure to higher education (Watts and Zinneck-er, 1987). Finally, the decline in the numbers of young people may be counterbalanced by changes among other constituent elements within the electorate. One example here is the heightened propensity of women to vote for anti-Conservative candidates, as illustrated in the 1987 elec-tion. All these elements are highly problematic but no more so than the crude demographic determinism that posits the notion that a fall in the proportion of young voters will herald a dark age of reaction. In this context it is worth recalling the comment of Mannheim when questioning the assumption that youth is progressive by nature.

> When I was young it was the current belief . . . This has since proved to be a fallacy, since we have learned that conservative or reactionary movements can also build up Youth movements . . . Youth is neither progressive nor conservative by nature, but is a potentiality which is ready for any new start. (1942, p. 35)

As soon as this is understood, the tiresome and vacuous rhetoric, which has so long been the stock-in-trade of youth organisations and self-appointed spokespersons, that 'youth demands change' can be seen for the nonsense it so often is. Young people have never spoken with one voice. Entry into adolescence is no more a guarantee of acquiring a mantle of radicalism, than old age is of reaction.

Changing families and changing young people

The decrease in the absolute numbers of young people will inevitably have an impact upon the structure of the family. Among heterosexual young people the continuous fall in the age of first marriage, which had been a discernible trend since before the turn of the century, appears to have been in retreat since the 1970s. The rate of marriage for both single men and women has fallen for all age groups since 1971, but the decline has been most marked for those aged under 30. In the vanguard have been those in their teens, amongst whom the number has fallen to about a quarter of its earlier level for both sexes, and the rate for those aged 20 to 24 has more than halved (CSO, 1988a). Cohabitation has increased with, for example, almost a third of marriages taking place between individuals sharing the same address. It should be stressed that this is less a feature with those couples who are both marrying for the first time and where one or both are under 20 (Haskey & Coleman, 1986). What has emerged is an extension of the period of quasi-independence, long a key characteristic of adolescence, freedom from marital and family ties being lengthened for the majority.

Not only are individuals getting married later; they are also opting to delay having children for a longer period of time. In 1975 the average age of motherhood was 26 years; it is currently around 27, and by 1995 is expected to rise to 28 (OPCS, 1987c). Since the early 1980s there has been a small increase in the fertility of women over 30. The overall effect is to compress the age range of mothers. Just as women are choosing to have children later in life so they are self-evidently opting to have fewer. According to the research of Dunnell (1979), in 1967 a majority of women who had been married for 12 years thought that between three and four children was the ideal family size. His 1976 survey showed that this had fallen to between two and three children, with a clear majority, 65 per cent, perceiving the two-child family as the ideal and only 11 per cent opting for four. Thus, not only is the onset of responsibility for children being postponed, but also the overall length of time being devoted to that care diminished. For the median interval between the reduced number of children has remained approximately constant at around 30 months (Werner, 1988b). The young people may tend to remain in the home for longer periods, as a consequence of extended education and unemployment, but overall this is more than amply compensated for by the decline in the number of progeny. Thus as (Davies, 1987) points out a cohort of women who bear only 1·4 children on average, which is below the current British rate, but in excess of the West German one, will spend only about a fifth of their life with a child under the age of 20. This graphically contrasts with the situation in 1900 when 'one quarter of the married women were in childbirth every year' (Halsey, 1978, p. 96).

In addition, the escalation in divorce and separation rates has meant the re-creation of, for some, the periods of independence usually associated with 'youth', this often occurring in the early to late 20s, for the median length of marriages culminating in divorce is less than 9 years. Consequently, commercial, leisure and other agencies are finding that it is financially advantageous to eschew a focus upon a narrow age range, for example, those below 20. An additional demographic trend is likely to encourage this. The gender balance among young people is altering significantly. In the past male emigration, industrial accidents, differential infant mortality rates and armed conflict all contributed towards females being in the majority. According to the Finer Report this meant that 'in mid-Victorian England, almost one-third of the women aged 20 to 44 had to remain spinsters because differential mortality and large-scale emigration so depleted the reservoir of men that there were not enough to go round' (HMSO, 1974, p. 23). Since 1911 the balance has slowly shifted towards men being in the majority in the under-16 age group, a state of affairs that has filtered upwards into other age bands. For example, by mid-1986 in the 15–29 age group there were 238 000 more males than females. By 1993 the projected figure for the same age group will be 284 000.

The implications of this are difficult to predict. It could, as one pair of commentators postulate, promote higher levels of criminal and anti-social behaviour amongst so-called 'surplus' young males (Wilkie and Wilkie, 1975). Certainly it will result in many men staying single longer than they anticipated or preferred, and in a widening in the age gap between partners. Possibly, also, it may lead to more men partnering women older than themselves, many of whom are divorced or separated (Leete, 1979). This imbalance will clearly influence patterns of leisure among young people. For example, in the context of prevailing norms, it will encourage commercial ventures to seek actively to attract younger women in order to compensate for the imbalance and to 'draw in' older single males. Marriages may well be made in heaven, but the preliminaries rarely now commence in the school playground or youth club disco and are less likely to do so in the future. Consequently, research (see for example Emmett, 1977; Hendry, 1983; Leonard, 1980) which highlights the 'courting function', the opportunity to meet potential partners or establish relationships, as a unique feature of young peoples' leisure, may have diminishing applicability for the Youth Service.

The changing nature of the family itself has been extensively discussed elsewhere and space does not permit the material and debates to be re-worked in detail. However a number of key points need to be extracted in this context. Firstly, as regards the gender division of labour within mixed-sex households, in particular the extent to which traditional patterns have been usurped appears to have been depressingly minimal (Mansfield and Collard, 1988). The categorisation of men's and women's work within the home still sadly requires minimal elaboration. Available evidence also unambiguously argues that the division applies with as much rigour to the majority of young people as it does to their elders (Wallace, 1987). If the expansion of women's employment has in the main merely imposed upon them the dual functions and stress described by Mansfield and Collard, it should be recognised that young people have been substantive beneficiaries from this exploitation, not merely financially. The decrease in the size of the average family has freed more and more women to enter employment outside the home. It has also emancipated young people, especially young women, from a great deal of unpaid labour relating to the care of younger siblings, allowing many to remain within education beyond the statutory leaving age and reducing the time involuntarily spent within the home. Paradoxically, the reduction in the size of the family, alongside the absorption of an increasing number of women into the labour market and the rise in the number of single-parent families, has increased opportunities for the generation of income within the setting of the home. Released from obligation towards their own younger brothers and sisters, a growing army now secure paid employment caring for the children of others. Almost a quarter of young women are regularly employed as baby-sitters and child-minders (Finn, 1984). A cash nexus has replaced many of the old informal support networks for those with child-care responsibilities, with a reserve army of young people providing much of the support required to release others to enter the labour market or engage in leisure activities.

Reductions in the average size of the family unit, linked to an overall improvement in housing conditions, have re-formulated patterns of young people's leisure. It is important to stress the centrality of these changes in this context, for, at the age of 18, 90 per cent of young people are still living at home (Kiernan, 1985). Both the space per individual and that communally at the disposal of the household have grown measurably. The 'dramatic reduction' in over-crowding that has taken place since the 1950s flows, firstly, from the decline in the size of the family unit and secondly, from substantive improvements in the quality of housing stock (Brown and Green, 1986). By way of illustration, the attractiveness of the home as a site for leisure activity and relaxation has been enormously enhanced by the spread of central heating, which although now the norm was as recently as 1976 the exception (OPCS, 1986a). This not merely adds to the comfort of the home, but also increases the potential utilisation of the available space throughout the year. In turn this encourages investment in additional consumer durables for home leisure activity, such as the video and home computer, the availability of which has grown rapidly during the last decade. As a consequence young people have increasingly acquired a pattern of home-based leisure habits, hobbies and pursuits that embody a self-evident uniformity to that of their parents (DES, 1983b; Ashton & Maguire, 1987). Inevitably the attitudes of young people have been influenced by the process Pahl (1984) dubs 'home provisioning'. As the physical conditions improve within it, not least in relation to its ability to offer resources for leisure, relaxation and learning, so the home becomes a more attractive venue. Equally as the centrality of the home as a site for leisure grows so the need to 'improve', maintain and service it expands in the form of 'do-it-yourself' and other activities, the skills for this being largely learnt within the home.

'Home provisioning' means the demotion of the youth club, to the extent that it has overwhelmingly lost the historic role Evans envisaged for it in this not untypical quotation:

> Few young people have enough room or privacy in their own homes 'away from the kids', to make it possible to invite their friends in . . . and the youth centre should provide a place where warmth and gaiety are to be found, where they can meet their friends and enjoy their company . . . Many examples come to mind: the influence of the attractive young wife and that of her husband on a group of young people who accepted an invitation to her home one evening to drink coffee: the way the young people were received, the furnishing and arrangement of the house, the evening meal already laid, and the preparation of her young family for bed made a deep and valuable impact on the young visitors. (1965, p. 169)

No longer does the youth centre or club serve, except for a diminishing number, as a retreat from an overcrowded home, even as a haven of peace and quiet, let alone a pre-eminent point of reference for access to leisure activities that writers such as Evans (ibid.) and Morse (1965) imagined that it would. However, unlike the adult equivalent, the pub, it has only the most limited capacity to transform itself. Whereas the latter can translate itself into an all-age unit, the youth centre is by definition to a far greater degree trapped within its age-related function. Consequently it is likely to possess only the most tenuous hold on the future unless it can be transformed into wider-age units. Specialist youth provision may be offered within such a setting but this is unlikely to compromise more than a facet of the overall programme.

As a partial consequence of the increased requirements and expectations centred upon the family it has, as an institution, exhibited a growing tendency to wilt under the pressure. Divorce and separation rates offer a crude indicator of this. What this means for young people is that between one in five and one in six will now see their parents divorce before they reach the age of 16 and that only 71 per cent of 16- to 18-year-olds now reside with two natural parents (Roll, 1988, p. 18). In addition to this cognisance must be taken of a further trend. During the 1950s four per cent of births were to parents who were not married. By the mid-1980s this had risen to 21 per cent, although over 60 per cent of these births were registered to couples living at the same address. Among these aged under 20 there are now more illegitimate than legitimate births. However the gap between the rates for younger and older women is narrowing.

The 'broken' or single-parent home has long been taken, in the commonsense world of welfare practice, as an indicator of a propensity towards maladjustment, delinquency or anti-social behaviour on the part of young people. As Morgan states, 'there is now a substantial literature suggesting that delinquents are more likely to come from homes where the father is absent' (1986, p. 46). Widely accepted research has, for example, linked marital disruption to offending (Wadsworth, 1979), low educational achievement and disruptive behaviour. Youth work is in no way isolated from this form of deductionalism as our later discussion of the 'underclass' indicates (see Chapter 7). The problem with this analysis is that the evidence to sustain is less than convincing and needs to be set beside research indicating an alternative outcome. Riley and Shaw (1985), for example, found the prevalence of delinquency to be no higher among young people from single-parent households. Gladstone (1979) came to remarkably similar conclusions in relation to vandalism. The obsession with linking character deficiency and inadequate socialisation to the experiencing of a single-parent home life has for far too long served as a smokescreen, obscuring the serious problem of poverty among this group.

Evidence in this direction is unambiguous. Firstly, poverty and, to a lesser degree, unemployment fuel the probability that divorce or separation will take place (Thornes and Collard, 1979; Haskey, 1984; Maclean and Eekelaar, 1986). Secondly, divorce, separation or the birth of child to a single parent all dramatically increase the probability that a young person will experience poverty and disadvantage (Millar, 1987). The legal, tax and income maintenance systems combine with discrimination in the labour market against women, who constitute over 90 per cent of heads of single-parent households, to ensure that the young people and their carers are far more likely than is the norm to experience 'serious economic difficulties' (Maclean and Eekelaar, 1986, p. 54). Although the proportion in employment differs markedly between male- and female-headed single-parent families, 57 against 37 per cent (CSO, 1988a), with one-half in part-time work (Haskey, 1986b), the key indicator of poverty is the dependence on state benefits. Only 39 per cent cited earnings as the prime source of income, compared to 92 per cent of two-adult families (FPSC, 1987, p. 5). As a consequence young people from such families figure disproportionately among those experiencing unemployment (Bradshaw *et al.*, 1987), are less likely to remain in education beyond the school-leaving age (Cooke, 1986), more likely to stay in the family home for a longer period and when they do leave it to experience homelessness (Children's Society, 1987).

Overall, young people are staying in the parental home longer. The median age for leaving home having begun to rise during the 1980s, in 1984 it was 21·9 for men and 20 for women (Jones, 1987). As already noted, the reasons for this are highly variable and this should not be interpreted solely as a negative by-product of youth unemployment. Running counter to this trend there has occurred an apparent increase in homelessness among young people. Again no single cause can be isolated. It should be noted that the re-partnering of single parents, as well as divorce itself, may well have encouraged an apparent growth in the number of young people leaving home earlier. In this context it is important to note that a fifth of all dependent children involved in divorce proceedings are of secondary school age (Haskey, 1986a). The figures for those aged over 16 but living at home are not available but some indication that the number will be substantial can be gained from the data which show that almost a third of divorces involve women aged 35 to 49 (ibid.). Certainly the government's own research, *Single and Homeless*, found that 'very high proportions of the under 20s . . . had left because of family break-up (excluding parental dispute) . . . The under-20s and the 20-year-olds were also the most likely to have left because of parental dispute' (Department of Environment, 1981, p. 17). This may go some way towards explaining the paradox of heightened levels of homelessness existing alongside a greater propensity to remain in the parental home among the majority.

The changes in the structure of families outlined above will have a growing impact upon youth work. Many of the traditional assumptions within youth work practice will have to be reassessed. In particular, the poverty experienced by single-parent families, rather than bringing forth vague and often pious moralising regarding their status, should lead to mounting concern in youth work circles over rising levels of divorce. Solutions should be sought not in homilies about the value of the family *per se* but in the practical round of ensuring that sufficient financial and social support is available in order to minimise the long-term disadvantages currently experienced by far too many young people.

Mobility, regionalism and young people

The movement of young people between regions is hardly a recent phenomenon. During the early years of industrialisation, the expansion of new and existing towns and industries was sustained by an influx from rural areas. In this period a far higher proportion of young people lived away from their parental home than is currently the case (see, for example, Gillis, 1974). Concerns regarding the moral welfare and social condition of these youthful immigrants was a pre-eminent motivation for the establishment of early youth clubs and movements such as the YMCA and the YWCA. Inevitably, over time, the rural reservoirs 'were drained of their younger people, natural increases declined, especially due to falling births' (Lawton, 1977, p. 33). The haemorrhaging of the rural population, which is still the subject of concerned discussion, has a long history. Migration and population movement then, as now, disproportionately involved the young; with 'the category 15–24 by far the most mobile age group, with migration rates 35 per cent above the next most mobile group (25–34 years)' (ibid., p. 64). The direction, volume and composition of the movement, however, are in no way fixed.

The rapidity with which the direction changes can be disconcerting. During the early part of this century the growth and prosperity of coal-mining and heavy industry acted as a magnet, enticing young immigrants into areas such as the North-East and South Wales. Two decades later the collapse of the same industries reversed the direction, young people, including the sons and daughters of those erstwhile immigrants, now being encouraged, via government grants and schemes run by youth organisations, to relocate in the South-East and Midlands, where the new manufacturing and service jobs were to be found. As Williams notes of Wales, years of growth and expansion ended and within two decades half a million had departed, leaving a 'pall of neglect and depression, a collapse of social capital and a dismal legacy in bad housing, ill-health, poor environment. Whole areas of Wales became and have remained problem areas' (1985, p. 253). It was the young who left in search of work, dignity and independence, their loss compensated for only in part by an influx of 'largely elderly, often retired, *rentiers*, an overspill from an affluent elsewhere' (ibid.) heading for the coast and rural tranquility. Such movements continue, although to an extent subsequent regional policies, income maintenance programmes and the social wage of welfare have prevented a re-enactment on that scale and compressed into that period of time. Further, as noted in the previous chapter, wide variables in the cost of living between regions, particularly those relating to housing and accommodation, curtail or prevent the movement of young people. The agony of decline is now prolonged for the 'sub-standard and lop-sided regions', with the elongation of the time-scale.

The volume, dictated largely by the state of the economy and the consequent demand for labour, is likely to be as variable as the direction. In periods of upturn and growth the movement of young people is encouraged by employers offering the lure of high wages, training or cheap housing and accommodation. For it is generally held that 'the transformation and modernisation of the economy is difficult without young people' (Baker, 1986, p. 435). More recently, against the backcloth of a depressed economy, with unprecedented levels of youth unemployment occurring nationally, rather than regionally as was the case during the interwar years, the government has taken deliberate steps to impede the movement of young people. Board and lodging regulations, which specifically curtailed the period of time allowances could be claimed by those aged under 26, unambiguously sought to prevent the movement of young people in search of work and independence (Matthews, 1986; Malpass, 1985; Davies, 1986). Income support, similarly, was adjusted, by reducing the rate for those aged under 26, the better to tie those without an independent income to the parental home (see Chapter 7). As the Report of the Social Security Advisory Committee commented, 'differential benefit rates for these young adults will make it difficult for young men and women to leave home' (Social Security Advisory Committee, 1988, p. 10). Youth work interventions have also sought, in contrast to the *modus operandi* previously adopted in periods of youth unemployment, to discourage the movement of young people. Strenuous efforts have been made to highlight the disadvantages, dangers and costs of heading south in search of employment. In the South-East advice and detached workers often concentrated on helping the new arrivals to return 'home' rather than settle in.

Externally the door was shut ever tighter by the government in order to curtail the immigration which had been so attractive in the years of labour shortage, when young workers, cost-effectively, arrived with the expenses of childhood ready met. The rapid falling away in the numbers of young people is beginning to change that scenario. The EEC decision to allow the free movement of labour between member states after 1992 is clearly designed to encourage young labour to move to where the demand is greatest and enable the growth areas to draw more easily upon the surplus in the periphery – Eire, Portugal, Greece and the impoverished outer regions of the United Kingdom. Also the next generation of external feeder states are being identified, and the problems of importation addressed with the wisdom of hindsight. Now it appears that the cheap labour is likely to come from Africa rather than Asia and the Caribbean (EEC, 1986).

Variations in the composition of mobile labour also need to be noted. In the nineteenth century young women were more mobile than men, a factor relating to their pattern of employment, especially service (Lawton, 1977). Divergence in relation to gender now appears to be insignificant, although the growth in service employment may reassert it. Other characteristics remain marked. Kiernan (1977) in her longitudinal study found that 23 per cent of people aged 17 to 26 had moved between regions. Among these the higher the educational qualifications the greater the propensity to move. In particular it was young women who had left school with the minimum who were the least mobile. A correlation also emerged in relation to social class, with working-class young people still in the main leaving the parental home to get married or move in with other relatives, rather than for reasons linked to employment or education. Those from professional and middle-class backgrounds were far more likely to leave in pursuit of post-school education or work. According to Jones (1987) of the 60 per cent of males and around 50 per cent of females who do leave home for reasons other than marriage, around one-half return.

Like the canary in a coal mine, the movement of young people from a locality or region provides a clear indication that all is not well. As the most flexible and volatile section of the labour force, they, as do immigrants from overseas, move to and seek out, with unerring accuracy, the epicentres of growth and prosperity. Indeed the long-term economic decline of certain areas can be illustrated by the absence of people from ethnic minorities in given localities. Whereas immigrants from Europe, the Irish Republic and elsewhere moved to Central Scotland, South Wales and the North-East 80 years ago, those who have arrived since 1950 overwhelmingly avoided those regions. The distribution of ethnic minority groups graphically reflects the economic vibrance of a locality at a given time. But, as already noted, prosperity is a will-o'-the-wisp. As large numbers of black young people have learnt, many of the localities to which their parents moved, such as West and South Yorkshire and the West Midlands, have subsequently experienced disproportionately high levels of job loss. This forced many, within the space of a generation, to move on in order to secure employment. Where this does occur the movement has a cumulative impact upon the population profile of a given region or locality. As with the rural–urban movement, where the trend continues for any length of time the new arrivals provide the basis for the generation of further age imbalance. For their presence raises the birth rate in that locality, as surely as their absence depresses it in the areas they vacated. The impact of this movement is reflected in the wide variations between regions in relation to the decline in the number of 16- to 24-year-olds in the labour force (Figure 2.2).

Inter-regional movements hide many localised ones. Young people do not merely move between regions and nation states in search of employment, housing, education and independence; they also decamp from adjacent neighbourhood to neighbourhood, city centres to new suburbs. According to Kiernan (1977), 24 per cent move within their county, but outside their local authority. The result is, in many ways, a miniaturisation of the inter-regional shifts. As Wallace (1987) showed in her study of one small area of the South-East, those young people who succeed in the jobs market tend to rapidly put physical distance between themselves and those who fail, by moving out to better housing and 'locations'.

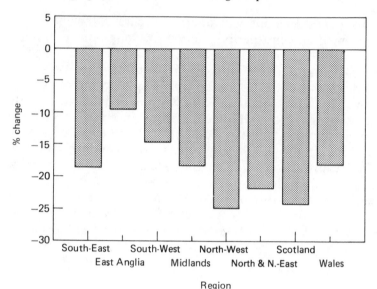

Source: Figures extracted from National Economic Development Office/Training Commission (1988) table 3.2.

Figure 2.2   *Regional changes in the number of 16- to 24-year-olds in the labour force, 1987–95*

Also, just as regions and cities, such as Newcastle and Sheffield, are 'greying' as a result of the outflow of young people, so are many of the 'new towns' and suburbs of the 1950s and early 1960s. In urban settings it is the most densely populated wards that have experienced the sharpest falls in population during the last decade as young people, young families and many of the better-off elderly have fled to the suburbs or in the case of the latter to the coast (Craig, 1986). As a consequence, Britain is becoming more ghettoised, not merely in relation to the physical separation of the rich from the poor, the employed from the unemployed, but also in terms of age. It is a process that has been under way longer in the United States than in the United Kingdom, but the results have been much the same, for, 'as city neighbourhoods have become more differentiated by price, and desirability, there is evidence that the elderly have become increasingly segregated from other age groups' (Fitzpatrick and Logan, 1985, p. 107). Fewer and fewer young people now, during the course of the daily round, interact with the elderly. Grandparents, for example, become people a car journey away or visitors who inconveniently take over your bedroom, not near neighbours to call in on. As speculative developers begin more energetically to exploit the Golconda of elderly property-owners with the lure of purpose-built specialist retirement villages, homes and developments, and variable house prices entice others to relocate to the coast or countryside and 'pocket the difference'; as house design becomes ever more age-orientated – the family dwelling, the singles development, the retirement home, the sheltered unit – so the physical estrangement of young from old gathers pace. And with that physical segregation comes, in its wake, the social and intellectual isolation of age groups breeding tensions, indifference and intolerance.

Discussion of the inequalities between regions must, from the onset, acknowledge that islands of prosperity exist in the relatively deprived areas and pockets of acute deprivation occur in the areas of prosperity. Things are never as clear-cut as the rhetoric of the North–South divide might lead us to believe. A judiciously organised tour of the North centring on Harrogate or Kendal, a carefully managed holiday in the North of Ireland operating out of Ballymena or Hillsborough, could leave a myopic tourist puzzled as to why anyone in those regions bemoans their lot. Similar deceptions could be wrought upon the unwary in the affluent South. To quote one young person living in the inner-city area of Southampton, with 25 per cent unemployment on their door-step, 'They've always thought we are all rich down here . . . the problem of course is that it's always been the same – the wealth is in the South, but that doesn't fucking do anything for me' (Irving and Whitmore, 1987, p. 13). Also, whether the region is prosperous or deprived, young people living in rural areas with deficient public transport are likely to be seriously disadvantaged in terms of access to leisure employment opportunities (McNabb *et al.*, 1979; Akehurst, 1983; Kennedy, 1984; Nicholson, 1985; Coles, 1986). Allowing for all the foregoing caveats, the evidence reveals the North–South divide to be more than a journalistic device and it is one which is getting wider. For example, in the ranking of 280 towns and cities on the basis of general prosperity and the rate at which each is improving or declining, the 35 highest scoring were all in the southern half of the country (Champion & Green, 1988). Similarly the divide can be illustrated with reference to housing conditions, earnings, ownership of consumer durables, levels of educational achievement and staying on beyond the statutory leaving age or share-ownership (for a summary see Winyard, 1987). In relation to the life chances of young people it is most graphically encapsulated in the contrasting rates of unemployment.

These variations, which have remained remarkably constant, reflecting long-term trends, have accelerated in recent years. In Great Britain employment fell between 1979 and 1983 by over two million, but losses in the North (North and North-West England, Yorkshire, Humberside, Wales and Scotland) were at twice the national rate. Subsequent growth has been concentrated almost entirely in the South-East (MacInnes, 1988). These regional disparities are not merely an historical anachronism that will be swept aside by progress. Rather they reflect a

> relocation of power with the removal from some regions, and the concentration in others, of the more powerful, conceptual and strategic levels of control over production . . . the organisation of production and the organisation of space go hand in hand. Particular forms of geographical inequality have as a necessary condition particular forms of organisation of production. (Massey, 1984, p. 112)

The old ruling classes have largely deserted the peripheral regions except for leisure purposes, or been supplemented by the new multinationals (Nairn, 1981). In the British context this has meant that:

> Relations of production are increasingly centralised in the south and east of the country. There is a growing geographical, as well as social division between conception and execution. The continuing elements of sectorial differentiation only serve to reinforce this dichotomy. The growth of the new 'hi-tech' industries – biotechnology is a prime example – is largely in the already

favoured areas. This is the new spatial division of labour, and it brings with it a new north–south divide. This time between the 'sunbelt' and the rest, where the 'rest' consists of relatively decentralised employment and great pools of unemployment where production used to be. (Massey, 1984, p. 296)

Monitoring the well-being of seals and birds of prey at the end of a particular food chain is a recognised litmus test for the effects of environmental pollution. Likewise young people – their poverty, their levels of unemployment, their rates of homelessness, and their patterns of mobility – provide a key indicator of the economic and social health of a region or locality. It might be said that they reside at the end of the employment and poverty chain. Where you grow up, as much as anything else, increasingly determines whether or not, for example, you will do so in a home blighted by unemployment; '80 per cent of young people in Chelmsford (aged 17 and 18) live with two parents (including step-parents) where the father is in employment, but the proportion is 61 per cent in Walsall and only 51 per cent in Liverpool' (Roll, 1988, p. 18). Individual characteristics play a part in determining who does and who does not secure work: 'being the right colour and choosing your parents and where you live very carefully may help. It also helps if you do not suffer from physical or mental disability, do not have a police record or are the appropriate gender' (Allen and Waton, 1986, p. 9) and in Northern Ireland having the right religion counts. Without devaluing the significance of those factors it needs to be stressed that the impact of all these upon the life chances of the individual are transmitted through a filter of regional differences.

The cultural and social impact of the locality have consistently influenced aspects of youth work practice; indeed it would be impossible to ignore them. Comparisons between Adams's (1982) account of growing up in Catholic Belfast and Jenkins's (1983a, 1983b) of the experiences of young people in a Protestant heartland forcefully illustrate the significance of locality. Similarly Coffield *et al.* (1986) highlighted the impact of regional decline. The question remains unanswered as to whether the continued 'internationalization of the British economy' (Nairn, 1981, p. 382) and the consequent 'general class and territorial disequilibrium of UK state' (ibid., p. 387), which has been under way since the turn of the century, will generate compensatory nationalism and regionalism. Will the economic disparities and divisions become translated into ever sharper and disparate regional differences, generating in Scotland and Wales among young people cultural and political nationalism, and in the English periphery a sullen loathing of all things metropolitan? The answer is not readily to hand, but it is hardly feasible to imagine that the current trends can continue without engendering just such reactions, so that the longer the economic and social divisions are expressed in spatial and regional dimensions, so these will come to acquire sharper cultural and social forms.

This can have a positive impact upon youth work practice. The myth of there being some common or universal mass practice has for too long obstructed the creative exploitation of regional and local differences. Different traditions of practice, diverse cultures and languages, and the experience of divergent material and environmental conditions provide both the possibility and the necessity for alternative visions of practice (Smith, 1988). Regionalism, locality and nationalism are not simple backcloths providing local colour to practice. They cannot be wished away, nor should they be. Within the lexicon of youth work, nationalism has predominantly been equated with reaction and racism. However this betrays a crude metropolitanism and ethnocentrism, one that denies the radical, reforming and internationalist strands within the resurgent nationalism that has evolved in Wales, Scotland and Ireland (Adams, 1986; Nairn, 1981; Williams, 1985). These strands, combined with the relative political and cultural autonomy demanded by the ideology of nationalism, have found their way into youth work practice. Such oppositional and 'peripheral' practice has flourished in certain areas, yet has remained unseen and unsung within a 'mainstream' discourse dominated by the priorities, interests and needs of an increasingly centralised state and metropolis-orientated bourgeoisie. Youth work is overcast by parochialism, not the much despised parochialism of the parish pump and Celtic fringe, but the parochialism of the centre.

Conclusion: demographic change and the youth service

As we have already argued elsewhere (Jeffs & Smith, 1988), the Youth Service faces an uncertain future. With the development of parallel forms of welfare provision, shifts in welfare ideology, and the expansion and differentiation of commercial leisure, there are serious questions as to what its distinctive and substantive contribution may be. This chapter has given us the opportunity to assess at greater length another element within the equation. The demographic trends outlined here will have a profound impact on the Youth Service and youth work.

Class (see Chapter 7), and here regionalism and nationalism, we argue, must serve as organising ideas to underpin practice. Not unexpectedly, these have been meticulously avoided, where possible, by those agencies responsible for agenda setting, training and policy formulation. Neither resides comfortably in the liberal framework. Further, age, which has served for so long as a unifying feature and justification for intervention, is losing much of its historical and self-evident significance. There are deep questions concerning the very notions of adolescence and youth, and the degree to which such ideas will continue to have any unique meaning in the experiences of those at which youth work has been aimed. It may be that Youth Services, youth organisations and practitioners can avoid addressing such fundamental questions in the short term. After all, they have, overwhelmingly, managed to by-pass sustained attention to questions of purpose, identity and theory for many decades. With fingers crossed, another moral panic or 'needy group' will be delivered ready, warmed and watered. Failure to deal with, or address, the structural issues beneath one moral panic, or the needs of the group temporarily in the spotlight, are brushed from the memory by the exhilarating arrival of their replacements. So the roller-coaster sustains momentum. The problem with demographic change is that it is like coastal erosion. Its movements often remain unnoticed, but then there is the realisation of dramatic change: the cliff collapses, the inland floods, peninsulas become islands. It may well be that local and national youth services will come to resemble so many of the Cinque Ports. The sea deserted their harbours, and the ships outgrew their facilities. Yet their courts and ceremonials continue, quaint reminders of purposes lost and roles transferred.

3

Youth Work and Gender

JEAN SPENCE

It has taken a decade and more of determined effort to establish the comprehensive validity of gender questions within youth work. Practice and analysis which initially emerged as a feminist-inspired response to the lack of involvement of girls in the Youth Service have grown into a movement which asserts that the issue of sexism affects both female and male managers, workers and young people. Moreover, it has become apparent that gender questions cannot be fully addressed unless they become part of an integrated curriculum which also deals with other structural inequalities, such as those discussed elsewhere in this book.

While it is apparent that, in general, the Youth Service has conspicuously failed to adopt such a curriculum, some uneven but recognisable gains have been won, most particularly within girls' work. Indeed girls' work is mentioned as significant in the *Thompson Report* (HMSO, 1982). More recently it has become an object of inquiry for the National Advisory Council for the Youth Service (NACYS), who, during 1987, set up a sub-committee on Youth Work with Girls and Young Women. This was 'to consider "the adequacy and appropriateness" of Youth Service provision for girls and young women' (NACYS, 1988b). The committee's report was published in 1989 (NACYS, 1989b). This formal, national response reflects the impact and success of the face to face work undertaken with girls and young women. However these gains should not give rise to complacency. They are neither adequate in terms of what a fully gender-conscious approach requires, nor are they necessarily permanent. The sudden closure of National Association of Youth Clubs (NAYC) Girl's Work Unit in 1987 (WWG Newsletter, 1987) illustrates the unevenness of progress and the potential impermanence of any gain. The implementation of the notorious 'Clause 28' of the Local Government Act which seeks to prevent the 'promotion' of homosexuality (Kent-Baguley, 1988) demonstrates the very real boundaries which deny the full expression of anti-sexist youth work.

If the more recent, sustained work with young women and girls is to bear fruit, it is important that gains be identified, acknowledged and analysed. If anti-sexist work is to progress, it is important that boundaries and barriers are seen as legitimate targets for struggle, and strategies be devised to effect this struggle. In order to complete this task, the relationship between girls' work and a gender-conscious or anti-sexist practice must be understood within the context and objectives of the Youth Service in general.

Leisure and the masculine connotations of youth work

From its inception the Youth Service has operated within the contradictory concerns to control and elighten. Its controlling function is predicated upon an understanding that any time which is not appropriated by the socialising institutions of home, school and work is time beset with danger for the individual young person and for society. This view is informed largely by the visible behaviour of young working-class male peer groups. The enlightening function of the service is dependent upon the assumption that the learning achieved at home, school and work is insufficient for a satisfactory progression to maturity and that other institutions do not necessarily provide an environment wherein young people can realise their full potential. This understanding is limited in gender terms by what is perceived to be the full potential of masculinity and of femininity.

For working-class young men and women, any time not dedicated to formal education and work is limited primarily by its relationship to the family. The conventional patriarchal family intervenes in the leisure time of its members in forms of gender–role expectations (Smith, 1968; Parker 1974; Hemmings, 1982). In consequence, it intrudes upon the freedom of young women more than that of young men, encouraging in or demanding of females that they participate more fully in its activities and duties in anticipation of their expected adult role. Education, work and self-defined leisure are commonly understood as secondary concerns for young women. Such expectations do not apply to young men whose adult roles are perceived as supportive of the family from without, rather than from within. Thus it is often the case that, while for young men leisure time is more fully their own, young women find their time constricted by family demands and responsibilities.

Family-defined limitations continue to exert authority over the activities of young women outside the home environment. Whatever the reality of female lives, it is conventionally assumed that women's role is focussed around husband, home and family. The achievement of adulthood for girls is associated with this condition. In accepting this definition of themselves, it is essential that young women project and emphasise their feminine sexuality in order to attract a suitable male partner. Yet the projection of feminine heterosexuality is fraught with sexual danger if it is unsupervised (Hudson, 1983). Thus when young women go out they are often expected to return home at a given hour, to indulge only in acceptable 'feminine' behaviour and to spend the time at an approved venue, in approved company. Conversely, if the leisure time of young men is unregulated, it poses problems which are mainly of public concern. Young men are not generally presumed to be in heterosexual danger from the street, but the community senses a danger to itself from groups of young men whose visibility and unrestrained behaviour, if not actually criminal, implies the possibility of criminality.

For boys, the achievement of adulthood implies the rewards of the control, power and superiority of masculinity (Parker, 1974; Taylor, 1984). This is most obviously achieved at a practical level through the world of work. Yet even when paid work is absent, the ideological connotations of masculinity persist. Whilst some young men might experience withdrawal and confusion and some might question the validity of masculinity in the face of unemployment, there are others whose response is to seek other expressions of masculine power. As many youth workers will confirm, masculinity is sometimes emphasised and exaggerated more aggressively when removed from the restraints which are imposed via the work situation. Such young men tend to socialise in loosely-knit but sometimes very large peer groups which act both as a challenge to their members to sustain their dominant masculine image, and as a self-fulfilling confirmation of the power of masculinity. Indeed they continue with, and tend to acquire, behaviour and survival tactics initially developed in opposition to the control of school (Corrigan, 1979; Willis, 1977).

It is such aggressive males and working-class social groupings which so often attract the attention of youth workers and a concerned public. It is towards such groups that much of the social control aspect of youth work is directed and it is in relation to such groups that most ideas about youth in general and the nature of working-class youth subcultures in particular have been developed (McRobbie and Garber, 1976; McRobbie, 1980).

As a general concept, youth is defined primarily in terms of its differences from childhood and adulthood. While this approach is of some value in indicating the broad issues of relevance to young people's lives (Mungham & Pearson, 1976) and often encourages a sympathetic and understanding approach by workers, it does nothing which enables policy makers and workers to respond to other conditions which cut across the age category. Structural divisions of class, race, disability, gender and sexuality tend to be subsumed and are uncritically accepted as 'given' in 'youth-in-general' approaches.

Youth work practice which focuses myopically upon the age experience deals typically with the masculine rather than the feminine experience of youth. For young men, youth implies a freedom from the restraints and dependence of childhood without the burden of the responsibilities of manhood. It is a time to explore the possibilities of male power, control and domination, to challenge authority, to test how much of the world they can claim as their own and to indulge in sexual experiment. For young women, the situation is entirely different. Adolescent femininity involves, not a freedom from the restraints of childhood, but acceptance of 'the apparent inevitability of subordination' (Nava, 1984). It involves additional restraints consequent upon feminine heterosexuality (Lees, 1986) and further responsibilities for family and personal life (Marshall & Borrill, 1984). It involves a transference of dependence from the parental family towards young men and a limitation upon the possibilities of them exploring their own sexuality, pleasures and interests (Barker & Allen, 1976).

Age-related analyses premised upon a universal and essential idea of 'youth' reinforce masculinity as the reference point for intervention and detract from a complete understanding of the way in which important issues affect young women differently from young men. In this way, the *Thompson Report*, for instance, can say in relation to unemployment: 'Throughout his or her conscious life, work will have been held up as the essential badge of adulthood. It stands for the end of dependence and the beginnings of real possibility and freedom' (HMSO, 1982). This statement completely ignores the relationship between female adult life and the family. It fails to observe the dependence and lack of freedom inherent in the adoption of a feminine identity. It fails to recognise that, for many young women, it is marriage and, in particular, motherhood which signifies inclusion in the world of adult women. Consequently, although the Report carefully includes the female pronoun, it misses the real significance of unemployment for young women. An analysis which integrated gender difference would not fail to notice that the lack of employment possibilities for young women tightens the grip of femininity upon them. While the opportunity of paid employment intervenes in the continuous progression from dependent childhood to dependent adulthood within the family and provides some small chance of subverting this progression, its absence propels some young women even more quickly towards the inevitability of marriage and/or motherhood. In not recognising this, the Youth Service fails to provide facilities which might counter the lure of the heterosexual relationship as the only acceptable leisure pursuit for young women and as the only appropriate avenue to adulthood. It also renders young mothers and young lesbians invisible and excludes them from its frame of reference. Thus even youth work practice which goes beyond the recreational approach, which is politically motivated in relation to issues which affect young people, and which sees itself as challenging, radical practice, is limited in relation to the young women. Any positive gains achieved by such work will be primarily gains for young men. Young women enjoy the consequences largely as an accidental by-product.

For young women, the period of youth is often experienced as one of restriction and repression. The successful achievement of femininity depends upon the sublimation of personal needs and interests and upon the acceptance of attitudes, values and interests which conform to the traditional female role (Lees, 1986). This is relative to the male role. Their desire and the pressure upon them to attract a suitable male partner leads many young women into a situation where they drop any personal interests and underplay any skills they might have in favour of interests associated with the projection of feminine heterosexuality.

> You get status when you go out with a boy – and girls are made to feel there's something wrong with them if they are not. When all my girlfriends go out for an evening together, everyone gets a bit depressed if they don't meet any boys. Somehow they feel it's not very exciting and only light up when they are flirting and getting the attention of men . . . (Hemmings, 1982)

The result of this emphasis upon the needs of those other than yourself is that young women tend to underachieve in education and employment (Byrne, 1978; Deem, 1978; Spender, 1982). They restrict their ability to participate fully in strenuous activity, conforming to the dictates of dress, style and feminine image, and they prioritise friendships with young men rather than with their female peers. In the search for a male partner, young women compete with each other and thus fail to develop a strong female group identity. Instead, they tend to socialise in 'best-friend' pairs. Larger groupings are often temporary, unstable and easily fragmented.

It is apparent that young women do not generally have a threatening public image, nor do they present a public problem of control in their leisure time (Hudson, 1983). Their relationship with youth work agencies is, therefore, less obviously immediate and pressing. It is often the case that youth workers, who do not perceive the underlying focus structuring the behaviour of the sexes, react to the superficial situation, interpreting the needs of young women only as secondary and in relation to those of young men.

The public image of youth work, whatever arguments to the contrary may claim, is predominantly that of 'keeping the kids off the street'. Failure to perform this controlling function involves a loss of credibility and by extension a possible loss of resources. The pressure to co-opt and control in relation to young men has led to the adoption of methods of work and activities which will prove attractive to them. These are primarily recreational in character and reinforce the masculine equation that leisure equals recreation.

This equation has dominated the approach of male youth workers more than that of females. It provides a convenient context for the participation of large numbers of young people under the supervision of the minimum number of workers. It panders to the masculine ego of the male worker, creating an environment wherein he can develop relationships with young men without undermining the 'leadership' role of the worker and without implicating him in a deeper emotional commitment for which masculinity is ill-fitted (Taylor, 1984). At the same time, such activity is concrete, visible and apparently politically neutral. Its results for young people can be measured in terms of cups, medals and the acquisition of physical prowess. Recreational, activities-based youth work is thus inherently biased towards a particular stereotyped conception of masculinity and is a self-fulfilling system for the colonisation of the space, time, energy and resources of youth work (Graydon,

1983; Van Dyke, 1984a, 1984b, Leaman, 1984). This is not to say that recreational work should not be a feature of youth work. It is rather to assert that, as presently constructed, such work fails to account for the social situation of girls.

Youth workers have intermittently noted the failure of girls to participate in the recreational aspect of mixed youth work (Working with Girls Newsletter, 12, 1982, pp. 4–11; Smith, N., 1984) but traditionally the tendency has been to respond by introducing special activities for girls which reinforce their familial and sexual roles. Hence the catalogue of cookery, sewing, craftwork, make-up, hairdressing, beauty and hygiene sessions, with the occasional foray into netball and dance. Most of these activities are not truly recreational in that they are directed towards relationships and to women's role in the family. Again, this is not to say that such activities are illegitimate or that young women and female youth workers should not demand the opportunity to develop their skill in these areas. However to encourage such pastimes for girls in a way which does not raise issues about their connection with the repressive aspects of femininity is simply to reinforce gender stereotypes. Moreover the introduction of female-defined activities in a mixed environment is always subject to masculine domination of space and resources and to problems of controlling the boys:

> . . . we used to come to the club on Tuesdays when it was mixed, boys and girls. It was chaos, pure chaos. The boys rushed around all over the place. They jump over the counter into the kitchen. When you tell them to stop, they say no, you don't own the club. They push and hit you. They think they own the gym – kicking footballs around all night, you just can't go in there unless you want to play too, and then they call you a tomboy. (quoted in Hemmings, 1982)

Despite the rhetoric of 'social education' which represents the higher ideals of enlightenment within youth work, practice remains severely restricted by the necessity of controlling young people, particularly young males, who use mixed facilities. A positive, coherent programme of education which might challenge gender and sex stereotypes is extremely difficult to achieve in the conditions under which most youth workers operate. There is an inevitable tension between theories of education and the practicalities of working in an under-resourced, leisure-based service. This leads many agencies to proceed at the level of the lowest common denominator, whereby all structured activity and every intervention by the adult youth worker is justified in loose educational terms. In this, the tried and true tradition-al methods of control through the organisation of recreation-al activity continue to predominate.

The very fact that the facilities of the Youth Service are offered as a public resource open to all young people relates to the masculine claim to public space which mitigates against the full participation of weaker groups. Clubs, coffee bars and drop-in projects are continuously subject to take-over by able-bodied, local male groups and unless the energies of such young men are controlled and directed, the job of the worker can degenerate into that of merely policing and protecting a building. When young women and girls do use Youth Service buildings, they are forced to seek out their own 'safe' spaces. They are thus often found behind coffee bars or congregating around the female lavatories. Because they participate in fewer numbers and in smaller groups, they are less visible and pose much less of a problem of control for the workers. Occasionally there is an eruption of 'trouble' among them and sometimes they are implicated in disturbances involving the boys. However there is virtually always more immediate pressure to contain the male partici-pants.

The most obvious effect of this is that a majority of worker time is spent with young men (Smith, N., 1984). The often poor ratio of workers to young people, and the difficulties of controlling space in Youth Service buildings, leaves little time available for small group work or for those young people – usually girls – who are not inclined to disruption. Allowing a worker to spend a concentrated period of time chatting 'casually' to one or two girls behind a coffee bar is not usually understood as effective use of that time. Workers who adopt such low-key methods are often the object of criticism from others who feel that they are not 'pulling their weight'. Such workers can lay no claim on funds and make no contribution to public relations. Work with individuals or small numbers is only recognised if it is dealing with a 'crisis', helping a young person solve a problem, or explicitly organised around discussion of a particular theme. Some young women key into the 'welfare' and 'counselling' orientation of the work as the only means available to elicit the attention of workers and yet, in so doing, help confirm the notion of female as problem. If any more creative and positive work is to be accomplished with young women, as single-sex work with them has illustrated, it is essential that some workers be freed from responsibilities for control and organisation of activities.

A second, and less obvious, effect relates to some of the controlling methods used. Feminist workers have occasionally described experiences of working in mixed situations wherein they have perceived their own methods to be overwhelmed by those of their male colleagues (Hamilton, 1981). The stereotypical case, which nevertheless contains some truth, is that of the male worker who relies on the authority of a strong, loud voice backed up by physical strength. Such male workers often presume the incompetence of women who are ill-at-ease with physical power. These men fail to recognise the value of more subtle and diversionary tactics in relation to questions of control. In this way, many male workers who are wedded to masculine methods tend to mistrust and underestimate the abilities of their female counterparts. They take upon their own shoulders the weight of responsibility for organisation and control while at the same time resenting the unequal distribution of labour which this seems to involve. This sometimes leads to tension and conflict in gender relations between workers, in which the argument of female workers, who are forced into a defensive position, can rarely prevail.

A third effect of the need to attract, control and direct young men has far-reaching consequences in limiting the possibility for youth work practice to develop beyond the theme of recreation in mixed settings. Activity organised as a reaction to problems of control fails to question social control as an issue, or to investigate why it is young men who seem to need such control. At the same time, it tends to promote those qualities of masculinity which make young men, in particular, a social threat in the first place.

To question why some young people are perceived as in need of control would involve criticism of their social situation, raising issues of social inequality, and implies a political challenge. Most workers are very wary of biting the hand that feeds them. To ask why young men often indulge in disruptive behaviour in the youth club is to raise questions about the nature of masculinity which would challenge the dominant position of male workers in the service. Many workers are afraid of taking a critical perspective which is both more difficult to implement, and less proven in its results, than activities-based work. While the leisure time of young people is interpreted as a problem to be solved by the Youth Service, it will continue to be dominated by men and boys and to promote a masculine view of the world.

Adult norms and the aims of youth work

A great deal of youth work rhetoric concentrates upon the idea of participation and upon devising appropriate approaches to implement this ideal. However, the reality of youth work organisation and practice on the whole defies the possibility of the full realisation of participation. The service's aims are premised on the adult understanding that young people are striving for the benefits of adulthood and are consequent upon what adult policy makers and practitioners perceived to be the appropriate attributes of maturity.

The Youth Service, no less than other agencies and enterprises, reflects the position of men and women in relation to the labour market and the family. Although there is evidence to show that women are training for, and becoming, full-time workers in increasing numbers, they are still failing to enter the statutory sector at the same rate as men (Holmes, 1986; Sawbridge & Spence, 1988). Similarly, although family patterns are changing and many more women are combining paid work with the home and family life, it is still generally the case that the major burden of responsibility and guilt in relation to the family is shouldered by women whose own socialisation, whatever their current beliefs, provokes contradictions between the demands of home and working life. These circumstances are particularly acute in relation to youth work.

The unsocial hours of work for full-time workers and the heavy commitment of time and energy required in field work mitigate against the development of a fully equal status for male and female workers. Only those women who are without pressing family responsibilities can hope to participate at the same level or in the same way as men. Such women tend to be concentrated in the younger age group and consequently at the lower end of the hierarchy. For women youth workers with families to care for, particularly those with young children, a full-time youth work post is fraught with difficulties and compromises. Often the only satisfactory resolution to this is either to leave the work completely or to take a part-time position, although in some cases, particularly in the non-statutory sector, job-share schemes have been arranged. Older women returning to, or starting, a career in youth work as their responsiblities for child care diminish often find opportunities for attaining senior positions circumstribed by male competition. Again, although the situation is changing slowly, and partly in response to the feminist challenge, youth officers, trainees and full-time 'leaders-in-charge' are predominantly male (Smith, N., 1984; Carpenter, Hart & Salvat, 1982; Sawbridge & Spence, 1988). It is, therefore, largely men who make the major decisions regarding policy, funding and methods. While feminism has questioned, criticised and to some degree influenced the nature of the work this has been achieved in an often hostile atmosphere. It is still predominantly white men who, in the main, define the aims and objectives of youth work as it is currently practised. Female youth workers find themselves constrained to work within a system which only infrequently takes cognisance of the needs of women and girls. This is even more the case for black and Asian women and girls (Parmar, 1985; 1988).

This situation is exacerbated by both formal and informal decision-making processes within the service. The formal bureaucratic structure depends largely upon committees wherein, for the same reasons of family responsibility, women tend to be outnumbered by men and where, more often than not, the chairperson is a chairman. Within the committee structure the voice of the female participant is often unheard or unheeded (Spender, 1980; Cameron, 1985) – particularly if she is expressing concerns based upon inequalities of gender. That women tend to distrust formal committee structures and feel uncomfortable within them is partly a result of a history of their marginalisation within them which is self-perpetuating. It is also partly owing to women's absence from the processes of informal decision making which provide the background to the committee meeting. No committee meets in a vacuum and few decisions are made without reference to informal discussion. Outside the working environment itself, this process takes place through social networks and usually in pubs. A great deal of information is exchanged and numerous alliances sealed over a pint. Such circumstances tend to reinforce the masculine power structure. If women workers wish to be involved, they must sacrifice their own time to what is essentially male society.

In relation to the actual work with young people, male and female workers are thus operating in a context defined by masculinity. Only in exceptional circumstances do men not hold the balance of power. Even the most sympathetic male worker is liable to define his own experience of the world as normal. His concern regarding gender can extend to sympathy but not empathy with women and girls, and his support, no matter how genuine, is therefore limited in its application. Mixed youth work is practised in buildings designed, constructed and organised by men. It engages with young people in a manner which corresponds with masculine ideas about what and who young people are and to what they should be aspiring. It is, therefore, hardly surprising that the majority of the clientele of mixed youth organisations is male. For young men experience their interests and gender position as consistent with the activities and structures offered by the Youth Service. It is largely in the interests of men and boys that full participation of young people in the Youth Service is denied. To institute democratic practices would not only deprive adult men of their role as 'leaders' but would also involve young men in a process incommensurate with the freedom and lack of responsibility of youthful masculinity. When attempts are made to involve young people in the decision-making processes of youth work it is often young women who become most involved. This not only provides them with a role within the service, but also corresponds with their assumption of the characteristic responsibility of female adulthood. To fully provide young people with the power to contribute towards defining the programmes and purposes of the Youth Service could possibly lead to a challenge to male control and influence. It would certainly provide the opportunity for young women to experience a power which is otherwise largely denied them, which would challenge the limits of femininity and, by extension, lead them towards developing skills and interests beyond their sexually prescribed role.

The intervention of feminist youth work

The philosophy and understanding mobilised by feminist youth workers is explicitly political in intent. It recognises the subordinate position of women, refuses to accept this as naturally ordained and challenges gender inequality as part of a social system founded upon economic, institutional and ideological division. Feminism defines the difficulties in the relationship of girls and women with the Youth Service not as a problem of females themselves, but as a feature of social and institutional practices which work towards the reproduction of inequality and which lead women to collude in their own oppression.

The feminist intervention in youth work has two main aims. Firstly, it looks to the Youth Service and attempts to change those features which exclude and marginalise women and girls. Secondly, it looks to the social construction of gender and seeks to develop practices with young people which will question received 'truths'. In doing this, it has begun to assert a radical methodology which is applicable to the Youth Service in general and which implies politicisation around all issues of social division.

Changes in the Youth Service

Although the participation of young women in the activities of the Youth Service is generally limited by family-oriented restrictions on their leisure time, the masculine basis of the service itself precludes their full involvement during what free time they do have (Hanmer, 1964; Smith, N., 1984). The mixed environment in its traditional organisation and practice is simply unattractive to girls, except in terms of their relationship with boys. The common excuse of those workers defending their lack of commitment to developing girls' work that 'the girls aren't interested in anything anyway, they only come here for the boys', is superficially true. In opposition to such commonsense beliefs, feminist work has shown that girls can be and are interested in pursuing a wide variety of opportunities and activities, not necessarily associated with their femininity (Carpenter and Young, 1986). However discovery of these interests can only begin by removing or decentralising masculinity in the youth work approach. The most obvious and immediately practical way of doing this is to remove the male presence, to provide female-only time and space within the Youth Service where-in female workers and young people can begin to explore their own needs, their own skills and their own potential in an atmosphere unfettered by masculine demands and domination.

Single-sex work with girls has been a fundamental element of the feminist strategy. Drawing upon the positive experiences of female-only organisation in the Women's Movement and looking to each other for encouragement, support and information, women workers have instituted girls-only events, activities, groups and clubs, often in the teeth of hostility and to the cries of 'What about the boys, we mustn't forget the boys!' Usually, before even beginning single-sex work with girls it has been necessary to prove empirically its potential in terms which conform to the traditional concerns of the Youth Service. This has involved women workers in a commitment over and above their normal responsibilities and has implied a requirement of 'success' beyond the normal expectations of youth work. Although this has put additional pressure on female workers, the achievements of events such as Girls' Days has unequivocally demonstrated, in terms of participating numbers and productivity, the willingness of girls to participate in structured activities given suitable conditions. It has provided women workers with the evidence to support the argument that mixed work is essentially boy's work.

The success of large-scale events and the support systems developed by feminist workers have created a framework within which more intensive, longer-term work with girls and young men has proceeded. While there are very few situations wherein single-sex work has achieved pre-eminence, there has been some Youth Service response to the demands of girls and women which has allowed for the creation of regular girls' nights, girls' clubs and girls' groups. This is not to say that positive support has always been forthcoming in terms of finance, resources or back-up work, or that women workers have not had to continue to argue the case for such work and provide evidence for their claims in terms not necessarily appropriate to the aims of female-defined work. For such work stands a constant challenge to the *status quo*. However it does suggest that there is a growing, if limited acceptance that the single-sex environment is an appropriate means of attracting and involving young women and that, if the Youth Service is to justify its claim to be relevant and accessible to all young people, then it is essential that it makes some adjustment to the demonstrated demands of girls and young women.

The *Thompson Report* (HMSO, 1982) actually recognised the importance of girls' work. Yet it stops far short of the overall demands of feminist workers. It recommends that single-sex work with girls only be promoted as a step towards the full integration of young women in mixed activity or as an optional extra mainstream provision. Nevertheless it does acknowledge that there is at present a need for such work and accepts that the Youth Service as a whole must seek to challenge its inherent sexism before girls can hope to achieve equality of opportunity in mixed provision. Such institutional awareness, however limited, and however unlikely to be operationalised as statutory policy, reflects the manner in which feminist work has highlighted the inadequacies of the service and has forced a recognisation that the problem of girls and young women for youth work is not one of feminine pathology but one consequent upon the way in which the Youth Service reproduces gender inequalities. In so far as it can be demonstrated that girls are not receiving a fair share of available resources, Thompson provided a degree of support for workers who are struggling to establish female-only facilities.

What the *Thompson Report* did not do, and here it represents not only the limits of the dominant masculine perspective but also the limited degree to which the feminist position has been integrated into mainstream thinking (DES, 1988a), is to identify in any clear and detailed fashion how anti-sexist practice can become a central element of mixed provision. Failure to identify appropriate methods of achieving this implies a failure to recognise that the issue is one of power and control; that the nature of mixed work can only change through pressure from women and girls themselves; and that it is only possible for them to exert such pressure and articulate clear demands from the basis of self-defined organisation and practice wherein they can explore the limits of their femininity and gender-stereotyping and discover avenues for change. In other words, the suggestion that female-only work should be short-term or optional is inadequate in the face of continuing gender socialisation in other social institutions. While moves towards anti-sexist practice in mixed provision must clearly be part of the feminist approach, it is also essential to maintain and expand girls-only work as an integral and important part of a long-term strategy. Women workers are limited in numbers, time and energy. There is little surplus for engaging in anti-sexist work with young men. Such work requires a male commitment and training. Only by consciously developing female-only provision can the Youth Service begin to deal with the specific situation and interests of different groups of girls and young women. Only by doing so can it encourage young women to challenge the collusion of femininity in masculine domination.

An approach which fully supports equality of opportunity demands more than the limited financial support envisaged by Thompson. It requires that funding sources be reassessed so as both to adequately service existing work with girls and positively encourage its development. Not only are current funding arrangements skewed disproportionately towards male single-sex organisations (Smith, N., 1984) but all finances which are available for mixed work are, because of masculine bias in methodology and aims, directed primarily towards work with young men. Feminist workers have consistently encountered financial obstacles to the development of their work. A great deal of such work has been forced to rely on charitable trusts (see Jeffs & Smith, 1988, pp. 76–83). While such trusts are helpful, the process of applying for grants is both time-consuming and uncertain in its outcome. Workers who have attempted to divert mainstream youth work funding towards work with girls have found that they are constantly required to justify the single-sex arrangement and must often fit their projects into categories which are not directly relevant. For example, taking a group of young mothers on holiday with their children requires facilities over and above what are generally considered suitable for young people and does not fit easily into criteria which the Youth Service has developed for funding 'residentials'.

In order to secure a redistribution of finance in support of work with girls and young women, it is essential that the Youth Service constructs a positive policy for such work (DES, 1988a, p. 13). This must draw on an understanding of the social circumstances of young women, recognise the tensions of the relationship between masculinity and femininity, acknowledge that the population of young women is differentiated and apply itself to the structures, methods and theoretical assumptions of the service. As yet, despite the efforts of feminist workers and the rhetoric of the *Thompson*

Report (HMSO, 1982), there is little sign in any but the most forward-looking local authorities of intentions to seriously articulate a girls' work policy for the statutory sector (DES, 1988a). This is not so surprising when the implementation of such policy would require a fundamental reorganisation of the Youth Service, threatening the power and control of men within it.

The absence of major reorganisation, or of moves in that direction, implies that the progress of work with young women is destined to continue to depend mainly upon the energy and commitment of feminist workers. The strategies and tactics which have emerged over the last decade to cope with and challenge the *status quo* continue to be of relevance. Such strategies place emphasis upon the national and local organisations of women workers, upon the development of training initiatives and the establishment of support, communication and informal networks. Within this, it has been possible not only to introduce, promote and publicise girls' work but also to begin to identify and confront some of the difficulties and challenges of a feminist and anti-sexist approach to work with all young people.

On a national level, both NAYC (which started life as the National Organisation of Girls' Clubs and has, since 1987, become Youth Clubs UK), and to a lesser extent the National Youth Bureau (NYB) made some limited concessions to girls' work during the early 1980s as a response to the demands of female field workers and their own female employees. In spite of the prevailing attitudes of NAYC (Carpenter and Rowley, 1985), and the subsequent events of 1987 when the NAYC Girls Work Unit was closed, the workers summarily dismissed and the Newsletter stopped, the unit was crucial to the introduction, promotion and communication of gender issues in youth work. The organisation of an annual conference of feminist workers between 1979 and 1983 under the auspices of the Association was of central importance in providing feminists with the opportunity to discuss their work and the issues arising from it. This conference was instrumental in developing the *Working with Girls Newsletter* which, between 1981 and 1987 was vital for the growth of a national network, for the recording of work, the dissemination of ideas and in providing support and information for otherwise isolated individuals in the field. The conference also led to the creation in 1981 of an independent National Organisation for Work with Girls and Young Women, which provides a network through a system of regional representation for women workers and users groups and the organisation of conferences and meetings in various parts of the country. The independence of this organisation holds some promise for its growth and development in the future, although it has experienced some funding difficulties.

Despite the implicit assumptions regarding the nature of youth which inform standard youth work practice across the board, in the matter of detail, the Youth Service has traditionally been a loosely-knit, diverse body lacking tight central policy initiatives. As such, it is prone to unevenness in its response to issues and susceptible to prevailing trends and fashions in its methods and target groups. This has sometimes worked to the advantage of those concerned with gender issues. For instance, the openness and lack of clear policy has left the space for women workers to fill gaps and silences, to organise at field-work level, and to translate this into demands upon local authorities and national organisations. The response might not generally have been positive, but presentation of the demands stimulated discussion and debate, and has raised the profile of girls' work. Such a situation can be used by workers seeking to promote work of this kind. However, this *ad hoc* strategy is ultimately lacking in long-term security. It results in a patchy response which is subject to regression if pressure is not sustained from below. Although exploitation of policy weaknesses has enabled significant inroads to be made in some areas and thus provided a basis for the development of new work, it is ultimately no substitute for a clear Youth Service policy which fully recognises gender divisions and inequalities and promotes methods of overcoming them.

The non-uniformed voluntary sector has arguably provided a more flexible and conductive environment for the development of feminist work than has the statutory sector. This is particularly true of 'independent' projects established to develop community-based youth work in decaying and

disadvantaged urban environments. The community emphasis, the positive objective to develop approaches relevant to
local needs and the efforts to encourage local participation
in these projects have led to some acknowledgement of the
political nature of this work and to identification of indica-
tors of structural division and inequality. Within this, some
awareness of the significance of gender and race has been
almost unavoidable. At the same time freedom from the
restrictions of purpose-built, expensive buildings has encouraged experimental and flexible approaches to the work.
This has highlighted group work and detached work with a
high level of youth participation and control as particularly
relevant to girls, and suitable to the skills of women workers.
The very possibility of attempting non-traditional methods
and the flexible working context from within these projects
(Holmes, 1986) has attracted women workers, and it is here
that some of the most successful and innovative aspects of
girls' work has been nurtured. Although some of these
projects are subject to short-term funding the work within
them has been of such substance and so relevant to the
otherwise rhetorical aims and ideals of the Youth Service as
a whole that it has been almost impossible for their achievements to be ignored.

The connections of feminist workers across the board,
based on their interest in promoting girls' work, the successful organisation of cross-organisational events such as Girls'
Days, the level of debate, discussion and education fostered
within the girls' work movement and the enthusiastic response of young women and girls have provided women
workers within the more traditional and conservative youth
organisations and local authorities with the evidence and
arguments to begin to confront the bureaucracy and make
an impact beyond field-work level. It has forced an acknowledgement that the issue of gender is one which cannot be
ignored, is not just the hobby-horse of a few extremists and
will not go away. Work with girls is thus very slowly gaining
respectability as part of the youth work brief.

However this respectability leaves no room for com-
placency. The gains so far do not extend to a national or
unified commitment to the creation and support of all girls'
organisations and projects, or to the provision of suitable

facilities for girls and young women. They do not necessitate any fundamental adjustments to the methods used with young men or challenge the masculine perspective of the service as a whole. If changes are to be wrought in these areas, it is essential that women workers continue to identify the barriers to feminist practice, risk transgressing traditional boundaries and engage with male workers, managers and policy makers in order to communicate the inadequacy of their concessions. Unless this pressure is sustained, girls' work is destined to remain a marginal trend in the service. At the same time, it is essential that the girls' work movement continues to be reflective and self-critical and constantly seeks to identify the shortcomings of its own practices. Only by doing so can it hope not to be bought off by the provision of concessions for a few. Provision for white working-class girls does not necessarily imply provision for black working-class girls (Parmar, 1985); provision for able-bodied girls does nothing for those with disabilities. Girls' work involves an infinite range of interests, some of which can all too easily be lost in the success of making gains for one particular group. Unless women workers are alert to the relationships between gender and other structural inequalities, then their work can not only be marginalised, but it can also be contained, neutralised and co-opted by the establishment.

Feminist field-work practice

In devising methods for engaging the interests of girls and young women, feminist workers have attempted both to utilise and to challenge femininity. Feminism does not, (as is sometimes assumed) involve a denigration of all things feminine, but seeks rather to promote the positive aspects and to transcend those characteristics of femininity which are repressive and inhibiting of independence, self-awareness, confidence and activity. Feminist practice begins with a recognition of the conditions and relationships within which young women live their lives and from which they construct their understanding of themselves. In so far as young women live their lives in different circumstances, so feminist youth work practice will differ in its approach. This practice seeks both to emphasise and to sympathise with the actual situation of girls while at the same time questioning and investigating opportunities for the exploration of alternatives.

In order to make contact with young women, it is essential to relate to their actual material situation. Traditional approaches based upon the school–leisure/ (un)employment–leisure models are constructed in relation to the material basis of the lives of working-class young men. In omitting the family/community emphasis of working-class female life, this model decentralises young women, particularly those of post-school age. The absence of women from public life, their invisibility to practitioners and commentators within the Youth Service, is largely a result of the increasing privatisation of their lives at this stage (Marshall and Borrill, 1984). Their adult power base, which is secondary to the power base of men, has its heart in the family and neighbourhood and their concerns are increasingly directed towards solidifying this base.

It is possible to attract school-age girls to Youth Service facilities by offering them the chance to participate in a female-only environment in activities and events from which they would otherwise be precluded by the domination of boys and young men. If contact has not been made and relationships developed with youth workers at this stage, it is unlikely that they will find much in the Youth Service to attract them at a later stage. Not surprisingly, because most youth workers, whatever their philosophical approach might be, are constrained by the limitations of their own working base, most female-centred, building-based youth work has been undertaken with girls of school age. Where the work has been successful with this age group, relationships have sometimes been sustained, but even then it is often impossible to maintain regular contact through traditional approaches. Unless working methods are adjusted to include a community perspective and unless the leisure orientation is decentralised, the Youth Service will continue to be irrelevant to young women after they leave school.

Making and maintaining contact with young women in the community implies an element of detached work whose brief is wider than that of simply 'hanging around with the kids'. It suggests that the worker must attempt to become involved in the local female networks which include older women and children, and must be willing and able to react positively to issues and concerns which are often personal in expression, but which also relate to conditions in the locality such as poor housing, welfare rights, poverty and lack of community facilities relevant to women. Such work, of necessity, involves the worker in visiting homes and in liaison with other services and organisations. Traditional building-based youth work denies the possibility of proceeding in this manner, while the application of strict age limits and the political sensitivity of most youth work agencies limit the potential for developing young women's participation in campaigns centred upon their material circumstances. There are, therefore, few situations wherein work with young women has achieved its potential. However, in projects which have worked with girls over an extended period, which have included a high level of participation from the girls in organising their own involvement and which are flexible enough to adjust to changing needs and conditions, some headway is being made with the older age group. As a result of their earlier positive experience in all-female youth work they have greater awareness of their situation and greater confidence in expressing their own needs and interests. Such young women are often key figures in providing the female youth worker with a wider circle of contacts.

In many building-based situations, there is little time or flexibility for engaging with the local community in a coherent way and here the most likely hope of attracting young women lies in the adjustment of opening times, of activities and of environment and facilities. The provision of a place to relax, to talk, to seek relevant advice and information, to learn a skill or to find a way of becoming involved in the day-to-day work of the centre, the organisation of crèche or play facilities and the accessibility without the interference of workers are especially relevant to young women. Unless building-based workers pay some attention to these details and provide opportunities for regular, unstructured, female-only drop-in times staffed by sensitive female workers, young women will be more likely to be found in the local cafe than in the youth club. Some centre-based workers have managed to make inroads at this level and develop young women's groups and individual relationships, but, once again, such developments depend upon long-term strategy. They also require the sympathy and co-operation of other workers and managers and a commitment from all those concerned to restrict the access of young men during such times.

Approaches to contact and follow-up work with girls and young women are thus dependent upon recognition of the dichotomy created by the school-leaving age which propels young women in the older age range into a different social situation and therefore into a different relationship with the Youth Service, from those of school age. The feminist perspective of those struggling to establish work with girls has proposed that the issue is not simply one of attracting more girls and indicates that the underlying models, structures and methods which characterise present practice require a significant shift in focus.

Methods of feminist work

The methods which have been used to engage the interests of girls and young women and to challenge feminine stereotypes and masculine hegemony are many and varied. They include the recreational, welfare and educational approaches which are found throughout youth work practice, but are distinct in that the emphasis is placed upon process rather than content, upon participation rather than control, upon questioning rather than conforming. The manner in which youth work is practised rather than the activities which it organises is of greatest importance in feminist work.

Thus attention has been given to the actual social situation of young women, which involves particularising not only their feminity, but also other social factors which influence their lives. Within this, the question of power is central and feminist workers are engaged in questioning all power relations and in a process of facilitating the realisation of the potential power of girls and young women. The badge slogan 'Girls Are Powerful' and the conference title 'Girls Rule O.K.' represent a fundamental tenet of feminist practice which includes workers in a process of attempting to relinquish their power as 'leaders' and looking towards the greater involvement and control of young women themselves. In accepting the political implications of its approach, successful feminist work has been able to present a challenge to non-feminist practice, illustrating the hidden political agenda of methods which fail to confront the question of power.

To organise young women around their social situation, feminist workers initially paid attention almost exclusively to gender and to the female exclusion from the majority of Youth Service activity. Girls' clubs, girls' nights, girls' conferences and girls' days have all been and continue to be of significance in providing opportunities for illustrating the socially constructed gender basis of female exclusion. They have enabled female workers and young people to explore the possibilities of achieving success and competence in activities otherwise denied them or practised in the competitive and inhibiting masculine environment.

However the most successful working structure has proved to be that of the small all-female group which concedes that there are differences among women and girls themselves and which focuses upon interests (which can be almost anything from motorbikes to cookery) or upon different social circumstances (such as motherhood, or living in a particular locality) (Carpenter & Young, 1986). While complementing the tendency of women and girls to socialise in small groups, the sensitively devised group can be instrumental in facilitating communication and mutual identity among its members, emphasising the benefits of co-operation in a way which begins to redress the tendency towards the isolation inherent in women's family role. Rather than simply lumping all young people together and assuming that their interests are undifferentiated and defined by age alone, female group work allows for the realities of other differences and divisions and provides the context wherein these divisions can be identified and articulated. This can be particularly important as a mechanism of politicisation, de-individualising problems and concerns and providing the potential for relating them to a broader analysis of social conditions and values. Of course, not all groups achieve these ideals and girls'/young women's groups are as prone as other groups to problems and contradictions. In addition, many heterosexual dominated young women's groups have degenerated or disintegrated as individual young women abandon them in favour of the lure of a sexual relationship. Nevertheless sensitively organised girls and young women's groups have without doubt been established as the most effective vehicle for implementing the ideals of feminist youth work.

Women workers have found that, when it has been possible for them to practise youth work in the context of the small female group, unfettered by masculine interruption and disruption, the need to control has been largely removed from the agenda. When control is no longer an issue, then the potential of youth work as a method of informal education is more apparent. Feminist work with girls has illustrated that it is indeed possible to apply the appellation 'education' to most activities when these activities are organised with reference to the real needs and desires of the young people concerned, when they involve the young people themselves in the background and back-up work, and when they are accomplished in an atmosphere of questioning and criticism.

The content of feminist work sometimes utilises stereotyped feminine skills, sometimes gender-neutral skills and sometimes attempts to involve girls in what is otherwise stereotyped masculine activity. Female involvement in some activities is admittedly more challenging in itself to gender stereotypes than others, but whatever the content of the work, the greatest challenge comes from the methods used. Providing a group of girls with the opportunity to play football or to take part in woodwork classes is an instantly obvious method of questioning male domination of these activities. However it is often necessary for workers to use traditional feminine pursuits such as cooking and sewing in order to attract girls. If such activities are organised as a means simply to improve skills in these areas or to show that women and girls can become involved and that their traditional skills are important, then they are of some value. However, if they are used as a medium for discussion about the status of the activity, about why it is that female workers in dressmaking and catering receive such low wages, about why women do most cooking and sewing in this society yet men become chefs and famous dress designers, then work in this context probably has a more penetrating and long-term effect than football without questions.

Anti-sexist practice

The educative and democratic methods attempted by feminist workers are of wider relevance than work with girls and young women. However, as long as such work remains precisely that, and mixed work and work with boys and young men fails to grapple with the problem of masculinity both as they affect men themselves and as they deform gender relations, then the full benefits of feminist work and its implications will be lost to the service as a whole.

Feminist workers argue not only for 'work with girls' but for the establishment of anti-sexist approaches generally. For unless male youth work begins to perceive the issue of gender as important, even in an all-male setting, and begins to question the assumptions of masculine power, then feminist work with girls and mainstream practice will increasingly diverge. Heterosexual young women of necessity continue to develop relationships with men and continue to live in the framework of masculine domination in the family. If the lessons learned in the all-female setting are effective, the implications for men and for male–female relationships are far-reaching. If work with young men does not respond to the challenge of a gender-conscious practice, it limits the possibility of both young men and women developing into the mature, responsible adults so central to youth work aims.

Anti-sexist practice demands that all workers, whether in a single-sex or mixed setting, must begin to accommodate and attempt to understand gender-related issues as they affect themselves, their position in the service and their personal lives; as they affect their relationships with young people; and as they affect the circumstances and relationships of young people themselves. Such a practice must involve male youth workers in questioning their own power and the manner in which their masculinity not only restricts and limits female workers and young women, but also curtails the potential of their own youth work. It must, by extension, involve consciously relinquishing the power and control which is based only on masculinity and devising methods of working with young men which question, rather than reinforce, the masculine expectations of youth. Ultimately anti-sexist work with young men depends on the willingness of male workers to learn from their female colleagues and to engage in a dialogue which is critical of, and threatening to, their own position.

To date, while many male workers have applauded the achievements of feminist work, very few, with one or two notable exceptions (Taylor, 1984; Lloyd, 1985), have attempted to illuminate the difficulties for themselves or to incorporate its lessons into their own practice. Consequently, while feminist workers are delineating the problems of working with men and boys, drawing attention to the limits of a male-dominated service and practising an effective and critical youth work methodology with both sexes, the agenda for anti-sexist male youth work remains relatively open and obscure. There is little sign of this situation changing in the immediate future. Moreover, in so far as the development of such work must of necessity involve questioning sexuality and broaching issues of masculinity, heterosexuality and homosexuality, then the contemporary homophobic climate restricts possibilities further (see Chapter 4).

It is apparent that gender-conscious youth work has wide-ranging implications for the Youth Service and that it is, at present, in its infancy, despite the inroads which have been made by feminist workers. The practice of feminist work has succeeded in some areas. Feminist workers have created support systems among themselves which provide a working model for the possibilities of a democratically organised system. The development of this practice is restricted by the controlling needs of the state, by the lack of resources and by the intransigence of masculine power. However the flexibility and co-operation of some locally based voluntary agencies, the energy, commitment and power of feminist youth workers' organisation, and the achievements of the work developed, hold out the hope that the issue of gender will continue to influence practice and inform future changes in a way which can only be of benefit to all those involved in youth work.

4

Sexuality and Youth Work Practice

PETER KENT-BAGULEY

Making sense of our sexuality, sexual desires, behaviours and identities is a difficult process riddled with contradictions and explanatory cul de sacs. Sexuality is an intensely personal affair, but it is equally political. Sexual politics is still neither widely discussed not generally understood and perhaps the vast majority of people prefer the ostrich attitude of 'what we do in bed is our own affair'. This is an inadequate and unacceptable response for at least three reasons. First, simply because it is untrue. The state has assumed an interest through its legislative powers in what we do, with whom and under what circumstances. Second, such a response reduces sexuality to physical sexual activity, an obsessive if not exclusive concern with genitalia and orgasm. Third, it is really saying 'let us not talk about it': an unthinking acceptance of the prevailing essentialist perspective which holds that sex(uality) is natural and therefore we do what we have to do. This simplistic view ignores the social constructions of sexuality and leaves unexamined the range of possibilities and limitations of choice.

The essentialist or biological determinist perspective does not simply ignore but rejects social and historical factors. In short, it claims to be non-political but as Birke clearly and forcefully demonstrates: 'That there are policies that follow from biological arguments is one of the reasons why biological determinism is political' (1986, p. 35). Further, there surely can be no dispute that sexual attitudes change over time. The response to male masturbation is an excellent example, in terms of how it is conceived, and how it should be dealt with:

> It is a real disease ... When masturbation has been firmly established you can no more talk your patient out of masturbating than you can talk a child suffering from scabies out of scratching. The latter is caused by an irritation in the skin and the former by an irritation in the prostatic urethra. (Huhner, 1924, p. 15)

The cause was seen to be a simply physical medical problem and the cure was similarly a question of medical intervention: '... so definite is the disease, so specific is the treatment, and so positive is the cure, that it is not even necessary to obtain the patient's confidence and co-operation' (ibid.). Huhner's credentials were impeccable; head of the genito-urinary department of Mount Sinai hospital, New York, gynaecologist and member of the American Medical Association at the beginning of this century. He was confident that masturbation was a 'curable disease' after a course of silver nitrate injections syringed 'slowly and gently into the deep prostatic urethra' (Huhner, 1924, p. 32). After six months of such medical treatment he was invariably able to pronounce the patient cured. Fortunately for male masturbators, views have changed.

The prevalence, appeal and persistence of biological reductionism perpetuates the notion of personal pathology masking political power. Sin, sickness and deviance are individualised, the products of individual biological malfunctions and not the results of complex social and political relationships. But as Birke succinctly points out: 'It is a very long way from a protein molecule to playboy' (1986, p. 69). Views of sex, gender and sexuality are intimately bound up with the general ideological structure of society and biological determinism, the constant claim of what is natural and therefore inevitable, is itself a political ideological tool: '... biological determinism concerning gender, serves to legitimate existing inequalities by naturalising them' (ibid.).

Capitalism, racism and heterosexism

Three fundamental characteristics all human beings share are class, ethnicity and sexuality. We do not have to be capitalist, racist or heterosexist, for these are not inherently natural characteristics. However the pervasive power of capitalism, racism and heterosexism is such that choices necessitate sustained struggle. They define the parameters within which we conceptualise relationships and resultant ideologies are made to appear natural; thus production for profit is seen to be naturally inevitable; skin colour is seen to naturally justify discrimination; and homosexuality is seen to be a corruption of nature.

Excited and often angrily abusive disputes arise in political and academic spheres over the primacy of one over the others. My aim is not to elaborate upon those disputes but, by noting their existence, to emphasise the socially constructed nature of human activity and particularly that of sexuality. Just because we construct our social reality within given ground rules, for example, those of capitalism, we should not suppose that the construction is necessarily easy to comprehend nor that it is somehow perfectly rational and logical. On the contrary, social ideologies are complex and contradictory.

> Men make their own history, but they do not make it just as they please . . . they do not make it under circumstances chosen by themselves, but under circumstances directly encountered, given and transmitted from the past. The tradition of all the dead generations weighs like a nightmare on the brain of the living. (Marx, in Marx and Engels, 1973, p. 96)

For Marx, the 'circumstances directly encountered' were the social relationships of production and an appreciation of these is the key to the understanding of the entire society:

> It is always the direct relationship of the owners of the conditions of production to the direct producers . . . which reveals the innermost secret, the hidden basis of the entire social structure . . . This does not prevent the same economic basis – the same from the standpoint of its main conditions – due to innumerable

different empirical circumstances, natural environment, racial relations, external historical influences etc., from showing infinite variations and graduations in appearance . . . (Marx, 1974, p. 792)

Answering those who reduce Marx's materialist conception of history to a simplistic economic determinism, Engels stressed that the ultimately determining element in history is the production and reproduction of real life but anyone who says

> that the economic element is the only determining one, transforms that proposition into a meaningless, abstract, senseless phrase . . . [because] political, juristic, philosophical theories, religious views and their further development into systems of dogma also exercise their influence upon the course of historical struggles and in many cases preponderate in determining their form. (Engels in Marx & Engels, 1969, p. 682)

For me the strength of Marxist analyses is that they recognise and stress the reality of dynamic relationships in their quest for understanding social change, emphasising the relativity of phenomena compared with the idealistic emphasis on eternalised fixed definitions. For example, we all know that there have been societies where slavery was an acceptable part of the 'natural order'. Similarly, homosexual behaviour has been centrally acceptable in some societies but not in ours; masturbation was once a disease, now it is not.

The examination of prevailing economic structures and their related ideologies is a prerequisite to the creation of strategies for challenge and change. For example, economic inequality is inherent within capitalism; it is an unavoidable consequence. The form this takes will vary accordingly to conditions at any given time; the degree to which they may be improved will likewise depend upon the forms of state intervention, but amelioration is not obliteration. The further analysis departs from the economic sphere, the more it may reveal that capitalism relies heavily upon racism and heterosexism to maintain its hegemony. For fragmenting the working-class on the basis of race is one effective block against working-class solidarity. Heterosexism, which assumes that sexuality is formed 'naturally' rather than constructed in society, is another ideological tool dividing the working class.

Rather than asserting fundamental primacies of one dimension over the others it would seem politically sound for personal struggles concerned with class, racism and heterosexism to recognise their complex interrelatedness; that at some periods one may predominate over the others, but that in the reality of everyday struggle one cannot be prioritised. A radicalised united working class presupposes the dismantling of institutionalised racism and heterosexism and without that radical unity the working class will fail to challenge the oppression of capitalism.

Heterosexism: legislation and policy

As was implied in the previous section, whether or not the seeds of heterosexism emerged from capitalism or from an earlier mode of production is not especially significant for our current purposes. What is evident, whatever the causal links, is that heterosexism has monopolised our understanding of sexuality. The automatic presumption of heterosexuality is perpetuated through a socially constructed gender system which makes use of biologically given sex differences. Just as our individuality is constrained by our class and ethnic origins, it is constrained by our gender. Not only are women and men expected to relate sexually to each other, they are expected to conform to a whole host of characteristics which purportedly reflect inherent differences between the sexes. Just as our biological sex is ascribed at birth so too is our social gender. The element of choice is denied and only available for those prepared to struggle long and hard against the pervasive and powerful forces of heterosexism.

The family is the primary source of heterosexist indoctrination; its structure, as well as its processes, typifies heterosexism *par excellence*, and for the overwhelming majority of young lesbians and gays offers no support whatsoever. It is the nursery for the enforced grafting and growth of gendered sexuality, instructing females in their subservient roles and maintaining that lesbians and gays, if they exist at all, are always somewhere else. The media reinforce the myths daily, through the twin techniques of silence and stigma. One survey – the first of its kind – of lesbian and gay content on British television revealed that it was less than two per cent in actuality programmes, such as news and documentaries, and below five per cent in entertainment programmes. Over 90 per cent of that content was deemed to be negative (London Media Project, 1986).

Heterosexism cannot, and should not, be dismissed as so much more jargon:

> in a heterosexist society, the pressure is on right from childhood, through adolescence and into adult life, to 'choose' heterosexuality. So intense is that pressure that most heterosexuals do not even experience any sense of having made a choice, and so universal is that most do not even experience it as a pressure . . . If we could successfully challenge heterosexism – not just attitudes, but the entire way society is organised around sexuality and gender relations – lesbians' and gay men's lives would be considerably improved. Heterosexuals, too, might well find that the pressures to conform to stereotypical roles and patterns would be much rendered, and new perspectives would emerge on a range of equally valid sexual identities. The ways in which men and women formed relationships both in mixed and single-sex settings, as colleagues, friends and lovers, would have far more variety and possibilities. (GLC, 1986, p. 6)

When we come to examine the state of legislation and policy, the size of the problem becomes clear. For example, in an otherwise excellent publication. Wise repeats the myth that, 'as recently as 1967 the Sexual Offences Act finally put an end to the criminalisation of male homosexuality' (GLC, 1985, p. 5). In fact it did not, nor was it that Act's purpose. What the Act did was grudgingly to decriminalise 'homosexual behaviour' (in plain language, in the terms of the debate, buggery) between two consenting adults, both over 21, in private. It was, and still is, plainly heterosexist and, therefore, oppressively discriminatory. Of the major parties only

Labour, and that as recently as 1985, has committed itself to an age of consent for gay men equivalent to that of heterosexuals. It should be emphasised that the law does not directly recognise lesbianism, but the general view is that the age of consent, were it to be called into question, would be deemed to be the same as for heterosexuals. In addition to perpetuating the oppression of young gay men, the 1967 Act made it easier to secure prosecutions for the 'homosexual offence' of 'indecency between males' which does not concern a sexual act but the public expression of the sexuality of a person, such as embracing, kissing and holding hands. The entrenched heterosexism within the police and courts has ensured a vigorous harassment of gay men since 1967. A Home Office report has shown that 80 per cent of all persons convicted of homosexual offences were in fact consensual (Walmsley and White, 1979, p. 7). There seems little doubt that the law is protecting the hegemony of heterosexism rather than men from male assault.

It is not just legislation on sexual offences that enforces heterosexism. The Sex Discriminaton Act (1975), for example, makes no mention of sexuality, sexual orientation, sexual preferences or, more usefully explicit, lesbians and gays. Increasingly, employers, particularly local authorities, have adopted equal opportunities policies but relatively few explicitly name the groups selected for equality, for example, lesbians and gays. Some, such as Rugby, Sandwell and Stockport, have explicitly deleted lesbians and gays from the proposed policy during council debates, only restoring them as a result of sustained campaigns. Only two authorities outside London, the cities of Manchester and Nottingham, have lesbian and gay units within their equal opportunities programmes. Although 'it will take a long time to change things', as one of the Manchester lesbian officers reported (Grant, 1986, pp. 114–19), at least lesbians and gays in those cities have channels for influencing local policies.

There is no legal redress for lesbian or gay men dismissed from work solely on the grounds of their sexuality. Heterosexism's catch-all ideology not only presumes the unnaturalness of homosexuals, it also presumes that the natural may be corrupted; hence the myth that lesbians and gays 'corrupt the natural development of young people'. The strength of this myth makes it exceedingly difficult for lesbians and gays working with young people to be open about their sexuality. A specific example will illustrate the situation. A maintenance man employed at a Scottish camp attended by young people of both sexes between the ages of 10 and 18 'had been robbed by someone he met at a gay pub, well away from his workplace. He reported the incident to the local police and during his interview freely admitted that he was gay. Soon after, his employers were unofficially informed that he was homosexual' (Crane, 1982, p. 105). He was dismissed, even though all concerned accepted that none of the man's relationships had involved any residents at the camp. Even so, his employers wrote that: 'At a camp accommodating large numbers of schoolchildren and teenagers it is totally unsuitable to employ any person with such tendencies' and the Employment Appeal Tribunal observed that 'whether that view is scientifically sound may be open to question', but upheld the reasonableness of the dismissal 'as the only safe course' (Crane, 1982, p. 106).

The techniques of silence and stigma are employed to the full in the vast majority of schools, with teachers denying an overt and positive place in the curriculum for lesbians and gays, while at the same time colluding with the prevalence of negative images within the informal structures. Research conducted in London revealed that '60% of their sample of young lesbians and gays said that the topic of homosexuality was not mentioned in any lesson at school. Of those who said that the topic was talked about, 80% said that they did not find it helpful' (Trenchard & Warren, 1984, p. 56). Significantly, one of the least likely contexts for its discussion was sex education, which, one suspects, is a reflection of the subject's relative rarity and its obsession with the mechanics of heterosexual sex rather than relationships and sexuality in general. Not surprisingly, the majority of young lesbians and gays feel marginalised, isolated and unhappy at school, often feeling obliged to participate in queer-bashing talk to avoid self-revelation.

By 1988, only the Inner London Education Authority (ILEA) and the London Boroughs of Haringey and Ealing had begun to address the issue of heterosexism within their schools, but even their tentative beginnings evoked a massive media and Parliamentary backlash. Scared by the spectre of lesbians and gays being given positive images in the classroom the government allowed a last-minute amendment to its 1986 Education Act. Carried by 300 to 138, it ensured that sex education can only be taught if school governors approve. They also have the power to determine content, while pupils may be withdrawn from any sex education classes. Thus, the Act permits the possibility of school governors overriding the anti-sexist, anti-heterosexist policies of elected local education authorities. Furthermore Angela Rumbold, then a junior minister of education, declared that 'to teach homosexuality as being an acceptable way of life is not correct' and she expressed her 'concern' that 34 per cent of a representative sample of teachers believed that homosexuality should be discussed in schools and presented as an acceptable way of life (*TES*, 7 and 14 November 1986).

Subsequently ILEA retreated from its policies in the face of press and parliamentary hysteria and withdrew its excellent *Anti-Sexist Resources Guide*. It also destroyed the first edition of its booklet, *Positive Images* (ILEA, 1986b). Five months later, the second edition appeared, without the cover information that it had been 'compiled by the ILEA Relationships and Sexuality Project Resources Group'. Also deleted was the Group's introduction and the original ratings for the books and films such as 'excellent book for the library' and 'highly recommended'. *Jenny Lives with Eric and Martin* was removed from the listings, presumably because it had been the subject of vitriolic attack in the press and parliament. Not surprisingly, the Lesbians in Education Group wrote to all ILEA members pointing out the 'urgent need for a policy statement on heterosexism to run parallel with the statements on race, class and gender, as well as one covering discrimination on grounds of disability' (ILEA, 1986a). With the break-up of ILEA, this will have to be fought for again at borough level.

The catalogue of repressive legislation was augmented by the introduction, during the winter of 1987/8, of the now notorious 'Clause 28'. This clause was to be inserted after section 2 of the Local Government Act 1986. It stated that:

A local authority shall not –
(a) promote homosexuality or publish material for the promotion of homosexuality;
(b) promote the teaching in any maintained school of the acceptability of homosexuality as a pretended family relationship by the publication of such material or otherwise;
(c) give financial or other assistance to any person for either of the purposes referred to in paragraphs (a) or (b) above.

One of the important aspects of the debates was the way in which Labour's front bench avoided reference to their party policy and sought refuge in a cul de sac of supposed definitional problems concerning the word 'promote'. Labour's failure to orchestrate a viable and sustained opposition permitted the centre stage to be dominated by an arts lobby. Ironically this 'centralised' the marginality of lesbians and gays and perpetuated that marginality by allowing special pleading for homosexuality within the arts to be unconnected with homosexuality in everyday life. Heterosexism has always meant that Chelsea's chic ceramicist's 'homosexuality' is accepted, while Cannock's coalminer's 'queerness' is ridiculed. The interlock of class and heterosexism ensures that the margins of condescending tolerance are reserved for the privileged class. Chronic concern about the continued safety of homosexual characterisation in the arts gained widespread national and local media attention. Campaigns to defend the limited, hard-won rights of lesbians and gays in real life passed largely unreported (Kent-Baguley, 1988).

Subsequently, there was some debate as to the extent to which the Clause could actually be applied to schools, given that it is the governors, rather than the local authority, who have responsibility for curricular matters. Beyond this, legal opinion taken by the Association of London Authorities and the National Council for Civil Liberties (NCCL) suggests that the legislation does nothing to prevent teachers 'giving honest and factual explanations' of gay and lesbian relationships if this is to protect the welfare of a pupil (*Guardian*, 26 July 1988). The opinion rests on a narrower definition of 'to promote homosexuality' as involving active advocacy directed by local authorities towards individuals in order to persuade them to become homosexual, or to experiment with homosexual relationships. However, within a few weeks of the Act becoming law, one local authority had already banned a National Youth Bureau (NYB) guide to voluntary work as it included a section on lesbian and gay projects (*TES*, 20 May 1988). Interestingly, the guide had been approved by its funders, the Voluntary Services Unit in the Home Office.

AIDS: a medical problem versus a moral panic

An examination of the deployment of AIDS as a weapon against homosexuals facilitates an analysis of some of the major assumptions of heterosexist forms of oppression. The fundamental assumption underlying all of the various heterosexist rationalisations is simply the essentialist or biologically given naturalness of heterosexuality to the exclusion of any other manifestations of sexuality. The basis of the ideology is as simple as that. How remarkable, therefore,

> that so much effort and so many taboos and prohibitions are thought to be necessary to enforce the sexual norms of our society. The difference between masculine and feminine forms of behaviour are dinned into us all from the earliest age to ensure that we are capable of 'doing what comes naturally'. (Milligan, 1973, p. 4)

Armies of professional moralisers pontificate on the sinfulness, sickness and criminality of homosexuality. Claiming that the essential purpose of sexuality is procreation, and because lesbian and gay sexualities in themselves are non-procreative, they deem them to be unnatural. Heterosexist arguments seem to ignore the significant number of lesbian and gay parents. This indicates the heterosexist obsession with biological givens; you are either heterosexual or homosexual, sexuality being conceived as a static rather than a fluid phenomenon. Presumably people who identify as bisexual are seen to be simply awkward, as are homosexuals who choose to be 'like that' rather than being 'unfortunately born like that', as a local councillor recently put it to me. The afterthought of the role of choice overriding what is 'biologically determined' is, of course, always uppermost in the heterosexist mind. Hence the rationalisation for the absurd and unjustifiable setting of the age of consent for gay men at 21, so that young men may not be 'corrupted' with the 'contagious disease'. Heterosexists in Britain appear sublimely unaware of the much earlier ages of consent in most other EEC countries. In part, this reflects a view that lesbians and gays are unfit for working with young people and rearing their own children. For example, lesbians find it exceedingly difficult to gain custody of their own children in divorce cases although usually the mother is preferred to the father.

The emergence of AIDS, far from being divine retribution for the sins of homosexuality, has been a heaven-sent opportunity for bigots to re-emerge, realigned and re-straightened in their defence of heterosexism. That 'viruses know neither nationality nor sexuality' (Altman, 1986, p. 175) is a medical fact deliberately buried beneath moral myth. It was during the latter part of 1980 that the disease was first monitored by the USA Center for Disease Control in Atlanta. Since then there remain few countries in the world where the virus has not been identified, although some have been extremely reluctant to admit it. Furthermore, the virus has been prevalent in Central Africa for some considerable time, as much among heterosexuals as among homosexuals. However 'the fact that the first recorded cases were exclusively among gay men was to affect the whole future conceptualization of AIDS' (Altman, 1986, p. 33).

While knowledge of the disease has grown steadily, the moral panic has been fed by the media. The notion of the 'gay plague' has been sustained through sensationalised distortions with scaremongering headlines, particularly in the tabloids. Prison officers have refused to deal with inmates suspected of having the virus, refuse collectors have objected to calling at the London Lesbian and Gay Centre, licencees have turned away gay men, fire brigade workers have expressed fears about giving the kiss of life and some parents have objected to their children attending schools where it is known a pupil has the virus.

It was not until 1986 that the Government seriously began to consider a public information campaign with its newspaper, television and street boarding message: AIDS IS NOT PREJUDICED: IT CAN KILL ANYONE. At the same time every household in the country was sent a leaflet: AIDS: DON'T DIE OF IGNORANCE. Government material has been obsessed with penile penetration and the morality of monogomy; 'the more sexual partners you have, the greater the risk. It is safest to stick to one faithful partner. Unless you are sure of your partner, always use a condom.' The tone of the message is scary and dreary, in sharp contrast to Terrence Higgins Trust's advertisement in *Marxism Today* (January 1987) which reassures readers that 'SEX IS GOOD, IT'S FUN' and invites people to 'be inventive sexually.' As Tatchell points out, the choice is not 'between AIDS and abstinence but rather between AIDS and playing safely' (1986, p. 31). He goes on to lay the ghost that promiscuity in itself is the source of the disease: 'the key to playing safely and preventing AIDS is not how often people have sex or how many partners they have. It is the way people have sex'. Later he rightly makes the point that a 'society which places so many obstacles in the way of homosexual love has hardly any right to turn around and condemn gay promiscuity' (ibid., p. 106). Where Tatchell concentrates on crisis intervention and welfare policy, Fitzpatrick and Milligan (1987) focus their analysis on heterosexism: 'It is the *oppression of homosexuals* that allows HIV infection to spread among gay men.' They argue that 'Scaring straights is no way to protect gays from the anti-homosexual backlash generated around the fear of HIV contagion.'

It would be misleading to create the impression that only the popular tabloids were responsible for pushing the homosexualisation of AIDS: *The Times* (admittedly from the same stable as the *Sun*) published what became a notorious editorial claiming that: 'the infection's origins and means of propagation excite repugnance, moral and physical, at promiscuous male homosexuality – conduct which, tolerable in private circumstances, has with the advent of "gay liberation" become advertised, even glorified as acceptable public conduct, even a proud badge for public men to wear' (*The Times*, 21 November 1984). The editorial went on to note that in Queensland blood donors who failed to disclose their homosexual behaviour were liable to fines and/or imprisonment and that 'anticipatory thinking along such lines is surely needed' in Britain. The homophobic sinfulness, sickness and criminality syndrome is thus neatly encapsulated in one editorial.

Learning for liberation

It is hoped that the preceding sections have illustrated the pervasiveness of heterosexism and, therefore, the tremendous problems there are for people who wish to choose not to be heterosexist. The situation is the same within the Youth Service although enclaves of anti-sexism have been established, almost totally by female workers. The overwhelming majority of male workers have not begun to confront their sexist attitudes and behaviour and their dominance makes it exceedingly difficult for women workers to establish bases from which to work.

Tackling heterosexism has hardly begun and consequently young lesbians and gays feel awkward, unhappy and unwanted in the majority of youth clubs as Trenchard and Warren found in their interviews: 'Heterosexual relationships were pushed down your throat, and this made me feel really pissed off' (gay man, 20). And 'Anti-gay and anti-lesbian remarks were made by the workers. Things like "he looks like a real poof". If you were arm in arm with another girl they called you a "lezzie". The young people didn't really understand, so they copied the workers' (lesbian, 17) (Trenchard & Warren, 1985, p. 14). Such statements typify the experiences of most young lesbians and gays in the Youth Service.

Heterosexism and sexism are not the same things, but nor are they totally separate; both hold the biological determinist view of the naturalness and normality of maleness being masculinity and femaleness being femininity with man being powerful and woman powerless. Anti-sexist policies and practices have, to date, been limited to purportedly providing equal opportunities for women in a male-dominated world, and a heterosexist one at that. Such a policy (regardless of the actual intention) has about as much chance of success as the policy of educational equality of opportunity within a class-structured society.

Furthermore, even if it were possible for such a policy to be successful, this would be limited to an equalising of power between the sexes within a heterosexist structure. This constitutes a massive indictment of policies because there would still remain the lack of choice regarding sexuality. Heterosexism would continue to limit the choices available; women, for example, would continue to be pressurised into marriage and child bearing if not child rearing. Any anti-sexist programme devoid of the issues of homosexuality and gay rights must be woefully inadequate (Kent-Baguley, 1984). Heterosexism, therefore, must be tackled equally with sexism for they are intricately and inseparably bound together.

Not surprisingly, the anodyne *Review of the Youth Service* by Thompson failed to address the issues of heterosexism and sexuality. All that the six men and two women members of the Committee could muster on sexuality was that: 'for both sexes, sexual relations are a source of anxiety as well as bewilderment' (HMSO, 1982, p. 11). However, in view of their observations on girls' work, it may be just as well! Noting that the service is 'failing young women' the Report immediately and defensively claims that it is failing 'not of course from set intent but because it uncritically mirrors sexist attitudes in society'. The paragraph concludes by saying that 'it is necessary that the Service should take deliberate steps to put this situation right' (ibid., p. 63).

The Committee's strategy for such change reflects precisely the prevalent situation in the service; heterosexism is taken for granted and the patriarchal privilege boys and men enjoy is not to be challenged, but in some ill-defined, hazy way opened up for girls and women. The Committee did not 'believe that mainstream provision should be segregated. It is not as though girls want to do different things from boys or need a different curriculum' (ibid.). If we are talking about ping-pong, pool and party games they may well be right, but surely there are fundamental issues relating to social relationships to be addressed within the euphemistic 'curriculum'. But evidently not for Thompson, where segregation is forbidden by their fiat and separate provision reluctantly conceded as a final option, 'always depending on the local factors of geography, socio-economic conditions and so on' (ibid.).

Significantly, the Report totally ignored the existence of young lesbians and gays, despite their claim that 'the Youth Service has the duty to help all young people who have need of it' (ibid., p. 48). The anomaly was explained by Thompson himself who said that young gay people's organisations are not seen as part of the Youth Service (London Gay Teenage Group, 1982, p. 1). I have referred to Thompson, not for its merits, but as an illustration of the pervasiveness of heterosexism and the proliferation of meaningless platitudes designed to support the *status quo* while purporting to give tentative encouragement to some radical movements within the service. An approach so lacking in any form of rigorous analysis inevitably leads to the banal rhetoric the Report so richly displays.

If women, lesbians and gays are to overcome their oppression then sexism and heterosexism have to be challenged and consigned to history. That means men must change; they must relinquish their power to define themselves a superior social position which necessarily rejects lesbians and gays and ostracises women. It is not a question of whether we should permit segregation, as though it were a possible option; it is a pervasive fact. Nor is it a question of facilitating an equal rights approach, for clearly that is inherently impossible. Segregation is the practical outcome of the power relationships in society; separatism is a political response to that. The radical politics of sexuality has exposed the conservative, supposedly consensual, politics of heterosexism. Working for change and liberation invariably elicits a wide range of hostility and a sustained struggle is essential for recognition and resources. Incessant invalidatory responses such as 'there are other, more important issues for youth workers to get on with' are still common after a decade of developing action and publicity for lesbian and gay youth issues. Such responses are particularly nauseous since it is invariably the case that such respondents cannot even think of any alternative issue, whether more important or not. In fact, 'in almost every case, provision for young gay people has arisen from the efforts of young gays themselves, against the reluctance and hindrance of the Youth Service, not with its expressed support' (ibid., p. 7).

Without positive, separate provision, it is obvious that, 'far from having the opportunity to measure themselves against others, young gay people can often only measure themselves against popular prejudice and against insulting models set up by the mass media' (ibid., p. 8). The paternalistic, heterosexist and sexist structures of the existing Youth Service have been increasingly challenged or left behind during the past decade, reflecting the two distinctive developments for change. Lesbian and gay workers, mainly in London, some openly gay, began to organise in 1977, forming the Gay Youth Workers' Group and launching a Sexual Awareness in the Youth Service Campaign. Some of the Group had been involved with the establishment of the London Gay Teenage Group in 1976 which, after innumerable submissions and meetings, was formally recognised by the Inner London Education Authority (ILEA) in 1979. In the same year the National Joint Council for Gay Teenagers (JCGT) was established and, though not a youth membership organisation itself, its purpose was to facilitate the development of lesbian and gay youth groups throughout the country.

The JCGT published two booklets. The first, *I Know What I Am* was a response to the Home Office Working Paper on the age of consent in relation to sexual offences. It was a carefully argued response, liberally interspersed with comments from young lesbians and gays themselves and concluded unequivocally that:

> the only civilised answer . . . would be to remove consensual sexual acts altogether from the realm of the criminal law. Only then can hundreds of thousands of young gay people freely seek and receive the best help and advice, make relationships of their choosing without constant fear of sanction, and use their energies and skills fully to make the world a better, kinder place. Only then, too, can the heterosexual majority obtain the help and education it needs to live in harmony with gay women and men at home, at school and at work (JCGT, 1980, p. 14).

Breaking The Silence was the JCGT's second publication, issued in 1981, consisting of accounts from thirty-four young lesbians and gays of their experiences growing up in heterosexist environments. The cumulative impact is a powerful and vivid picture of a vast range of struggle, unhappiness and joy.

The struggle within the Youth Service, from a national point of view, remains very much in its infancy. The pioneering work of the Joint Council for Gay Teenagers and the London Gay Teenage Group are invaluable foundations. The latter's recognition by ILEA along with subsequently formed lesbian and gay London youth groups was undoubtedly important groundwork. It led to the appointment by ILEA in 1985 of a lesbian youth and community advisory officer with the specific remit 'to support and facilitate the development of lesbian and gay youth groups'. The London Gay Teenage Group also secured GLC funding for a year-long research project in 1982 which resulted in the publication of four more booklets on the experiences of young lesbians and gays. Although centred on London, the research findings typically represent the difficulties of the vast majority of young people throughout the country who choose to identify their sexuality with someone of the same sex.

In view of the unwillingness of most local bureaucracies to adopt positive policies and practices for lesbians and gays, it is not surprising that many have spurned the authorities and adults and organised themselves. This self-help movement emerged at roughly the same time that some lesbian and gay youth workers began to organise within the service, but during the late 1970s worked very much in tandem with the workers through the Joint Council. However, by 1981, the Gay Youth Movement was holding its first annual general meeting and was sufficiently strong to be asserting stridently its autonomy, rejecting adult interference and announcing its distrust of formal organisations, including gay ones. The Lesbian and Gay Youth Movement Magazine (L & GYM) often provides vital reminders to older and, to greater or lesser extents, bureaucratised lesbian and gay workers, of the dangers of becoming institutionalised in our struggle against heterosexism, and consequently assuming a condescending approach to young lesbians and gays. The magazine's reviewer of Lorraine Trenchard's booklet, *Talking About Lesbians*, for example, notes:

> At times Lorraine's comments in the book read like the Blue Peter annual . . . worthy lines included: 'the young lesbians have shown themselves to be aware and worthy of admiration' and 'I have come to know a number of these young lesbians and have developed a great respect for them.' I know that her intentions behind the book were good but it's hard to find any justifications for its sickly social-work style or for why funding for the book didn't go directly to young lesbians. (*Lesbian and Gay Youth Magazine*, 1985, p. 8)

In view of the opposition in L & GYM encounters from lesbian and gay organisations it is understandable that they have no intention of devoting their energies to working within heterosexist bureaucracies. Also eschewing pragmatism, Fitzpatrick and Milligan make a scathing attack on the bureaucratised professional lesbian and gay workers. This is the outcome of an analysis which uncompromisingly rejects co-option by the state: 'In return for fat salaries and token campaigns, the radicals of the seventies accepted and reduced horizons dictated by their Labour paymasters . . . In return for a few grants for lesbian and gay centres and 'phone lines, they put off to the future the struggle against the criminalisation of homosexuality and the brutalisation of homosexuals' (Fitzpatrick and Milligan, 1987).

A perennial issue facing progressive movements is when, how and to what extent they work within the structures they struggle to subvert. Progressive movements are seldom, if ever, composed of look-alike identikit people; heterogeneity, not homogeneity, is as much a characteristic of such movements as it is of the powerful. Only crude, simplistic generalisations produce notions of the 'minority' and the 'majority' being homogeneous, self-contained entities. Such unthinking slogans are merely substitutes for complex analysis. Thus it is that those people with a blind heterosexism not only regard all 'homosexuals' as being the same, but even fail to clarify what they mean by 'homosexual'. Lesbians and gays are therefore forced to struggle with what it means for them to be lesbian and gay and that continuing process, not surprisingly, has produced and continues to produce a rich variety of cultural styles. Different styles, influenced by, among many factors, sex, class, ethnicity and age, give rise to a variety of political strategies.

The Lesbian and Gay Youth Movement best illustrates those working autonomously, suspicious of, and uninterested in, working within existing heterosexist bureaucracies, such as political parties, local authorities and the Youth Service. Other, usually older lesbians and gays, largely because of their location within the social structure (and therefore able to work within existing structures) perceive a need for initiating change from within. On a pragmatic level the two need not be antagonistic; it is not a question of one or other strategy. Liberation struggles have to cope with numerous targets at numerous levels; there is scope for all approaches.

> Lesbian and gay equal opportunities units provide an indispensable stamp of legitimacy for our struggle . . . and indeed at the current time perhaps a pre-requisite for change, we need to remember that they are a beginning, a means and not the end of lesbian and gay rights [for] even lesbian and gay workers are not immune to the tentacles of professionalism . . . the professional invariably being the antidote to the political. (Kent-Baguley, 1986, p. 12)

The vast majority of workers, and youth and community workers are no exception, are still colluding with the oppression of heterosexism. It is time they recognised that and began the long, discomforting and painful process of analysis for change and stopped pretending that they treat everyone 'as people'. For such a view is, at best, charitable, idealistic and divorced from reality and, at worst, a conscious lie to avoid being challenged. It denies both the differences people are trying to express and the oppression they experience for their struggled expression. There is no soft option; you either join the struggle against heterosexist oppression or remain an oppressor.

5

Youth Work and Race

KEITH POPPLE

The purpose of this chapter is to unravel and clarify some of the experiences and needs of black young people, particularly in relation to youth work; and to examine theories and methods of challenging young white people's racism while validating their experiences in a society that has offered many of them an insecure job market and little or no economic power.

Before beginning there is a need to clarify some points of terminology. The word 'black' is used as a shorthand term for Afro-Caribbean, Asian, Chinese, Vietnamese, and many other so-called 'ethnic minority' groups. It is recognised that there are obvious and specific differences in the cultural processes of these groups but they do possess similarities in the way that white society has received and treated them. They all suffer structural and racial disadvantages and discrimination in British society. More specifically the term 'Afro-Caribbean' is used rather than 'West Indian' because the former describes more accurately the links with Africa while the latter has its roots in the colonial past and is a label coined by white colonisers.

'Racism' is referred to throughout this chapter. This is a shorthand term for the theory that the world's population is divisible into unequal and hierarchical categories based on physical differences, particularly skin colour. The dominating powerful groups, which are largely white, impose their conceptions on the rest of society. This is sometimes simplistically shortened to 'prejudice plus power equals racism'.

For a more detailed description of the term, the reader should refer to Rex (1986).

The reader will note that the term 'first generation' is used to describe those black migrants who came to Britain as part of the postwar labour immigration. As Fryer (1984) describes in his comprehensive study of black people's history in Britain, the migration of black people to this country is not a recent phenomenon. Africans and Asians and their descendants have been living in Britain for nearly 500 years, with many thousands of black young people brought to Britain against their wishes to work as domestic slaves. Other blacks came of their own accord, contributing 'to the rise of British capitalism and, in particular, to the accumulation of wealth that fuelled the industrial revolution' (Fryer, 1984, p. xi).

Large-scale immigration began in the late 1940s from the Caribbean islands, followed by immigration from the South Asian countries of India, Pakistan (and later Bangladesh) and Ceylon (Sri Lanka). These migrants established their home in Britain and in due course brought up children who are frequently referred to in race relations literature as the 'second generation'. These are the black youth referred to throughout this work.

The reader should note that shortage of space has prevented this chapter from addressing other significant groups residing in Britain: the Irish, the Jewish and the East European communities.

Colonisation and migrant labour

To understand the experiences of second-generation blacks in British society it is important to refer to postwar labour migration. From 1945 Europe and the USA were rapidly rebuilding their economic infrastructures. Britain experienced an expanding and booming economy while suffering a chronic labour shortage. Employers, both public and private, significantly encouraged blacks to migrate to Britain. It cannot be left unstated that, as a junior minister, Enoch Powell actively encouraged Afro-Caribbean nurses to

work in the National Health Service (NHS).

The jobs the immigrants filled were largely low-waged and semi-skilled, and often located in declining areas of large conurbations, particularly in the South-East. Immigrants were also attracted to work in the textile mills of the North-West, and the manufacturing industries of the Midlands (Runnymede Trust, 1980, p. 5). Black workers are still concentrated in industries and services characterised by unsocial hours, shift working, low pay and a poor working environment (PSI, 1984; Hamnett and Randolph, 1988). As Phizacklea and Miles state, 'black labour tends to be replacement labour, employed in socially undesirable jobs vacated in the context of full employment by white indigenous labour' (1980, p. 19).

Black people's arrival in Britain is paralleled by labour migration from Wales, Northern England and Scotland towards the South and Midlands. There was also a move from manual work, that is from jobs termed undesirable (Bohning, 1981) or inferior (Castles and Kosack, 1981), towards white-collar occupations. Married women and migrant workers tended to be taken into these jobs, many of which had been abandoned by those moving up the employment hierarchy.

It is difficult to appreciate the devastating experiences of those who travelled to Britain for work. Most immigrants regarded British society with some respect even if the reality of British rule in the Caribbean and Asian sub-continent had been less than liberal. Some came believing it was a promised land that provided opportunities of wealth, and certainly acceptance for themselves and later their children. Migration from the Caribbean and South Asia had long been a logical route for escape from the interrelated difficulties of over-population and under-employment.

When migrants arrived they found no facilities or assistance to ease their change from a life style moulded thousands of miles away to that needed to sustain living in a developed industrial society. They found no co-ordination of educational, housing or welfare services, nor specialist help from the various welfare agencies. Patterson's (1963) work indicates that initial contact with whites proved a bitter disappointment (see also Lawrence, 1974, p. 30). The labour and housing markets led to migrants being concentrated in some of the worst housing in Britain's declining inner-city areas (Rex and Moore, 1967). How the immigrants settled in Britain with all the attendant problems of racism, exclusion and injustice is now becoming a well-documented chapter in British postwar history (see, for example Ramdin, 1987).

Unemployment and immigration controls

Since the 1960s, as unemployment increased, successive governments have been closing the door on further immigration from the New Commonwealth. It is now almost impossible for Afro-Caribbeans or South Asians to settle in Britain unless their next of kin is already residing here. As Peach (1968) notes, the level of migration to Britain was responsive to the domestic labour market and it is questionable whether immigration controls have done little more than accede to white people's fear of being 'swamped' by migrants. Entry into the EEC has allowed access to EEC nationals seeking work here. Little wonder immigration legislation and practices are considered to be examples of institutional racism. Immigration laws have been devised to keep blacks out but allow whites in.

Many first-generation blacks have experienced a decline in their economic position while living in Britain. Like all members of the working class they gained from the postwar expansion and, although initially victimised in the housing market, a substantial proportion were able gradually to move from private rented accommodation into council tenancies and owner occupation. When Britain's economy faltered in the 1970s migrants began to experience the effects of structural unemployment.

Young blacks and job opportunities

The 1985 Labour Force Survey indicates that unemployment rates were, in general, appreciably higher among blacks than whites. While white female unemployment was around 10 per cent (11 per cent for men), for Afro-Caribbeans it is nearly double this rate at 19 per cent (23 per cent for men), and for Pakistanis and Bangladeshis the figure was 44 per cent (28 per cent for men). Unemployment among Indian females stood at 15 per cent (18 per cent for men) (OPCS, 1987b, p. 22). According to Youthaid, the plight of black young people is likely to be substantially worse (1985, p. 3). Figures produced by Roll (1988) appear to confirm higher unemployment rates among black and Asian young people and a considerable degree of 'hiding' from unemployment in education and training (see Chapter 7, Figure 7.3).

The inbalance in unemployment rates is the result of two principal factors, apart from the impact of class (see Chapter 7). Firstly, young people continually encounter direct discrimination when applying for jobs. CRE (1982) research confirmed that 50 per cent of all employers discriminated against applications from ethnic minorities, although this was outlawed by the 1976 Race Relations Act. Hubbuck and Carter (1980) showed that, in 48 per cent of the situation tests in which Afro-Caribbean, Asian and white candidates, with equal educational qualifications, applied for the same job, either or both of the non-white candidates were refused an interview, unlike their white colleague. In six per cent of cases the reverse happened.

Secondly, black young people are subject to indirect discrimination in the labour market. On the whole this is more pervasive and undefinable. Workers in the industrial field are often recruited informally or by 'word of mouth'. Frequently firms do not advertise or use Job Centres. Jenkins (1982) indicates that such recruitment policies have definite advantages for the employer. The status or reputation of the employee recommending the applicant helps the employer to 'assess' the applicant's ability; those introducing the newcomer will also assist in ensuring their acceptable behaviour; this fosters healthy industrial relations; it is a cheap form of recruitment when there are hundreds of job seekers; and it assists in keeping the number of applicants down to manageable proportions. Jenkins's work, and Lee and Wrench's study (1983), show that this informal recruitment disadvantages ethnic minorities.

For those in employment there are appreciable differences between work undertaken by whites, Asians and Afro-Caribbeans. Overall whites undertake work of a higher level than blacks, but there are large variations between men and women, and between different sections of the black population. The PSI survey (1984) found that 83 per cent of Afro-Caribbean male workers are engaged in manual jobs, compared with 73 per cent of Asian men and 58 per cent of white men. The survey also found that 19 per cent of white male workers are employers, managers and professional workers, with 13 per cent of Asians in the same category, but only 5 per cent of Afro-Caribbeans. The proportion of white men in 'other manual' work is double that for blacks. Variations exist between the different Asian groups with job levels much higher for African Asians than for others. In other groupings, nearly 70 per cent of Bangladeshi employees are in semi-skilled or unskilled work, compared with 40 per cent of Indian and Pakistani employees and 25 per cent of African Asian employees. These figures are generally supported by data from the labour force survey (OPCS, 1987b).

In the case of women, there is a larger proportion of non-manual workers among whites. The percentage of Asians in professional and managerial employment approximate to that of whites. The percentage of 'other non-manual' workers is equal between Afro-Caribbean and whites, with Asians registering a lower percentage. According to the PSI survey (1984) the semi-skilled account for a larger section of the manual work-force among blacks than among whites and there is a higher percentage of unskilled workers among whites. The report argues that this is mainly because of the higher percentage of white women in part-time employment.

Qualifications have played a limited part in explaining job levels. The PSI survey (1984) found that seven per cent of Asians who had gained qualifications of A level standard or above were employed in semi-skilled or unskilled manual jobs, compared with two per cent of whites. 84 per cent of whites with these higher educational qualifications undertake non-manual jobs, compared with 75 per cent of Asians. The survey shows that there has been a recent development of Asian males under the age of 25 years being engaged as professionals, employers of managers. As many as 18 per cent of Asian males aged between 16 and 25 are in this category. This compares with seven per cent of white men of the same age and four per cent of Afro-Caribbeans. Asians are under-represented in the second highest category, 'other non-manual', with 11 per cent compared with 30 per cent of whites and 27 per cent of Afro-Caribbeans. Asians are highly represented in the low category of semi-skilled manual with 30 per cent compared with 11 per cent of whites and 23 per cent of Afro-Caribbeans. The job levels of white and Afro-Caribbean women under 25 years of age are similar although Asian young women are twice as likely to be in semi-skilled manual jobs compared with whites and Afro-Caribbeans, and the total proportion in white-collar employment is significantly smaller.

Education for the few

Young blacks similarly experience difficulties in the education system. The *Swann Report* (HMSO, 1985) confirmed the findings of the *Rampton Report* (HMSO, 1981a) that Afro-Caribbean children were on average under-achieving at school and are more likely than white children to acquire poor or average examination results. It broadly replicated a survey undertaken by Rampton of 1978/9 school leavers from LEAs which had high concentrations of children from black groups who, between them, were thought to account for approximately one-half of all black school leavers. Swann showed that Afro-Caribbean leavers had secured a slight improvement in their relative performance over the period but they were still under-achieving markedly in comparison with their peers. Asian children show on average a pattern of achievement which resembles that of white children, although there is a variation between different Asian groups; Bangladeshi children in particular are shown to be seriously under-achieving. While inter-ethnic comparisons of attainment can lead to an over-simplified and distorted view of black students' performance (particularly Afro-Caribbean) (Troyna, 1984), the gaps in analysis are illuminating.

Neither the Rampton nor the Swann Committee provides a breakdown in the differences between gender, although the work of Driver (1977, 1981) and Fuller (1981, 1982) shows that Afro-Caribbean girls achieved better examination results than Afro-Caribbean boys and their white counterparts. Fuller believes that the girls, aware of their double disadvantage of being both black and female are determined to achieve academic qualifications. This could be regarded as a form of resistance to racism, although it would be incorrect to assume that such girls are likely to become members of a privileged labour elite. As Fuller remarks,

A labour markes which is largely sex-segregated and which operates differential rates of pay from women and men means that the only edge which the black girls may have over black boys is that their paper qualifications may give them the option of obtaining their lower wages through shorter hours of work and in possibly more congenial working conditions. (1982, p. 98)

Evidence relating to the level of qualification attainment for Asian girls is limited. Research is emerging from white feminists concerning white girls' schooling but relatively little attention has been given to black girls' and in particular Asian girls' education, which in itself is a reflection of the way in which their needs have been marginalised or ignored (among the exceptions, see Griffin, 1985; Wright 1987). There seems little attempt to address the positions of black girls other than as part of generalised observations and this is often as appendages to the concerns of all girls or to those of black boys. Parmar argues that much of race relations literature is gender-blind or examines black women in terms of their family life, which in relation to Asian women 'reproduces commonsense ideas about their passivity, the role of husbands, and religious rules' (1982, p. 238).

One of the few studies that relate to Asian girls is that by

Driver and Ballard (1979) whose work found that Asian pupils achieved higher average examination results than did white pupils attending the same school. Their qualification to this conclusion was that the mean level of achievement was low in relation to pupils in other schools. They further concluded that Asian girls had a better record of 'school persistence' than the boys or white pupils and the stereotype of Asian girls as cowed and downtrodden was incorrect.

It is generally assumed that socio-economic factors such as poor housing and poverty are connected with poor attainment in school, and that certain groups of black students may suffer disproportionately as a result (HMSO, 1985, pp. 81–2). However this should not be taken as indicating that the school is powerless in this respect. Wright's (1987) investigation suggests a strong association between school processes and the educational attainment of Afro-Caribbean students. Such processes, which include streaming, selection, pedagogy, classroom control and extramural activity, not only have an impact on attainment, but also profoundly influence the broader learning and socialisation that students experience.

Recognising the needs

The Youth Service's first official recognition of the needs of black young people was in the *Hunt Report* (DES, 1967) which was concerned with the ways in which the Service could assist in the absorption of young immigrants into British society. The report was compiled at a time when just over one million blacks lived in Britain, or under two per cent of the population, of whom only a small proportion had been born in the United Kingdom. The report accepted a small degree of separation as a temporary measure, with separate black clubs tolerated 'on the grounds that they might be better than nothing, but would still hope that they might become integrated later' (ibid., p. 47). Overall, the Hunt Committee rejected the notion of separate youth provision and concluded that the service should attempt to bring black, Asian and white young people together in youth projects and clubs.

Despite the Hunt Committee's general warnings that appropriate action had to be taken to assist young blacks if the service were to avoid possible difficulties, little happened at an official level for several years (YSIC, 1972). One important development established during the 1970s was the *Youth and Race in the Inner City Project* located at the National Association of Youth Clubs (NAYC), which was sponsored by the DES and the Voluntary Service Unit of the Home Office. This action research project sought to describe the response by voluntary and statutory youth agencies to the situation of young black people living in inner cities. In 1973 the project director questioned the Hunt Report's concern with integration:

> Do we subscribe willy-nilly, and despite all that has gone on since the Hunt Committee reported, to the integration consensus in which the youth service continues to trade? I suggest that youth work with black youth given the evidence from within the youth service over the last few years clouds the reality of their everyday experience and attempts to control and contain the effects of that experience on them by engaging in massive irrelevancies as far as their needs are concerned. (John, 1981, p. 11)

A later Commission for Racial Equality (CRE) report on the problem facing youth in a multi-racial society and examined the services responsible for meeting them (1980). Published prior to the St Pauls, Brixton and Toxteth disturbances and the subsequent *Scarman Report* (HMSO, 1981b), the CRE's work proved to be a largely ignored warning of the plight of Afro-Caribbean and Asian young people. The Report was critical of local and central government's inadequate youth policy and pointed to white people refusing to appreciate the worsening conditions for black young people. Quoting figures that indicate the low take-up of youth provision by blacks, the CRE called for a radical review of the Youth Service to meet the needs of ethnic minorities and spelt out how an effective policy could be devised. The report was a distinct move from the integrationist themes of the Hunt Report with its acceptance of separate centres for young blacks and was to set something of the tone for later debates.

Youth provision for young blacks in the mid- and late 1980s

The *Thompson Report* (HMSO, 1982) recognised, with the benefit of hindsight, the naivety of the Hunt Committee's recommendation that there should be integrated youth club work which encompassed all young people in a particular area regardless of ethnic background. Instead the Thompson Review Group suggested that youth provision should reflect the values and attitudes of the neighbourhoods from which the young people came. Thompson signified a positive shift in the understanding of young black people's needs and one that reflected the opinions of many workers. Evidence from the DES (1983b) indicates that current usage of youth clubs is significantly higher among Afro-Caribbean young people than white young people with some 52 per cent currently attending one or more club. However the same survey reveals that Asians are least likely to use youth clubs (20 per cent), the exception being sports centres and school clubs where it is thought parental constraints do not operate as strongly. The survey found only 45 per cent of Asian young people had ever attended a youth club. A more detailed survey undertaken by Willis and colleagues (1985) for the Wolverhampton Borough Council found that, in an authority where one-third of 16- to 24-year-olds were unemployed, the young jobless were more likely in general to go to the youth clubs. On closer scrutiny one can see that this is largely accounted for by the very high attendance among young Afro-Caribbeans.

The use of youth clubs by young Afro-Caribbeans is an interesting phenomenon and can be explained partly in socio-economic class terms. Proportionately more working-class young people attend youth clubs, than do middle class (see Chapter 7). Since Afro-Caribbean young people are more likely to come from working-class backgrounds than Asians or whites, one would expect them to be attending youth clubs in higher proportions. A further explanation is the Afro-Caribbean community's reaction to the racism of white youth clubs which has led to the establishment (with financial assistance from the CRE and certain LEAs) of a network of clubs and centres which tend in general to cater specifically for Afro-Caribbean young people (CRE, 1981). Here we should also note possible differences in perception:

> Black young people see youth clubs much less as clubs in the traditional sense, and much more as territory within which they could give expression to cultural preferences and political options, and establish an identity as young blacks and resist the repressive attempts of the state. (John, 1981, p. 38)

Financial support for local youth projects has come from central government who can provide a 75 per cent grant to local authorities for specific work. This funding under Section 11 of the 1966 Local Government Act is restricted to areas where two per cent or more of the population are from the New Commonwealth. Similarly the Urban Aid programme which was initiated in 1968 provides a 75 per cent grant for particular projects, but unlike Section 11 finance it can be used for capital expenditure and is not restricted to a requirement of a designated ethnic population. The drawback to both these schemes lies in the nature of short-term funding which makes a project's life precarious and workers insecure. Further, Section 11 'is firmly rooted in a policy tradition that prefers voluntarism to compulsion, inexplicitness to explicitness, assimilation to anti-racism, marginal rather than mainstream spending, and is preoccupied with racial disadvantage rather than racial discrimination (Dorn and Hibbert, 1987, p. 60).

The Scout Association, which claims it is strongly committed to a 'multi-cultural society', launched a Scoutreach development programme to encourage young blacks to join local scout groups. The results have yet to be fully analysed although the overall level of black participation in the scouts is still low. By October 1985, Afro-Caribbeans made up only 0·30 per cent of the total scout membership and Asians 0·58 per cent. These figures have to be compared with those available for 1974 which show that there has been a rise of 107 per cent in 11 years in the scout membership of Hindus, Sikhs, Muslims and Buddhists. Figures relating to Afro-Caribbeans in 1974 are not available (Scout Association, 1985). Overall it appears there was a growth in young black boys joining the scouts, but as a percentage of all scouts this was still small, and as a percentage of all black young males it was marginal.

The recent upturn in young black's affiliation is in stark contrast to evidence collected over the years that black young people have not taken up conventional Youth Service provision because of hostility and fears of rejections. A study by Cross (1977) found that only 33 per cent of black youths had used youth clubs, and at the time of the study only 10 per cent were still attending. Asians were found to be less likely to use the facilities than Afro-Caribbean youth and the problem was identified as being not one of lack of familiarity with the institutions. Interviews revealed that black youths were unable to use their local youth clubs because they were made unwelcome by young white people. The CRC conducted a number of follow-up seminars with youth workers and policy makers and found the latter claimed to be operating within certain financial and staffing constraints. The workers experienced a sense of low morale and isolation when confronted with black young people who were themselves victims of racial abuse, homelessness, unemployment and conflict with the police (CRC, 1977). The youth workers concluded that the Youth Service was not relevant to many of the difficulties that young people in multi-racial areas encountered and, more seriously, was never intended to be. As one report noted, 'Black youths are being debarred from certain Community Centres, not expressively but subtly and unobstructively on the grounds that they love too much reggae, "would not conform" and were "too noisy". It is being noted that because of their "life styles" black youth should be given their own centres' (Birmingham CRC, 1980, p. 36).

In those areas that do often have youth clubs serving the local black population there can often be a need for youth workers and management committees to consider the programme. An HMI Report on three youth clubs in Lambeth suggested that they could offer their accommodation and resources to specific black groups, as well as providing programmes to 'promote wider understanding between young people of different ethnic origins' (DES, 1983a, p. 18). Overall the report is critical of the clubs inspected and thought they could be clearer in their objectives in relation to the community. As it was, the clubs were 'characterised by individual and *ad hoc* responses' (ibid., p. 23). While some of the particular criticisms were disputed by ILEA, the general argument contains a degree of truth. Williams (1988) has subsequently asserted that much provision used by black young people dismally fails to meet their needs, a point also made by Brown (1987). The former writer argues that: 'One of the most important and pressing roles which the youth service in general, and black clubs in particular, must assume is the politicization of black young people, especially that faction which drifts into crime' (1988, pp. 61–2). Significantly, he takes his analysis substantially beyond much of the literature's fascination with what Intermediate Treatment (IT) workers tend to label 'the heavy end'. He contends that there have been major developments in youth provision within black communities. Here we might focus on the work with the young people undertaken by black churches and churchpeople (see Garrett, 1986). This is hardly a new phenomenon, interventions of this form certainly dating back to the 1920s (Smith, 1988, p. 31). However what is becoming clear is that the scale, scope and nature of provision is still to be fully appreciated, particularly in respect of provision within Asian religious organisations. In a similar way it is important to appreciate the development of work with Afro-Caribbean and Asian young women and girls (see, for example, Jamdagni, 1980; Lee-Sang, 1982; Parmar, 1988). It often involves exploring rather different forms of intervention, as Dennis has shown with regard to work with young black women with children. Such work

cannot be centre-based because centres don't have anything to offer them. Fitting in with their lifestyle means accepting their definition of themselves – and their attitude towards 'professionals'. They are used to the interest of 'professionals' – have often been bombarded by them – and to being seen by them as 'problems'. Young Black women are not 'problems' to themselves; they do not see themselves in this way. (Dennis, 1982, p. 10)

Within and beyond such provision, Williams argues that practice must be cultivated in respect of the sizeable proportion of black young people who 'are trying to "make it" in the white system' (1988, p. 69); and that particular attention must be paid to the growing number who are defining themselves as 'black British' and are trying to work out exactly what this means (Williams, 1989). In terms of the old debates about welfare and the working class, it is being argued that it is necessary to focus upon the 'respectables' as well as the 'roughs'.

Working-class exclusiveness

The 'rough' and 'respectable' distinction has also made something of a come-back in furthering our understanding of working-class racism. Cohen has suggested that there is a 'rough' racism:

> centred on territorial rivalries and the perceived threat of Jewish/Irish/Blacks invading 'our' areas. This is largely a racism of male youth. There is also a respectable racism organised around moral panics concerning 'outrages to public propriety' supposedly committed by ethnic minority communities elders. (1988, p. 34)

The working class have always used communities to protect themselves from the difficulties and harshness of life, traditionally establishing informal systems of mutual support and co-operation which have acted as a protective wall for those inside and a repellant to outsiders. Engels (1969) discussed its importance against a set of social relationships where alienation and deprivation defined nearly all the ways in which people related to one another. One of the cornerstones of capitalism has been the ensuring that men and women compete against each other for work, housing, goods and services. Community life and groupings can be a reaction to this system of competitive social and economic relationships which separates individuals from one another. However the contradictory manner in which capitalism operates ensures that, although the working class are forced to compete with one another, they do learn from each other. Without romanticising aspects of working-class culture, there is an element of its functioning built up over the years which results in its people assisting one another at a time of individual hardship or misfortune, or when family units are under pressure.

Community, therefore, is one of the most important cultural ways in which the urban working class have over the years attempted to improve their lives. Working-class culture is, though, constantly evolving and it has been claimed that working-class community life has been eroded in the last fifteen years or so (Seabrook, 1982). It is still a powerful force in its relationship to outsiders, particularly migrant workers. In the nineteenth century the Irish migrant workers experienced verbal and physical abuse by such communities, almost parallel to that experienced by black immigrants in the latter half of the twentieth century. Engels makes reference to the Irish workers as an exploited group in English society, but believed the racial mix of English and Irish working people would hasten the class confrontation with the bourgeoisie (Engels, 1969, p. 153).

Attacks against racial minorities have been historical features of working-class communities, from the violence directed against the Irish in the nineteenth century, to the attacks on Jews in London's East End in the 1930s and the attacks on Asians in the 1970s and 1980s. This violent xenophobia can be a direct result of keeping working-class people ignorant of the reasons for migrants' presence in their communities and placing them in competition with each other. Moreover, in recent times, numerous whites have associated the physical decline of their area with the influx of blacks, something right-wing groups like the National Front and politicians including Enoch Powell have been quick to exploit. Yet, at the same time, the sense of community has also acted against 'outsiders' seeking to attack minorities, for example, the anti-Fascist actions of the 1930s (see Cohen, 1988, p. 37).

The extent to which there had been an increase in violence on blacks by whites is documented by Klug (1982), with Asians particularly vulnerable to physical attack. A report from a Home Office (1981) study found that there could be as many as 7000 racially motivated attacks a year, with Asians 50 times more likely to be victims than whites, with other black people 36 times more vulnerable. *Hansard* (23 July 1985) showed that there were 691 reported cases of racial attacks and harassment in London for the first six months of 1985. The Newham Monitoring Project logged 1200 cases of racist attacks in five years and believed there is major under-reporting of attacks to the Metropolitan Police (GLC, 1985).

It would be wrong to conclude that all white working-class communities are engaged in warfare against black people. This is plainly not the case. The underlying resentment towards black people's presence is, however, fed by myths, prejudice and misinformation conveyed through the major social institutions, particularly the media and the education system. British white culture has its own dynamic force that perpetuates racism. There has also been a danger of focussing on working-class responses and so ignoring the ideology of racism created and sustained by the middle classes in order to support their position and enterprises (see Fryer, 1984, pp. 133–90).

Black young people's reaction and response

Working-class exclusivity has taken its toll on black young people. As we have seen, until recently blacks were generally finding youth clubs and their members hostile and unfriendly towards their presence. The development of Afro-Caribbean and Asian self-help youth projects is a result of this exclusivity, as much as it is a response to the lack of specific provision for black young people. Working-class exclusivity has led black people to protect their interests by relying on their strong cultural groupings to act as a barrier against racism and discrimination. As individuals, blacks are not immune to the abuse and harassment they receive from white society, but by establishing and maintaining groupings they are able to develop their own material forms which have acted as a counter to racism and provide an opportunity to encourage cultural formations in their own right. In a highly complex and interwoven system of cultural overlap, black people have sustained and generated cultures and formations that not only react to discrimination and inequality but also create processes that have an identity and vitality of their own, independent of hostility from the dominant group.

Within the black, as within any community, there are generational differences. Parents who often had a direct experience of the Asian sub-continent or Caribbean island, drew strength from experiencing their culture in their homeland, and had a secure knowledge of their own language. Castles *et al.* indicate that migrants did not form a homogeneous group, coming to Britain from 'different historical and political backgrounds, and from different classes within their own societies' (1984, p. 42). For instance, would-be Pakistani migrants were screened in order to secure the labour of those with wealth and skills, while some of the Indians who migrated to work in the West Midlands foundries were from the old colonial administrative class in the Punjab. Although they all suffered different forms of racism, they have perhaps experienced less harassment than their children. Unlike their children, they did not attend British schools, which have largely provided inappropriate education for black children (Stone, 1981), and they have not been subjected to the high levels of unemployment experienced by their offspring.

Although at a different stage in history, young black's experiences of Britain are similar to those of their parents, yet they have created ways of resisting aspects of racism and discrimination. Some have formed strong cultural groups of their own which are often in conflict with their parents. For instance, a small but significant section of Afro-Caribbean young people have found within Rastafarianism a complete new identity and pride in their cultural links with Africa. Cashmore (1983) discusses the issue of the older Afro-Caribbean generation finding the movement disquietening, with black Christians regarding it as heretical. He states that, as nearly all Rastas come from conventional Christian homes, there were inevitable parent–child conflicts over belief; 'In practically all cases tensions had caused either temporary or permanent rifts, with the youth leaving home after disagreements had grown to a head' (ibid., p. 193). For the black youth involved, Rastafarianism can provide a greater sense of resilience and purpose. Recently media attention has falsely suggested a relationship between Rastafarianism and criminal activity. Cashmore shows that, although the belief system of Rastas is 'broadly based and amenable to differential interpretation, adaption, supplementation and abridgement' (ibid., p. 7) it is engaged in providing its followers with opportunities to 'revive the true self' (ibid., p. 171), not in street crime.

Other Afro-Caribbean young people have similar feelings of resentment to their parents' commitment to unrewarding, poorly paid hard labour, and have, through necessity, engaged in 'hustling', a throw-back to life in the Caribbean islands (Pryce, 1979). This is, arguably, a 'realistic' solution to an economically unjust situation. It can also be argued that this individualistic and competitive activity demonstrates both a vibrance of culture, as well as a disdain and arrogance towards the victims of hustling. That energy, being contained within a criminalised sphere, is also denied to the political struggle (Williams, 1988). In general black young people have demonstrated an ability to survive, use and identify, rather than internalise aspects of many cultures (Kahn, 1982). This ability to manipulate more than one culture is never seen by white society as a source of strength and ability, but posed as a cause of stress and conflict. The negotiation of young blacks' culture can be seen in many forms. Black young people often do not want to disinherit all their parents' cultures, in which they have pride, but they do demand change. Jamdagni (1980) provides evidence of the way in which Asian teenage girls become aware of the differences between Asian culture and dominant white society. Asian girls are often acutely aware of their parents' need to cling to family and cultural ties as a reaction to a frequently hostile environment. They can feel that they are 'missing out' on a youth culture that their parents believe should be out of bounds to their daughter. The ensuing struggle between conflicting expectations and pressures placed upon Asian girls between their family and the dominant culture is one of concern to a number of youth workers. As a result, much of the 'mainstream' provision for Asian young women is predicated on notions of identity crisis, cultural conflict, language and communication problems (Parmar, 1988).

Jamdagni believes that the assumption that the problems of Asian girls is one of 'cultural conflict' ignores the external pressures on Asian families in Britain. Asian girls' experiences, therefore, have to be seen within the broader context of being members of an economically and socially disadvantaged group. Jamdagni points out that the notion of 'cultural conflict' presupposes that the problems facing Asian girls are related directly to them being *Asian*. Whereas 'cultural considerations are bound to be more relevant sometimes, it should be recognised that at other times the necessary issues are likely to be those which are applicable to adolescents in all cultures, e.g. conflict between different generations and personalities within families' (1980, p. 131).

The establishment of youth projects by the black community is a further example of the response to exclusion, while providing opportunities for young blacks to develop their own cultural formation. It is part of a wider movement that black people are engaged in, so enabling them to consolidate their social and cultural links while responding to the lack of specific provision. Young people using such clubs and resources frequently identify with their aims as well as exercising some control over their development. It has also been known for self-help youth projects to act as a focus for self-defence in reaction to particular local circumstances such as a Fascist march, a strike or a murder. It has been argued that Asian communities have traditionally identified self-help activity as part of its business enterprises. According to Scott (1982) it is possible to find youth

associations linked to entrepreneurial activities, a situation
not unlike the growth of youth clubs created by Lancashire
and Yorkshire mill owners in the nineteenth century. In
areas where Asians are to be found in larger concentrations,
the self-help organisations have been assisted by statutory
funding. Yet it also has to be recognised that younger
members of Asian communities have evolved their own
political organisation (Carey & Shukur, 1986; Mukherjee,
1988). These organisations often create tension and a challenge to both the dominant white society and the traditional
Asian community. Gilroy (1981) makes reference to this
tension, believing it is rooted in the political strategy rather
than 'aberrant familial practices'. He argues that these
conflicts are based on the fundamental unity of the community concerned and conducted in a manner which makes
dialogue possible. Gilroy provides the example of tension
between the Asian Youth Movement and the Indian Workers, Association, stating that this conflict is 'between corporate and autonomous modes of struggle in a complete
fashion, informed and affected by the peasant political
traditions in which both aspects of the movement have been
formed' (ibid., p. 214; see also Bains, 1988).

CRE-funded self-help black youth projects have attracted
criticism from some writers, including John (1981). He
agrees that such projects act as a bridge between young
black people and the various statutory agencies but believes
that the intermediaries, whether black or white, are selling
black young people short. These intermediaries are often
professional careerists ever willing to 'trade their "responsibility" as an antidote to the assertive, uncompromising
positions adopted by black youth' (ibid., p. 209). John
argues that these careerists have to be resisted as much as
the British State, a position also supported by Bryan *et al.*,
1985). Claims made concerning the success and desirability
of self-help schemes, particularly by the CRE itself, obscure
research experience which suggests that 'self-help schemes
with CRE patronage serve at best to confirm young blacks in
a position marginally within social and political life in this
society, and to frustrate their movement towards independent black organisations' (John, 1981, p. 246). John believes

blacks should not have to rely on a government-appointed body for patronage, but rather should deal directly with their local authorities and elected representatives. As he points out, the Youth Service is one feature in young black people's lives in which they are attempting to respond to their subjective condition of being racially oppressed.

The case for black youth workers

At present there are few black full-time youth workers in Britain and it is only in the last few years that there has been more than a trickle of blacks attenting full-time training courses. It is argued that black youth workers are needed in order that black young people can relate easily and securely to people they trust and subsequently make increased demands on the Youth Service to meet their particular needs. This process has been endorsed by the *Thompson Report* (1982, pp. 59–62). Yet, as Williams (1988) has noted, there can exist considerable tension between black workers and young people, rooted in variables of ideology, culture, gender and experience. Fisher and Day argue that the black youth worker shares with black people a common history, experiences and certain identities and associations. For a black youth worker:

> may be the reference that some people need, and by virtue of his/her skill, position and commitment can assist with personal as well as other problems. The evidence from social psychology seems to indicate that black children achieve higher self-esteem and a positive self-identity when there are appropriate role models for them to emmulate. In other words black youth need black workers. (Fisher and Day, 1983, p. 78)

This argument is taken up by Parmar who emphasises the possibility of non-patronising and non-racist dialogue with young people and their parents (1988, p. 208).

The case for black youth workers should not be confined to full-time positions and much needs to be undertaken in the recruitment and training of black part-time and voluntary youth workers. John (1984) argues that without changes in the structure and nature of the training of both black and white full-time and part-time workers there is a danger that they can work against the interests of black young people. He puts forward a convincing argument that all youth workers are in danger of reinforcing oppression and the label of 'trained' adds further weight to a worker's impact.

In an analysis of the power relations in the Youth Service, John reveals the differentials in pay and conditions of full-time and part-time workers which determine the latters' position in the hierarchical youth work setting. Consequently black part-time workers operating under the direction of a full-time youth worker may find their experiences and skills dismissed on the grounds of race and their position in the power structure. John concludes that the shared experience of blackness and racial identification between worker and young person does not offer sufficient understanding of a complex situation where power relationships operate on a number of different levels.

Anti-racist youth work

Challenging racism among young people has to be set in the context of the years of socialisation which have encouraged white young people to believe that black people are in some way less human or less real or less anything than themselves. To expect any immediate and permanent change among young whites exposed to anti-racist youth work, however utopian and well intentioned, is unrealistic. Undertaking anti-racist youth work with many young whites can be as productive as cultivating oranges in the Arctic Circle. However, this does not diminish the hope youth workers see in the different methods of anti-racist practice which, if used in a collaborative manner, could make some long-term inroads and encourage white young people to take responsibility for their racism.

In the face of limited documented responses to the issue of racism, Ritchie and Marken (1984) provide a useful commentary on strategies which might be used to combat racism. These are: providing the facts; multi-cultural education; political and cultural education; making rules; and confrontation. They admit that these divisions are crude but their work does offer descriptions and critiques which, although not mutually exclusive, do provide youth workers with practical guidance. As a contribution to this debate it is my intention to build upon Ritchie and Marken's ideas with the reservation that, as such work is an emerging practice, this cannot be definitive.

Condemnatory approach

One method of tackling racism that is occasionally used by youth workers is the condemnatory approach. This involves shaming young white people by suggesting that they are a major part of the problem and that racism is wicked and must be eradicated. The condemnatory approach is based on the theory of individual pathology that has informed much social and psychiatric work. It is a worrying aspect that some youth workers who claim to practise anti-racist work hold to the view that the working class need to be shocked or bullied into understanding racism and that the same working class need to change their ideas for their own good. In reality much of this approach is the product of an anti-working class attitude. The youth worker is in effect holding a 'holier than thou' view which makes no connection between oppressions, whether they be based on class, race or gender, and by omission her/his analysis believes that racism resides within the individual rather than recognising that the individual is largely a product of a racist society. This approach must be considered to be counter-productive for it is more likely in the long run to turn young people away from considering the complexity of the issue. In effect it is oppressing white young people rather than liberating them. Indeed it may make the racism of the playground and street all the more virulent (Cohen, 1988, p. 93).

Multi-cultural youth work

Work can be undertaken to introduce white young people to

other cultures. Young people may be unaware of the variety of different cultures in Britain, let alone the rest of the world and could benefit from meeting young people from other races and experiencing other kinds of life styles. If this is to take place it has to be worked upon in a systematic manner. It may be possible to develop programmes within youth clubs or projects which begin to examine young people's own culture and those of others. This needs to be set alongside an extensive educational programme, so that the young people may learn about the culture and beliefs of their neighbours and the nature of the racism they encounter.

The multi-cultural approach has been criticised by a number of writers, including Mullard (1984) and the National Anti-Racist Movement in Education (NAME), anxious to shift the focus from the differences between black and white people, which is sometimes epitomised by samosas and steel bands, to an approach that recognises the issue as being one primarily of structures that both unite and separate people. Cultural differences can be perceived by young white people as further proof of their supremacy as they do not, in their own words, wear 'strange clothes' or worship 'odd-looking gods'. For the multi-cultural approach to have any success it demands a high level of skill and commitment on the part of the youth worker. However it is important to recognise its limitations; as Mullard notes, multi-cultural education is located within a social base of white, middle-class relations. One of its characteristics is to maintain a plural cultural order which continues the reconstruction of colonialism during a crisis of capital. He goes on to argue that multi-culturalism's allegiance is to whites first and then to black groups. Multi-cultural education is 'about the reproduction of culturally defined equality within a situation of the production of structurally defined inequality' (Mullard, 1984, p. 15). Many of the doubts about multi-culturalism are well summed up by Sivanandan:

> While multi-cultural studies may, in expanding differences in customs and culture, help to modity attitudes, such studies are primarily an extension of existing educational techniques and

methods and, as such, allow racism within society, and within the educational system, to pass unchallenged. And education itself comes to be seen in terms of an adjustment process within a racist society and not as a force for changing the values that make the society racist. Ethnic minorities do not suffer disabilities because of ethnic differences, but because such differences are given differential weightage in a system of racial hierarchy. (1985, p. iv)

Educational approach

The main thrust of this form of practice is to provide facts and figures on the black population on the assumption that if young people are in receipt of the correct information they will be able to appreciate more fully the position of the minority groups in Britain. They in turn will become 'teachers' and will counter ignorance in other white young people. This is a popular form of anti-racist work and there are a number of publications that, with adaptations, serve well for this purpose (CVS, 1982; ALTARF, 1984; Dickinson, 1982). There are, however, limitations to this approach, as there is no guarantee that *by itself* a set of facts and figures will change people's deep-seated views. Young people might on face value appear to agree with the youth worker who is communicating the information, but in the privacy of their front room, or on the terraces of the local football club they may well revert to their comfortable myths and stereotypes. Consequently the educational approach is valuable if used in conjunction with other methods.

Race or Racism Awareness Training (RAT)

This approach seeks to confront white people with their institutional and attitudinal racism through structured activities which are designed to heighten personal awareness and encourage a commitment to anti-racist practice. RAT has usually been employed as a preliminary for those who wish to develop anti-racist work, and consequently has been used mainly with adults. Advocates of RAT claim that some black participants gain opportunities in a supportive atmosphere to give vent to feelings of oppression and discrimination, whilst white participants may acquire a clearer understanding, and become more sensitive to the all-pervading nature of racism, as well as an awareness of the action they need to engage in to readicate it (Flynn and Miller, 1984).

One of RAT's sternest critics has been Gurnah (1984). He is critical of Katz (1978), a central exponent of RAT, for her reductionist analysis which implies that racism mentally affects black and whites in the same way. Gurnah is critical of the slogan 'racism is a white problem' which is used throughout RAT. This, he believes, obliges RAT to focus on the individual in the faint hope of changing structural inequalities. Further, Gurnah argues that the tone of the work is often accusatory and highly moralistic, its objective to 'guilt-trip the white workers into action against racism' (1984, p. 15), noting that there are serious negative consequences to RAT, especially in that it provides whites with an acceptable language of anti-racism which can disarm black critics. He argues that such work with members of the petty bourgeoisie is misdirected, as it will never lead to action. For 'it is as if by feeling guilty compensates them for their involvement in the capitalist system. Then the petty bourgeoisie can busily pursue his/her individual political and self-interest, so long as he/she honestly express his/her involvement with the system: it is a kind of altruistic egoism, typical of classical liberalism' (ibid., p. 17). Gurnah does accept that RAT has enabled modest advances to be made, particularly in bringing many blacks into prominence as trainers. However his central criticism remains that RAT is not doing enough to advance black unity.

Carpenter is suspicious of arguments that RAT is not the real struggle but a diversion into guilt-tripping and navel-gazing. She argues that the criticisms of RAT are often in an intellectualised form 'reading like a political tract that needs translating for most people. All this tells me is that its critics are the very people who fear "the people"' (1985, p. 5). She then goes on to say that she is weary of the 'real' revolutionaries who are obsessed by the revolution but are not engaged in the major changes they can make in their own life. Carpenter believes RAT has given her a number of insights, which has led to her wanting to develop strategies for change. She proclaims 'Training itself cannot create change. But people can' (ibid., p. 5).

It would appear that RAT works best when its partici- pants are encouraged to establish links with each other in order to provide continual support. RAT demands that white workers actually *do* something with their new-found understanding and sensitivity. Gurnah's argument that effort is misdirected when working with the petty bourgeoisie appears to deflect attention from the commit- ment and energy many youth workers make to anti-racist practice after undertaking a RAT course. He gives little credit for the major moves made by practitioners who often come from traditions and practices steeped in racism. Work- ers with these positive commitments provide some of the greatest hopes for influencing the take-up of anti-racist practice and the resultant impact on young people: a point ignored by Gurnah.

Cultural and political education

Cultural and political education has been used to engage in an examination of the influential and powerful relationships between nations and people and to build upon the similar- ities facing black and white young people, rather than emphasising the differences. Such an approach takes into account the relationship of young people with the labour market and attempts to place their attitudes and action within a framework that analyses economic and social trends in the wider society. Youth workers engaging in this form of work have, therefore, to appreciate many of the differences that separate black from white in a class society. Yet workers will need to centre their practice around common experiences encompassing both black and white, for inst- ance in unemployment, homelessness and schooling. As Ritchie and Marken note, 'The attempt to discover racial and ethnic themes within the fabric of local urban life promises to be a slow and hesitant process but one which offers the possibility of creating alliances' (1984, p. 17).

In this context, cultural and political education attempts

to make connections between institutional discriminations and inequalities of race, class and gender. It is a liberating form of education, being engaged in understanding forms of oppression as well as creating and transmitting the appropriate knowledge that will assist young people to shed some of the shackles of racism (Smith, M., 1987).

Youth workers who are engaged in cultural and political education have to contend with real, as well as imagined, concerns about black people which often turn on the issue of competition for scarce resources. It is black people who are perceived as a problem, not the context which has created and perpetuated the difficulties facing all the working class, whether black or white. As we have seen, racism is a central strand within working-class culture and must be faced as such by youth workers. However, such are the contradictions within capitalism that racism can be viewed as an issue around which class struggle could be played out. We have witnessed black young people's resistance in the face of racism and discrimination, which has led for many to a growing political understanding of their position within a stratified society. The experiences of black youth are now being replicated at a different point of history in relation to white youth. The rationalisation of production, the realities of unemployment, declining wages and reduced welfare and health services are to some degree experienced by all youth. White and black young people live side by side sharing common and similar experiences of disadvantage. In these circumstances, there may be opportunities for youth workers to engage in cultural and political education which attempts to make links for young people between their daily experiences and the factors that create them. However, it would be naive to believe that an effective strategy is possible without support and commitment by a whole range of workers and administrators. This should not mean a 'freezing' of action but rather a spur to devise appropriate cultural and political strategies.

Developing positive practice

In some accounts of educational efforts to counter racial inequality, what might be called 'multi-cultural' approaches are placed at the other end of a continuum from what are labelled 'anti-racist' approaches. For example, Grinter (1985) has argued that multi-culturalists seek reforms within existing structures, whereas anti-racists seek to transform them. As Troyna has commented, this is an over-simplified picture; 'Closer scrutiny of the themes and concerns of anti-racist educational policy statements reveals a continuity and commonality with earlier multicultural imperatives' (Troyna, 1987, p. 7). The distinction between the models, he argues, can be seen at its sharpest in the contributions from black writers such as Parmar (1982), Mullard (1984) and John (1981). It is a theme that Cohen also takes up:

> The liberal or multi-cultural position rightly resists the compul-
> sory morality of 'positive images' but fails to recognise the forms
> of hidden persuasion which exist in the educational system and
> the wider society. Anti-racists are much better at highlighting
> these dimensions of hegemony, but if they use the most sophisti-
> cated theoretical work to expose the hidden ideological man-
> oeuvres of racism, they no less strenuously exempt their own
> practices of propaganda from similar critical scrutiny. (1988, p.
> 96)

Cohen argues that one way through is to attempt to connect that which is progressive in both anti-racist and multi-cultural approaches with what might be called a cultural perspective. This takes popular culture and the way different groups of people see and understand the world as its starting-point. In many respects it parallels Smith's (1988) advocacy of informal education, mutual aid and popular practice within youth work (see also Jeffs and Smith, 1989).

One final area requires attention before the chapter is concluded – that is the questioning of the need for such practice by white workers operating in areas where there are few black people. Taylor (1984) found widespread com-placency in the 'White Highlands', among both workers and young people, and that these areas had not been forthcoming in formulating strategies to tackle racism. He argues that racism is not confined to areas where black people live. For example, he relates an exercise in getting trainee youth workers in such an area to approach a number of 13-, 16- and 19-year-olds to describe their feelings about black people living in Britain. The exercise found that 13-year-olds were generally consistent in being either indifferent to blacks or welcoming of an opportunity to have black friends. The older teenagers were less tolerant and felt black young people were competitors for sexual partners, jobs and so forth. The 19-year-olds, particularly the unemployed, used black people as scapegoats. If these results are typical of young 'White Highlander' attitudes, then there is much to be done in developing anti-racist youth work programmes, as 'all white areas' are an integral part of a multi-racial Britain.

The reader will be aware by now that the issue of youth and race is a complex one and, in tackling it within broad parameters, I have been unable to develop some ideas as fully as one may wish. I hope this proves to be a strength, as this chapter aims to engage the reader in taking their thinking and practice further, for lack of action on race and racism is an acceptance of the dispiriting state of affairs we have at present; a situation that allows racism to continue unabated.

Youth work appears a marginal activity when related to the social and economic change needed to overcome the problem facing black and white young people in Britain. Youth work may have an important impact on the micro-level affairs of many people and it has been my intention that this chapter will provide a critical analysis of the issues surrounding young people, the role and practice of the youth worker and the Youth Service.

Positively responding to the issue of young people and race will always appear an uphill task in a society that does not prioritise young people, but any disheartening effect this may have should be checked against the fact that there is now more exciting, inventive and, it is hoped, effective work with black young people and anti-racist youth work than existed even five years ago. Encouragingly there has been a growth in progressive youth work where the needs of black young people and anti-racism have shifted centre stage. The task now is to keep the issue central to *practice*.

Acknowledgements

I am grateful to the many people, colleagues and friends, who have given me critical advice, information and support when writing this chapter. My thanks are particularly due to Shahin Popple who has been a great support for my work. Any inaccuracies, omissions or glaring mistakes can be credited to me.

6

Young People, Youth Work and Disability

DON BLACKBURN

The only acceptable forms of debate about disability are those which examine ideologies and practices towards those who have been categorised as disabled. The questions which should be raised concern stereotyping and stigmatisation, together with the institutional practices regarding the construction of the category of disability. Any analysis of the responses to disability should move away from an individualistic psychological focus relating to coping and attitudes, towards a consideration of the central issue of power. Questions of powerlessness are well illustrated by the lack of opportunity afforded disabled people to argue their own case. The dominance of professionals speaking on behalf of those with disabilities often muffles and distorts the voices of those living beneath a blanket of professional care: an experience not unknown in the Youth Service.

The definition and categorisation of people as disabled is an institutional and social practice and for most young people so categorised the main institution involved has been the school. An appreciation of the role of the school is central to an understanding of the representation of disability in regard to young people. It is not only the main institution involved in placing young people in such categories but, as Apple indicates, its perceptions of young people are used by other agencies, for 'the school occupies the central position in a large network of other institutions' (1979, p. 138). Thus, in the first part of this chapter, we will focus on schooling. From there we will go on to examine the youth work response.

Schooling and special needs

Since the advent of compulsion following the Education Acts of the 1870s, schools have sought to exclude those who it was thought would not or could not benefit from institutional provision. The perceived need to identify pupils who would fail to benefit has led, for most of this century, to the development of practices which would aid this task of detection. For those young people who were deaf or blind or had a physical disability, identification at the turn of the century was relatively easy, since their disabilities made them particularly visible within an institution or social group. For others the task of detection was more difficult. There appeared to be a group of young people who, to all intents and purposes, looked like the rest of the school population but who resolutely failed to meet the expectations of the system in terms of school progress. The apparent efficiency of the school system required that these pupils be identified and special measures taken to cater for this form of disability, that is, 'educational backwardness'.

The Report of the Departmental Committee on Defective and Epileptic Children (1898) recommended distinguishing between those who would benefit from special classes ('feeble minded') and those who would not ('idiots'). The following year the Elementary Education (Defective and Epileptic Children) Act enabled local authorities to provide special educational facilities for this group of young people if they wished. Thus the policy of exclusion of these young people was given statutory approval. Separate provision for deaf and blind children had been similarly approved in Scotland in 1890 and in England and Wales in 1893. The difficulty of identifying this group persisted despite the best endeavours of eminent members of the medical and educational worlds. Some felt that clues could be gained as to the mental abilities of pupils from their physical appearance; that the way to facilitate identification was to search for some external 'stigmata of degeneracy' which indicated inner disturbance. This method was held to have a degree of plausibility since in the case of some young people with, for example, Down's syndrome (mongolism) or hypothyroidism (cretinism) there were quite obvious physical characteristics which accompanied the intellectual disabilities. However, in the case of other educationally 'backward' children, the signs were assumed to be correspondingly more difficult to recognise. A certain Dr Beech, giving evidence to the 1898 Committee, felt that in detecting the 'feeble minded' (the group between 'normal' children and 'idiots') 'there were not more than six doctors in England capable of discriminating between imbeciles and feeble minded children' (quoted in Pritchard, 1963, p. 137).

The last decades of the nineteenth century and the early part of the twentieth saw an increasing state concern regarding Britain's position internationally. Competition between nations was seen as a Darwinian struggle and it was increasingly felt to be important that the 'efficiency' of the nation be improved to enhance the country's chances of survival. The British defeats in the Second Boer War heightened anxieties about these issues and in particular the 'low quality' of army recruits served to emphasise them. The school system was expected to play its part in the drive for national efficiency. It was therefore seen as important that those who would not benefit from mainstream provision should be segregated so that the schools could get on with the task of effectively educating the majority of the population. In France in 1905, Binet and Simon produced their first tests designed specifically for identifying young people in need of special education. According to Sutherland 'the effect was immediate and world wide . . . In California Lewis Terman and in Liverpool Cyril Burt began work on the standardisation of Binet's and Simon's tests on American and English school children respectively' (1977, p. 137). The problem of the identification of the 'feeble minded' appeared to have a solution: the intelligence quotient (IQ) test was born.

The proponents of mental testing believed that it was possible to construct relative scales of intellectual ability which could be used to compare individuals. The appearance of a 'scientific' method of grading people seemed to offer a technical solution to the problem of identifying those pupils who would not progress in school terms. Those categorised as feeble-minded were not only perceived as threats to the efficiency of the school system, but were also held to be a source of moral danger. It was believed, particularly by those in the Eugenics Movement, that intelligence was inherited and, in addition, that it was also linked with the ability to behave morally. It followed that morality could be passed on from generation to generation. Dugdale's (1877) purported study of a family called Jukes, and Goddard's (1912) equally suspect report on the 'Kallikak family' sought to demonstrate the relationship between feeble-mindedness, crime and poverty. This viewpoint was not restricted to the fringes of educational and political debate. In this country Cyril Burt was influential for over half a century in arguing the case for mental testing in schools. As an educational psychologist working for the London County Council, he not only had a platform for his theories, but could also influence policy and practice regarding the use of mental tests. The Spens Committee (1938) which reported on the secondary school system nationally, was also interested enough in Burt's views to call him as an expert witness. The Committee's recommendations of different types of school for different types of pupils reflected Burt's opinions. An indication of Burt's perception of the relationship between intellectual and moral qualities can be seen in the following extract:

> Backwardness is not merely an educational problem. From the ranks of the educationally subnormal most of our paupers, criminals and ne'er-do-wells are recruited. Even the few who do nothing to incur official condemnation 'can scarcely' as one writer puts it 'be deemed credible members of a democratic state'. (Burt, 1952, p. 16)

Thus the distribution of mental ability through the population was linked closely to the distribution of moral ability, with the 'feeble minded' at the lower end. Held to be a largely undetected repository of immorality and pauperism, their intellectual and moral backwardness, it was assumed, threatened dire consequences for the national stock if these characteristics were passed from generation to generation. The belief that moral worth and intellect were related in the way that Burt and others suggested appeared to offer legitimation to the differential treatment of individuals who had been labelled as 'feeble minded' or 'backward'. For if, as Burt seemed to suggest, they were hardly to be regarded as full members of a democratic society, then the implication was that they could be regarded as unable to benefit from the civil rights that the more intelligent deserved.

The policy of excluding those termed feeble-minded from the mainstream school not only seemed to have a scientific aura of respectability through the use of apparently technical (and by implication neutral) tests of mental ability, but was also justified by a moral rationality. The interests of this group could be safely determined by those who knew better, that is, doctors, teachers and psychologists. This assumption that individuals could be placed on an intellectual and moral continuum stretching from the least to the most able was a reflection of a similar paternalistic ideology which legitimised colonial expansion in the nineteenth and twentieth centuries. Britain was justified in colonising the Third World in order to ameliorate the moral and intellectual backwardness of the people living there. Societies, like young people, were held to be progressing from a less to a more moral and rational state. Until they could achieve the correct moral and rational maturity they could not be held to be capable of full citizenship.

This perspective depended for its power on the ability to compare individuals or nation states. The implicit model of maturity which was used for comparison was that of the white, bourgeois male, whose moral and intellectual status was unquestioned. In addition, in the explanations of educational backwardness, a homogenous concept of population was required in order for the technique of comparison to have effect. Ironically in a society which highlights individuality, comparisons between people can only have effect if there is some unifying relationship between the individuals concerned and others. 'Intelligence' only has meaning as a social attribute, and can only be 'measured' if the assumption is made that all individuals within a population demonstrate this quality to some extent or other.

Although mental testing gained credibility in the period prior to the Second World War there is some debate as to the degree to which IQ testing was used by education authorities. Sutherland (1984) has recently argued that, although there may have been a substantial debate about mental testing in some circles, in reality there were many obstacles to the widespread use of standardised tests for the purpose of selection. However one strand within the field of education, which developed alongside the testing movement and which complemented it, was the progressive school movement which argued for an education based on the 'needs' of young people. The classification of young people was not incompatible with the aims of 'progressive' educators who were influenced by Freudian ideas, since the individual 'needs' of the young person could be more clearly identified and matched with the correct type of teaching (Bowman, 1981). Indeed it was argued that, if the schooling was not matched to the needs of the young person, then 'maladjustment' would result. The categorisation and exclusion of young people from mainstream schooling could now be justified in terms of efficiency and morality and, in addition, be presented as being 'in the interests' of young people themselves.

The notion of matching 'types' of young people to 'types' of education received official backing with the publication of the *Spens Report* (HMSO, 1938) and the *Norwood Report* (HMSO, 1943). These influenced the establishment of the tripartite system (grammar, technical, secondary modern schools) after the 1944 Education Act, by its attendant regulations and through a particularly rigid reading of the Act which laid down 'education suitable to [the pupils] age, ability and aptitude' (HMSO, 1944, Part II, 36). Thus the ideology of educational classification was given form and substance.

The Handicapped Pupils and School Health Service Regulations of 1945 created eleven new categories of handicap in place of the four which had existed prior to the Second World War. These categories of disability were blind, partially sighted, deaf, partial hearing, delicate, diabetic, epileptic, physically handicapped, speech defects, maladjusted and educationally subnormal. Young people with severe mental handicaps continued to be excluded from the school system altogether since they were regarded as being ineducable. These categories remained in operation until the 1970s, except that young people with diabetes were included in the category of 'delicate' in 1953. By far the largest group of young people in these categories were those who were regarded as 'educationally subnormal', formerly the 'feeble-minded'. The criterion for selection to this group was that they were 'retarded' by more than 20 per cent in school performance, and in effect those who scored between 50 and 70 points in IQ tests were so categorised.

During the next twenty years the psychological arguments which legitimated the structure of the school system came increasingly under fire from a variety of sources. This attack predominantly took two forms; firstly the notion of a fixed intellectual ability from birth which could be measured by IQ tests was criticised (see, for example, Simon, 1971; Halsey and Gardner, 1953). Secondly it began to be argued that selecting young people at 11 for admission to different types of secondary school meant that a large pool of ability was not being tapped; for example, the chance of being selected for grammar school depended to a large extent on the number of places available rather than the individual abilities of young people. Arguments for modifications to the school system were increasingly couched within very similar terms to those used at the turn of the century – namely Britain's ability to compete in an increasingly technological environment. On this basis both the *Crowther Report* (HMSO, 1959) and the *Newsom Report* (HMSO, 1963) argued for the raising of the school leaving age. The efficiency of the selection process of the 11+ examination became a central issue in the arguments. However the debates in the early stages did not relate to the fundamental assumptions of mental testing but were more concerned to replace the rigid notion of the inherited nature of ability with one in which ability also depended on environment. If ability depended on environmental factors then it followed that changes to the environment, including the school, would result in changes in ability. It could be argued that what young people required was the equal opportunity to benefit from educational provision. The problem was not that abilities lay on a continuum, but that the rigidities of the school system prevented the efficient matching of ability and social position. The unspoken but implicit basis of the notion of equality of opportunity was that young people should compete for unequal status. In practice, as secondary education moved towards a common, comprehensive school, so the use of mental testing at 11 declined.

Until 1970 one group of young people, classified as 'severely educationally subnormal', had been excluded from the school system entirely. The categorisation of young people as 'educable' or 'ineducable', a practice which persisted in Northern Ireland until the mid-1980s, depended on which side of a tested IQ of 50 they lay. Those lower than 50 were accommodated in Junior Training Centres run by the NHS. The contradictions in this use of a continuum of ability to place young people in different categories became more apparent throughout the 1960s and the arbitrary nature of the cut-off point for admission to schooling appeared less defensible. This was coupled with the fact that the activities and methods of the Junior Training Centres and schools for 'educationally subnormal' pupils appeared to be very similar; as a result demands from teachers and parents grew for the inclusion of the severely handicapped within the school system. The 1970 Education Act was a response to this movement and the category of 'Educational Subnormality (Severe)' was added to the other ten.

The change in the administrative status of this group of young people marks a shift in the strategy of the State towards those classified as disabled. The undermining of the inherited notions of intelligence in the 1950s and 1960s, in pursuit of a restructuring of secondary schools, opened up the opportunity of intervening at the level of the social (that is, the environment) rather than concentrating on the individual. The *Plowden Report* (HMSO, 1967) encapsulated this argument in relation to primary schooling – children were 'handicapped' by adverse home conditions and extra resources should be made available to schools in deprived areas in order to counter these effects.

This reasoning was also applied to a range of other 'problem' areas such as delinquency and poverty. The problem still lay with the individual but was now seen to be due to faulty socialisation rather than innate pathology. The focus of action could be transferred from the individual to the community. In order for the community focus to act on the individual it was necessary to move from a policy of exclusion to incorporation within the community.

The idea of shifting the emphasis towards the community and away from institutions had a great deal of support from people involved in pressure groups. In 1977, MIND, an organisation campaigning in the area of mental health, was using the arguments of community (and economy) for shutting down long-stay mental hospitals in its evidence to Royal Commissions on the NHS. Arguments for using a concept of community as an organising principle could be seen to appeal to many individuals and groups. Certainly this movement towards community was reflected throughout the late 1960s and early 1970s in the field of special schooling. As the arguments for the tripartite system were undermined, the justification for segregating children from the community school appeared less and less defensible. The issue of integration of disabled pupils within mainstream schools became a central debate. The public face of this debate was reflected in Government White Papers, Education Acts and Reports during the 1970s. At the beginning of this period the arguments which brought the severely mentally handicapped within the ambit of the education service pointed to the arbitrary nature of an IQ score of 70 as the cut-off point from mainstream schooling for the moderately mentally handicapped.

The DES leaflet *The Last to Come In* emphasised the need for flexible approaches but also reinforced the idea of a 'mental continuum': 'The inclusion of mentally handicapped children within the category of "educationally subnormal" children gives recognition to the fact that mental handicap is a continuum; it will enable children to be moved from one kind of school to another without formality if their development shows the need for it' (DES, 1971, p. 3).

Quite clearly the issue of integration was linked to the process of assessment and categorisation of pupils. Consequently, in 1973, the DES asked five local education authorities (LEAs) to evaluate a new procedure for assessment, and in 1975 this was introduced for England and Wales. The new procedure was intended to be multi-disciplinary and to emphasise the prescription of appropriate education rather than categorisation. The ten statutory categories of disability were replaced by five areas of information dealing with: sensory skills and language; physical and medical attributes; cognitive development; emotional development; and home background and parental attitudes.

The relationship between the comprehensive school ideal and the notion of integration was underlined the following year with the 1976 Education Act. This was intended to increase the provision of comprehensive schools, but included Section 10 which changed the emphasis from the provision of special schooling to the use of ordinary schools by disabled young people. Section 10 was not implemented and it lay on the statute book until repealed by the Conservative Government in 1980. Shirley Williams, the Labour Secretary of State for Education after 1976, has argued in an interview that the delay in implementing Section 10 was due to the fact that the Committee of Enquiry into the Education of Handicapped Children and Young People (the Warnock Committee) was to issue its report in 1978. However it is clear that economic arguments loomed large in that delay (see Williams, quoted in Peter, 1977, p. 9).

The Warnock Committee had been appointed in 1974 and it raised expectations and fuelled the general debate about integration. When the report was published, among many recommendations it gave a rather more limited approval to the arguments for integration than some proponents expected. It recommended that the definition of young people in need of special education should be widened, since 'about one in six children at any one time and up to one in five children at some time in their school career will require

162   *Young People, Youth Work and Disability*

some form of special educational provision' (HMSO, 1978, p. 40). Of the 20 per cent who would need special education, 18 per cent were already in mainstream schools and two per cent in designated special schools. The report called for the replacement of the older categories of disability.

The categorisation of pupils by disability was officially ended by the 1981 Education Act and replaced by the *Warnock Report*'s more amorphous (and wider) concept of special educational needs. In addition the 1981 Act gave statutory approval to the notion of integration, although this approval can be seen to be largely cosmetic. The Act also said that integration must be consistent with the 'efficient use of resources'. Despite the problem of implementing the 1981 Act, over a period of ten to twelve years educational policy in relation to young people with disabilities underwent an ostensibly radical change. The commitment to exclusion based on official categorisation was abandoned as policy makers embraced the idea of integration. Whatever the practicalities of administering the policy change, whether from lack of will or assumed insolvency, the moral and rhetorical battle appeared to have been won by the pro-integration arguments.

The reality for young people during this transformation was paradoxically the reverse of the rhetorical debate. As the integration argument developed, the policy of exclusion continued unabated and in fact grew. Special schooling during the 1970s experienced growth, firstly through an increase in designated special schools for young people in the ten 'old' categories. The terminology and numbers here are rather less than precise, owing to the range of provision and the different estimates of the number of young people involved. Several observers have commented on the changing patterns of school populations (see Ford *et al.*, 1982; Galloway, 1982; Tomlinson, 1981, 1982; DES, 1978, pp. 121–2). Whereas some categories – for example sensory and physical disabilities and epilepsy – show a decline recently, other categories, such as educational subnormality and maladjustment, have increased.

In contrast to this expansion school populations have, overall, declined. Secondly, growth also occurred with the development of school-based and off-site units for 'disruptive' pupils and those with 'learning difficulties'. In this area there is rather more difficulty in obtaining figures. One source of information for units for behavioural problems is the HMI Survey of 96 English education authorities in 1978 (DES, 1978). This found that 239 units provided places for 3962 young people aged between four and 17 years and that the majority of units had been established in the period from 1973. The Advisory Centre for Education (ACE, 1980) found that 59 authorities were providing 439 units for 'disruptive' pupils. So throughout the 1970s and particularly during the deliberations of the Warnock Committee the rhetoric of integration contrasted strongly with reality.

The perspective of the *Warnock Report* has been influential in debates concerning special schooling both at the level of the DES and locally in schools and the LEAs. Within Warnock, as with the earlier *Plowden Report*, the compensatory mechanism of the school was explicitly argued for (HMSO, 1978, p. 81). There is no contradiction here between the notion of integration and the expansion of school provision. Indeed the report did much to popularise the view that there was a pool of disability whose needs were not being met, the opposite side of the coin from the pro-comprehensive arguments of the 1960s.

A major difficulty with this viewpoint is that it relies for its data concerning potential demand on information supplied by teachers. As Lewis and Vulliamy comment, 'To rely on the unexamined definitions which teachers give of their problems is to beg the question' (1980, p. 5). They go on to argue that the limitations of this approach can partly be seen in the way that issues involved in schooling have been tackled by the DES. The reliance on appointing committees of enquiry into aspects of the school system has resulted in a fragmented and piecemeal approach. Each report is seen as an opportunity to influence those in control of the distribution of resources. Consequently there has been a strong temptation to accept the terms of the agenda, in this case the existence of something called special needs, rather than questioning constructs such as maladjustment or educational subnormality. The problem of special schooling remains at the level of debate about integration in relation to the individual. The alternative question pertaining to the usefulness or justice of exclusion has not been widely posed. Nor has the focus markedly shifted to examine the resources and structures of mainstream schooling that militate against the acceptance of particular 'types' of young people. At a simple material level assumptions about the likely clientele of a given school operate against some young people having access, for example those with limited mobility. It may be a significant indicator of the level of genuine interest in integration that no useful economic analysis has been carried out of the relative costs of special education in mainstream and segregated settings.

The onus is often placed upon those outside the main provision to justify their inclusion and in a sense prove that the disabled would be better off within mainstream schools. The acceptance of this agenda supports the maintenance of an ideological position in relation to those young people categorised as disabled, by focusing on the problem of the individual as opposed to the problems of the institution and social structure. In addition the integration debate has concentrated on the ability of mainstream and special schools to develop the academic skills of young people. Consequently there has been a polarisation of opinion, with fingers being pointed at the supposed inadequacy of special schools by pro-integrationists, while opponents argue that integration is a romantic utopianism which ignores the realities of life in mainstream schooling. Whilst the development of literacy and numeracy is important, attempts to compare the relative efficacy of different types of school on the young people who attend them seem at best to be rooted in a rather static perspective, accepting the *status quo*. This kind of debate remains squarely within the tradition of matching 'types' of young people to a particular school style. In addition, the debate often ignores one of the crucial issues in this arena, namely the economic and social consequences of the process of categorisation for some young people irrespective of whether the skills are developed or not.

It is not the intention of this chapter to denigrate the work taking place in many special schools, nor is it informed by a rose-tinted perspective on mainstream schooling. It cannot be denied that some young people have immense difficulties in developing their skills and abilities, owing to pathological and biological conditions. But what is being argued is that, as well as schools being concerned with the consequences of young people gaining credentials from the system, equal attention should be paid to the negative effects of selection and categorisation as 'disabled' on the post-school life of young people. In a sense a category of disability acts as a negative credential for school leavers, regardless of whether academic qualifications are gained or skills of literacy and numeracy are acquired.

Beyond schooling

What then are the realities of life for young people categorised as disabled in the post-school period? For many disabled young people employment has always been a tenuous possibility and for others simply a non-option. Hard data on the extent of the difficulties experienced by young people in this area have always been difficult to come by but Walker's (1982) survey for the Warnock Committee went some way to rectify this state of affairs and gives a clear indication of the degree of disadvantage. Although many of the young people studied were capable of entering employment this group was five times more likely than others in the same age group to be under-employed. Not only were they less likely to get a job in the first place, but even where employment was found, it was more likely to be temporary or part-time. Where jobs were obtained they were within a very narrow choice range, characterised by low skill levels, poor conditions of employment, low pay and a high degree of insecurity. Young disabled women were even more likely to obtain low rates of pay. For some groups of young people, most notably those classified as having severe learning difficulties, the career of disability is continued by an almost automatic transfer from school into what are euphemistically called Adult Training Centres. These entail neither being treated as adults nor being offered any recognisable form of training. The rates of pay in the centres can be as low as 25p or 50p per week. The limitations of resources and staffing together with the overcrowding due to lack of places have led, in many cases, to institutions becoming over-stretched occupational custody facilities.

In some local authorities the centres have to some degree to be self-financing, with the pay and leisure facilities of the trainees depending on this extra finance. At one time the centres could rely on contract work from industry – carrying out labour-intensive tasks that it was not economically viable to mechanise. Has the reader ever wondered who puts the plastic pourers on salt containers or where cocktail sticks are bundled? As the recession has deepened even this source of alternative funding has declined. Many staff are badly paid and coping with intolerable conditions – in some cases, despite the odds, developing innovative practices relating to a high degree of self-determination by the disabled people attending the centre.

A movement for self-advocacy by people who are labelled as mentally handicapped has begun to develop in some areas. The first national conference of people in this group was organised in 1972 (Shearer, 1972) by the Campaign for Mentally Handicapped People (CMH). However the number of day centres where the self-advocacy movement has affected the reality of daily life for people is relatively small. Most centres are organised along strictly hierarchical lines, often maintaining discriminatory distinctions between staff and trainees; for example in separate toilet and dining facilities.

Some units are in the process of being renamed 'Social Education Centres' which at least reflects a rather more liberal concern for a broader conception of the facilities which the day centres should offer. Rather than simply focusing on work as a central concern the emphasis has in theory shifted to include education and leisure. In reality, the power relationships, in many cases, have remained unaltered.

Limited employment opportunities with poor pay turns young disabled people towards a reliance on welfare benefits in order to subsist. That those considered to be disabled are among the poorest in society has been emphasised time and again by social surveys (see Townsend, 1979, ch. 20; Layard *et al.*, 1978). In addition to those with disabilities tending to be drawn from manual as opposed to non-manual families, on almost every index of deprivation those people with 'disabilities' did worse than the 'non-disabled'. Even mild incapacity is linked to degrees of deprivation greater than for the rest of the population.

There has been some improvement in the benefit system for this group of people since 1970 but at the same time the complexity of the system has militated against effective claims (Baldwin *et al.*, 1981). A further problem is that there is some evidence that people are reluctant to be categorised as disabled in order to gain the benefits. Some benefits require that young people be examined by a medical panel to ascertain their degree of disability in order to qualify. The onus is on the disabled person or the family to demonstrate the deserving nature of their case.

One of the limited advantages of the Special School system is that the young person in one sense may have a means via which requests for benefits and allowances can be channelled. School staff can, and do, help and advise young people and their families in their contact with welfare agencies. The quality of this help is often related to the willingness or ability of individuals within particular schools, the level of awareness and training in welfare rights issues among school staff, and the guidance of the LEAs. In reality teachers are often placed in the position of doing an inadequate job, owing to the deficiencies in the welfare network which often stops just short of the school gates.

The fact that teachers can intervene on occasion on behalf of young people and their families illustrates the disparity that exists between the way that accounts of need are accorded different status. Acquiring benefits is not solely a matter of knowledge about what is available but is also dependent on how, and by whom, social need is defined. The young person's, or family's definition of need often requires 'authentication' from a member of the medical, educational or welfare professions.

The school leaving period is a time of heightened anxiety

for the families and the young people themselves. The uncertainties of the future are underlined by the transition from the security of the statutory school placement to the often discretionary provision, whether educational, employment or care. For the families of profoundly disabled young people the burden of the caring role may be emphasised by the increasingly visible prospect of the continuation of that role into the future. There may appear to be little chance of the young person having the opportunity of an independent life apart from the family.

Glendinning's (1983) study of the position of families of disabled young people underlines the disgraceful disparity of welfare provision for this group of people relating more to geography and the efforts of individual workers than to needs. In addition she puts forward the hypothesis that the growth of notions like community care may, paradoxically, have put more pressure on the families of disabled young people to maintain their caring task out of a sense of guilt. The concept of 'community' entails a blurring of the social reality for many groups but the notion of 'care' also adds mystification to the debate about the needs of many individuals and groups. In reality care and caring is not a sympathetic frame of mind which all good people should adopt. It is often hard manual work carried out in conditions of poverty or near poverty with the small personal rewards offset by large personal sacrifices on the part of those undertaking the caring.

The discrimination and disadvantage which disabled young people and their families suffer is not, in the main, due to massive conscious opposition by the majority of the population. It is the accumulation of small indignities and humiliations, often due to quite specific material disadvantages. Discrimination is sometimes due to callousness but is more often due to the wearying obstacle of having to overcome bureaucratic inertia. It must also be added that an almost pathological meanness of spirit colours the administration of welfare in this country. The fostering allowance gives a good illustration of this. While Personal Social Service departments are willing to pay extra grants to those prepared to foster disabled young people, at the same time there seems to be a curious blindness whereby parents are put in the position of having to justify their family's and children's needs in order to secure financial help.

Not surprisingly the main burden of care of disabled young people falls in many families on women. Baldwin's (1985) study showed the disparity between the effects on men and women. In particular the employment prospects of women were affected in comparison with other women with non-disabled children, and the disparity increased as the children grew older. Her study illustrates the complexity of the relationship between having a disabled child and patterns of family income and expenditure. The families she looked at were clearly dependent on a range of support, for 'the financial costs of caring for severely disabled children at home are considerably greater than existing support from cash benefits, services in kind and the Family Fund' (ibid., p. 167).

The inequities of the benefits system will in reality not be ameliorated by the changes introduced by the government. Whilst it is difficult to generalise about the effect of the changes to direct disability benefits, the replacement of special needs payments with a loan system will have seriously adverse effects upon disabled people and their families in relation to the provision of specific equipment or adaptations to living accommodation. In addition the reduction in housing subsidies will also affect disabled people disproportionately. The assumption seems to be that people are either disabled *or* poor, whereas in reality people are usually disabled *and* poor.

Leisure, personal life and youth work

Given the poor employment prospects that disabled young people face there have recently been calls for a realistic response to this lack of opportunity. It is argued that, since a life of enforced leisure is likely to be the lot of disabled young people, there should be a corresponding focus on the development of leisure facilities and the acquisition of leisure skills. Leaving aside for a moment the paternalism of this notion, this sort of suggestion ignores the possibility that the sources of disadvantage in employment may be the same as or linked to sources of disadvantage in leisure.

Apart from the fairly obvious constraints on taking part in leisure activities engendered by physical and sensory disabilities, there can also be extra problems relating to social isolation and lack of skills. The problem of isolation and lack of peer group friendships is particularly acute with this group of young people. It is reasonable to assume that attendance at a special school may actually exacerbate the problem. If young people are transported from their immediate neighbourhood to spend the day with other young people from a wide geographical area then this can interfere with the development of friendships in at least two ways. Firstly, the chance of making friends with someone from the same neighbourhood at school is obviously diminished. Secondly, if friendships are established at school, then it can be difficult to continue them after. Leisure costs money and, given the economic position of disabled people, this is a further and important constraint on the inclusion of this group in leisure activities.

Given the constraints we should not be startled to discover that the leisure activities of disabled young people tend to be passive and solitary rather than active and group-based, for example watching TV and listening to records (Cheseldine & Jeffree, 1981). This solitary passivity also has consequences for the possibility of developing sexual relationships with other people. It is not merely lack of opportunity which can be a restriction but also the mythology and misinformation which obscures any debate on sexuality in relation to disabled young people. This should not be too surprising in the light of the nonsense which enmeshes the theme of sexuality generally. The conjunction of sexuality with disabilities which are held to be mental in origin often stimulates half-hidden respectable fears of young men teetering on the edge of uncontrollable sexual frenzy. Or young women in a state of perpetual wantonness.

This picture may appear to be a caricature of reality; after all, are we not much more understanding, tolerant and humane than we used to be? It is true that the legal category of moral defective disappeared with the 1959 Mental Health Act which reduced somewhat the practice of locking up young mentally handicapped women for indeterminate periods for the 'crime' of having an illegitimate child. However, witness the knee-jerk response of groups of owner-occupiers to the establishment of community hostels; or hear for the umpteenth time girls as young as six referred to as 'man crazy'; or examine any large institution's response to masturbation; and it quickly becomes clear that the apparently caricatured beliefs of gentlefolk have a very concrete reality. In the case of young people with disabilities, questions relating to sexuality are often framed within much more rigorous criteria than for other members of the population.

Personal relationships for disabled people are assumed often to be part of the public domain which gives others the right to intervene. The option of saying 'mind your own business' to comments and queries about sexual behaviour is not often accorded to disabled young people. The activities of Ms Gillick and Ms Whitehouse illustrate that similar concerns in relation to the rest of the population are being resurrected by the New Right. The control of sexual behaviour is held to be the province of others, not the people concerned.

Given the disadvantages which disabled young people encounter in the realms of welfare, employment, leisure and personal life, it is worthwhile examining the response of various organisations. The rhetoric and public statements of organisations concerned with fulfilling young person's needs in this area give an impression that there exists a fair amount of provision for the young disabled person. However the gap between rhetoric and reality is rather wide. A study by Cheseldine and Jeffree found that twenty-six out of forty-two national organisations reported that they made 'some provision in the field of leisure time activities' for young people categorised as 'mentally handicapped' (1981, p. 50). The authors, having interviewed young people and their families, found a completely different picture to this apparently positive position. The view from the intended client/consumer group was of limited facilities and opportunities. It must be admitted that there has been a response to the needs of particular groups of disabled young people but this response has, in one sense, mirrored the situation in the schools.

As the rhetoric of integration has developed in conjunction with the expansion of special educational provision, so there has been a corresponding increase in clubs for those categorised as disabled. The two main organisations concerned are the Physically Handicapped and Able Bodied (PHAB) clubs and the Federation of Gateway Clubs. The PHAB clubs are intended to cater for those people who are physically handicapped, while Gateway clubs are for mentally handicapped people. The term 'youth club' is something of a misnomer in the case of both these organisations, since the age range of their membership can be from 15 to 75; a majority of the members are in fact well over 20 years of age. Both organisations have developed over the last two decades with growth particularly fast during the 1970s. PHAB developed from about 60 clubs in 1974 to 450 in 1989, while the Gateway Federation had grown to over 700 clubs by 1988. The existence and expansion of segregated club provision is justified in the case of the Gateway clubs in a pamphlet produced in 1982 by the National Society for Mentally Handicapped Children (Mencap); 'For only a very few retarded members would integration into a normal youth and community centre be feasible without resultant frustrations and subsequent lapse of membership if not on the part of the handicapped then of the normal members' (Stuart, 1982, p. 4). The confident tone of this pronouncement and others like it, which are made on behalf of the disabled young people, may lead us to overlook the fact that evidence is never produced in support of such bold assertions. It may be that, to the writers of such statements, the truth is self-evident, a matter of common sense, the Authoritative Voice needing no justification. Whatever the reasons, there is no indication from this arrogant paternalism that the members of Gateway clubs might have aspirations that conflict somewhat with the segregationist line followed by many of the clubs.

The stated aims of the PHAB clubs appear in contrast to

be rather less insular. The intention is that the clubs function as a kind of half-way house allowing for a development of understanding and friendship between able-bodied and disabled people. The clubs' function is to be a transition between segregated institutions and the community. Unfortunately, in reality, this intended aim has been rather modified as the clubs have developed. In a study of a sample of PHAB clubs, Lam (1982) found that the major objective of many of the club leaders was the expansion of membership, so rather than being seen as a means to an end, clubs have become an end in themselves for many of those involved. In addition, the recruitment policies of many of the leaders leave some doubt as to the commitment to the concept of integration. Forty-one of the fifty leaders interviewed by Lam opposed the admission of mentally handicapped young people to the club membership. This position was justified on the grounds that physically handicapped people do not want to be further stigmatised by contact with the mentally handicapped. In the quest for tolerance from society this argument represents a fine line in hypocrisy.

Despite the foregoing criticisms of provision for disabled young people it must be said that at least the people involved are doing something, however misguided some of us may feel those developments are. There is a certain irony in writing a chapter which criticises existing institutions, particularly the schools and specialist youth provision. It is almost an exercise in voyeurism whereby those in mainstream youth work who have done little or nothing for disabled young people can be presented with a critical view of those who have at least tried. It is no use sitting and getting angry or, more likely, cynically apathetic about others' practice if the onlookers are not prepared to alter their own. And there is no smug salvation in the rattle of collection tins; charitable Good Works for disabled young people are no substitute for political and social action with disabled young people.

At this point it is traditional to ask Lenin's question, *What is to be done?*, followed by an outline of the model programme. The critic has some responsibility for suggestions about better practice and this obligation will be accepted a little later. However no special originality nor privilege should be attached to such recommendations. It is not the author's intention to contribute to the mystification which envelopes the notion of disability by pointing to practices which will miraculously resolve the conflict, ambiguity, discrimination and lack of resources involved in this section of the social arena. There is no magic button for us to press. However there is one principle from which we can begin and that is the simple one of asking people themselves what they want. This raises a major problem for youth workers, since the structure of youth work itself may be one of source of difficulty.

The existence of separate youth provision for those categorised as disabled may mean that many mainstream workers do not come into contact with these particular young people. How can the young people themselves represent their needs to others without the filtering of those engaged in separate youth work? There is a responsibility here on youth workers in both mainstream and special provision to move towards the short-term objective of abandoning an increasingly indefensible form of segregation. This will then offer the opportunity of beginning to learn and work together on developing new modes of representation for disabled young people and an authentic voice which provides a channel for the various needs and interests of young people generally. This is not a comforting, tolerant and liberal argument. The process is likely to be messy, unpleasant, conflict-ridden and difficult for people to deal with. Disabled young people are not an homogeneous group, but one of the few common features which this group shares is their disadvantage, made worse by the majority. A further principle which has to be accepted is that they have the right of access which should not have to be earned; one which should not be delayed until extra resources appear on the horizon.

Once the principle of equal access has been established in practice then it is possible to see a range of work which could be developed. First, being involved with non-disabled young people offers the opportunity for those who have been segregated in special schooling to develop social skills through interaction with a broader spectrum of the population. This involvement might be aided and enhanced with a range of activities using role play, video, discussion and group work focusing on the development of self-awareness which emphasised the ability to judge and then make appropriate responses to other people.

This is not an argument for teaching a mechanistic set of 'skills' which are then used when the appropriate signal is given, as with animals in a circus act. Human interaction and the ability to respond to other peoples' needs and interests, as well as making our own needs and interests known to others, are learned in a constant process of negotiation. Social knowledge in this sense is in a constant state of flux and in reality is never complete. We need the opportunity to act socially with other people and learn how to monitor the process. For disabled young people this process is often not aided by the dependence that may be created in family and school experiences. How can people assess their own social behaviour if they seem to have little or no control over their own lives or even their own behaviour?

Second, the sense of deference linked with dependence which disabled people often develop might be attacked by specific assertiveness training. This kind of training has also proved to be of direct benefit to young people in the United States, for example in improved self-confidence when arguing for educational and welfare rights. In some ways young disabled people have a marginal advantage over other groups when it comes to struggles for resources and access. Legislators, when framing new statutes, have often made discretionary provision for those people regarded as disabled in order to be seen to be making a gesture in the direction of this disadvantage group without actually committing institutions or the state to concrete action. Consequently there is a multiplicity of local authority and national enabling legislation on the statute books which has not been adequately tested, quite apart from that statutory legislation which is not being enforced. A good example of this is the group of Oxfordshire parents who forced their LEA to provide FE opportunities for a group of disabled young people under a section of the 1944 Education Act. Quite clearly there is a role for youth workers here in the field of welfare and education which encompasses not only quite specific skill training (that is, assertiveness) but also a supportive advocacy, giving encouragement and help with welfare applications. In addition, there is a need for information and research on rights and benefits issues, and youth workers might contribute here, whether in conjunction with other agencies or as an alternative to them.

There is quite clearly a need in the area of leisure for the involvement of youth workers at a number of levels. Here access to youth facilities opens up a number of possibilities for disabled young people. The provision of skills training in a range of leisure and sports activities has been shown in itself to reduce the isolation of disabled young people. A combination of teaching specific skills and an awareness programme relating to leisure provision would be a fairly concrete and easily established first move. What may also be needed in the area of leisure, as with welfare, is a programme to enhance access to community facilities.

An initial step might be to examine the access policies of the local council leisure department. Do disabled young people have separate access times? Are all people welcomed at the cinema, theatre or bowling green? What physical constraints are there relating to doorways, toilets, stairs? And here again, as with welfare rights, a support and advocacy role may be needed from the youth worker in order to take action against the discrimination identified. A useful source of information and ideas about advocacy and self-advocacy, together with a history of its development, is to be found in Williams and Schoultz (1982), *We Can Speak for Ourselves*.

These kinds of approaches to youth work with disabled young people are not an argument for the sort of amorphous community policies practised by the old Liberal Party. They are an argument for an interventionist approach to youth work, but with the intervention focused squarely on the institutions and aimed at removing their restrictions. It is also interventionist in respect of the young people themselves, seeing youth work as enabling and educational rather than merely as reactive and pacific. This is not an argument, however, for maintaining young disabled people as the recipients of expertise and thus maintaining their powerlessness.

Conclusion

The suggestions which have been put forward are only part of the response that should take place to these issues. One part of the programme does indeed relate to the learning and help which young people with disabilities may need in removing disadvantage. Equally, if not more, important are the help and education which the rest of us need in order to reduce the problems which these young people face. The best place to get the help needed is in work and dialogue with young disabled people and that dialogue must be on level terms. Quite clearly there is a need to be informed about the extent of material disadvantage, but also we must question our own beliefs, assumptions and stereotypes about disability.

Discrimination against disabled young people has taken many forms and youth workers along with the rest of the population have a responsibility to resist it as actively as they do racism or sexism. The problem for youth workers, as with other workers in this field, is that these kinds of strategies require a commitment resulting in action, not merely debate or pious statements of intent.

One great problem for disabled people and one symptomatic of the discrimination encountered has been the difficulty of attracting support from others, not least socialists. Struggles by small groups of people at the local level over issues like access are regarded by some as distractions from the main task of 'defeating Capitalism' and are seen at best as marginal to the main cause. There is, in addition, both within institutions and outside them, an opposition from trades unions to developments relating to self-advocacy and decision making by disabled young people themselves. Trades unionists and socialists in education, social work, nursing and community care are suspicious of support centres set up with the aid of Community Programme (CP) funding and its successors.

This conflict may be perfectly understandable, given the cutbacks in public services and the growth of the private care sector. But it is not merely lack of resources which pushes disabled people and their families to set up separate facilities from those provided by the State – it is also the inability of the State provision to respond to the needs and wishes of those who use the institutions. One of the reasons that Thatcherism struck a chord with many working-class people flows from their experiences of the bureaucratic institutions of welfare and education. The treatment which young disabled people have suffered has really been a more extreme form of that meted out to other sections of the population.

The official procedures which define young disabled people for state school, welfare and legal systems are merely one set of categories which has been developed to manage people and their needs. The managerial approach to welfare which has developed throughout this century has been the responsibility of both major parties. Its reliance on expert advice and concern with organisational efficiency has resulted, almost inevitably, in a lack of concern to engage in genuinely democratic debate about resources and needs. Certainly one of the problems that disabled young people have had, and which will also face youth workers who engage with these young people in welfare and leisure issues, is that the people who decide upon these issues for them are often representatives and officials of the local state.

In arguing and acting to reduce discrimination for young disabled people, youth workers will inevitably be faced by their employers or source of funding. This is one of the central dilemmas faced by those working in social work, education, housing or welfare: the institutions within which they work are often the source of the discrimination from which their clients suffer.

7

Young People, Class Inequality and Youth Work

TONY JEFFS and MARK SMITH

While the policy documents and collective rhetoric of youth work often make some allusion to anti-racist or anti-sexist practice, less is said at present regarding the subordination of young people as a consequence of their class. This has not always been the case. Any historical survey of youth work shows that many workers and sponsors were acutely conscious of social class. Their reasons and motives for this varied, some being concerned about the welfare of the working-class young, seeing them as victims, while others sought to use youth work as a means of combating the rise of the working class as a social and political force (Blanch, 1979; Dyhouse, 1981; Springhall, 1977).

The more explicit references to class encountered in much earlier writing are no longer commonplace. Instead, in policy discussions of youth work, we have coded references to alienation, inner-city youth, disadvantage and unemployment, such allusions often being linked to the experiences of 'ethnic minority communities' (DES, 1987a; Jeffs & Smith, 1988, pp. 15–17). The focus is on discrete problems encountered by young people rather than on the underlying social divisions and forces that shape and infuse those difficulties. All is nicely sanitised in the technical language of the professional. As soon as the 'policy discussions' are examined in an honest way, then the problem of class emerges, to cause discomfort and embarrassment to the purveyors of bland Youth Service orthodoxy.

Farewell to class?

Possibly the lack of explicit reference to class today is a result of the fact that those who sponsor youth work feel secure behind other forms of socialisation such as schooling, the mass media and the family. Certainly the development of working-class political organisation in the form of unionism and the Labour Party has hardly posed a revolutionary threat to capitalism and to bourgeois privilege. Thus protected, the vast bulk of those who occupy dominant positions within society have sought to wish away the very concept of class. Indeed the very success of their venture gave rise to the social democratic consensus of the late 1950s, 1960s and early 1970s. It was assumed that:

> basic material problems had been solved; and that any difficulties and stresses which persisted were personal (arising out of character weaknesses or unforeseen individual tragedy), or social in the sense that they emanated from family failure or, at the widest, the disappearance of community. (Davies, 1986, p. 12)

Within such an ideological climate it was hardly surprising that those who held that class was central to any understanding of society often ended up being likened to Low's representation of the TUC as a plodding cart-horse. The idea of class, it was argued, related to another age.

This cosy social democratic vision came to be challenged, both politically and intellectually, as more critical perspectives emerged within the Labour movement in the late 1960s and in the 1970s. Further, the development of feminist and black political organisation led to a more extensive examination of what was held to be the dominant ideology. The vision was finally shattered by the rise of Thatcherism. The shift towards vocationalism and training; the continued development of treatment and policing initiatives; cut-backs in welfare funding; the privatisation of certain services; and the provisions to allow schools (and hence certain youth work activities) to opt out of the state system: all the foregoing have to be set beside the often highly-publicised grand gestures designed to massage opinion concerning the plight of young people. Thatcherism's affection for the market, and opposition to any impediments to its free functioning, has altered not just the environment in which youth work operates, but also its language. The new buzz words are choice, opportunity, enterprise, entrepreneurship, individualism and responsibility. These dovetail neatly with a reinvigorated and brash managerialism. Class considerations sit uneasily alongside this individualistic and managerial framework, and the related world-view which places a particular regard on leadership and the possession of certain individual qualities and credentials. According to this view it is 'natural' that those possessing the right background, wealth and/or higher educational qualifications should occupy positions of power. It is 'natural' that there is a ruling class who may act collectively. By implication a class or classes who oppose such interests become defined as 'abnormal' and dangerous.

Yet class, like the proverbial bad penny, keeps reappearing in empirical work. For example, Marshall *et al.* concluded that data from their major survey confirmed that class solidarities 'retain an importance that undermines recent accounts of the alleged demise of class consciousness and class politics, and associated rise of aggressive consumerism' (1988, p. 267). Britain remains a capitalist, class society. Class continues to exercise a profound and all-informing influence upon the life-chances and experiences of young people, be it in the spheres of education, health, employment and housing, or social experiences such as leisure and friendships. The evidence, as we will show, unambiguously spells out a message of class conflict, inequality and oppression.

Class divisions and the emergence of the new middle class

It is not intended here to embark upon a lengthy theoretical and conceptual discussion of class. Although attractive, it would do little to enhance the central argument. Voluminous literature already exists to which the reader can turn

(Marshall *et al.*, 1988; Goldthorpe *et al.*, 1987; Wright, 1985; Giddens and Held, 1982; Giddens, 1980; Parkin, 1979). However what we do need to state is our belief that the origins of class divisions lie in the unequal ownership and control of the means of production. Control over what is produced is more than simply an 'open sesame' to profit and wealth. It is a powerful and determining lever in vesting disproportionate control over the world of ideas, information and the formation of personal and public relationships. Ownership of the means of production, or effective control over it, is what enables individuals and groups to secure for themselves, their family and allies, social and political advantage. It is the absence of such ownership, or access to the largesse of those who do, that confines the majority to a lower order of economic existence. The ownership of wealth is neither fixed nor accidental, but the end-product both of enormous struggles between nations and peoples and of myriad personal and individual conflicts. Thus, although classes may appear fixed to the means of production, both the membership and power of them alters over time. This is because: 'Class domination is not simply a "fact": it is a process, a continuing endeavour on the part of the dominant class or classes to maintain, strengthen, and extend, or defend, their domination' (Miliband, 1977, p. 18). Youth work and youth workers cannot avoid being caught up with these struggles (Jeffs and Smith, 1988, pp. 7–10), not least because the needs, aspirations and behaviours of the young people they work with are deeply influenced by class relationships and conflicts.

Britain is stratified by relationships of superiority and subordination, where people at the top, 'because of their social position, have differentially favourable access to the scarce goods of the society' (Coates, 1984, p. 100). These scarce goods are not just material items, but also less tangible phenomena such as power, status and control. While there may be some movement over time, it is the case that those people with favourable access to the scarce goods of society are generally able to ensure that their offspring experience similar life chances. Extraordinary, not to say obscene, privilege remains remarkably concentrated. In this process, Giddens has argued, three sorts of market capacity are normally of importance:

> Ownership of property in the means of production- possession of educational or technical qualifications; and possession of manual labour-power. In so far as it is the case that these tend to be tied to closed patterns of inter- and intragenerational mobility, this yields the foundation of a basic three-class system in capitalist society: an 'upper', 'middle', or 'working' class. (1980, p. 107)

Analysis such as this points to one of the central features of advanced capitalist societies: the emergence of what might be called the 'new middle', 'service' (Goldthorpe, 1982) or 'professional–managerial' class (Ehrenreich and Ehrenreich, 1971). While we might want to question whether this grouping arises from the possession of a particular form of market capacity, there can be no denying that the class map of such societies has altered. A range of managerial groupings has emerged, including top executives, and middle managers and technocrats. In addition, there are a large number of other people who, while not necessarily managers, have a significant degree of control over how they do their work and what they produce. Examples of these are lecturers, teachers and researchers. Youth workers would also find themselves located here.

Managerial, professional and administrative employees such as we are discussing here may be seen as:

> typically engaged in the exercise of delegated authority or in the application of specialist knowledge and expertise, operat[ing] in their work tasks and roles with a distinctive degree of autonomy and discretion; and in a direct consequence of the element of trust that is thus necessarily involved in their relationship with their employing organisation, they are accorded conditions of employment which are also distinctive in both the level and kinds of rewards that are involved. (Goldthorpe, 1982, p. 169)

These employees can thus be differentiated from wage-workers. However there are also tensions and divisions within the 'service class'. For example, one of the key features of recent years has been the attempt by the state and its managers to limit the degree of discretion enjoyed by certain professional groupings such as teachers, social workers and youth workers. The latter, in particular, can be seen to occupy a somewhat contradictory position. 'On the one hand, they are like workers in being excluded from ownership of the means of production; on the other, they have interests opposed to workers because of their effective control of organisation and skill assets' (Wright, 1985, p. 87). As we have argued elsewhere, if youth workers sometimes display a measure of confusion and express ambivalence when trying to understand where they are located in a class society it is hardly surprising (Jeffs and Smith, 1988, p. 9).

Class inequality in Britain

The class structure of Britain is often mapped on the basis of occupation and income and, more particularly, wealth. These ways of approaching class provide us with a picture of different aspects of the situation. When we examine the structure of the population according to *occupation*, the change in the shape of the employed population is obvious (see Figure 7.1).

As might be expected from our earlier discussion, the dominant trend has been the growth in non-manual employment, with the proportion of managers and professionals growing from 12 to 25 per cent. Clerical and sales employment have increased a mere three per cent. All three categories of manual work have declined. By 1981, manual workers were a minority in the labour force, having fallen from 63 per cent in 1951 to 45 per cent. While we must be careful not to interpret these figures too literally, the criteria by which jobs are allocated to social class categories having altered, there is evidence that these trends have continued (OPCS, 1987b, p. 19).

All this might be taken to mean that the working class is in terminal decline as a major political and social force (Gorz, 1982; Bahro, 1982). However such an assertion is simplistic.

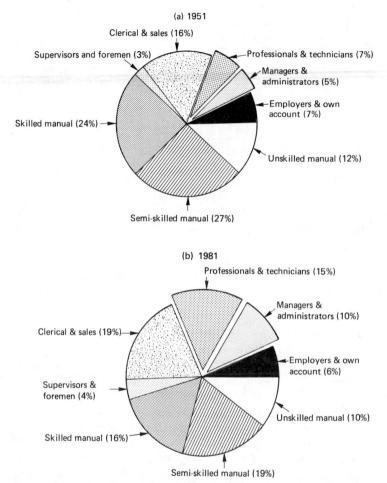

Source: Based on figures given in Heath. A. and S.-K. McDonald (1987) p. 365, and ultimately derived from census material.

Figure 7.1 *Distribution of the economically active population by occupational category: Great Britain, 1951–81*

Evidence from studies such as Marshall *et al.* indicates that class interests are still central to the political process (1988, p. 274). Furthermore careful attention has to be given to the way in which occupations are assigned to particular class categories. The nature of many white-collar and service jobs, which are usually portrayed as being outside the working class, is highly routinised in much the same way as those classified as manual. Also the bulk of workers within these sectors have only limited control over their direct activities and none regarding the overall operation of their organisation. While no claim is being made that routine sales and clerical workers are 'proletarian by temperament' (Marshall *et al.*, 1988, p. 136), it can be seen that 'the working class is neither swelling to compose a gigantic proletariat, nor is it on the verge of disappearing' (Giddens, 1987, p. 288; see also Gerry, 1985).

Classes in Britain, when defined in terms of occupation, can be seen to have qualitatively different life styles. When Reid (1981) brought together a wide range of contemporary research using occupational classification, he was able to conclude that:

> While the actual differences between the separate classes have varied in magnitude, an abiding impression must be of the very substantial extent of the differences between the middle (non-manual) and the working (manual) classes, and of the stark difference between the extremes – the professional and the unskilled manual classes. (Reid, 1981, p. 296)

He went on to compile a list of contrasting differences:

> We can state that middle-class people, in comparison with the working classes, enjoy better health; live longer; live in superior homes with more amenities; have more money to spend; work shorter hours; receive different and longer education, and are educationally more successful; marry later in life; rear fewer children; attend church more frequently; belong to clubs more often; have different tastes in the mass media and the arts; are politically more involved – to mention only a few examples. (Reid, 1981, p. 296)

In the face of such evidence it is difficult to deny that social class (as defined by occupation) is a useful concept. However what such schema do is simply to classify; what they do not do is to explore the antagonisms and connections between the various classes. Further, as Marsh (1986) has argued, there are two especially critical questions about such schema. Firstly, since the majority of people at any one time have no job, to whose occupational group should they be assigned? Here the standard response has been to designate people via the occupation of the 'head of household' or 'chief wage earner'. Thus it is not uncommon to find people in different occupational groupings within the same household, while designated only under one. This tends to leave women invisible, males largely being regarded as the 'head of household'.

What we must recognise here is that many women have a direct relationship with production through their own employment. In this sense, women in employment, for example, are not 'declassed' by marriage (Stanworth, 1984). In addition, even where they are not directly employed, the partners of those who are in employment perform important functions for capital. By contributing to the maintenance of their partners in the labour force they lower costs to the capitalist.

The second question concerning occupational classification schemes arises because any given individual tends to change occupations over a lifetime. Which job should be selected?

> Some jobs, like research fellowships, are held exclusively by people at particular stages of their careers and lifecycles, while others, like clerks, have different significance for different incumbents: they are springboards for careers when they are held by young men, but are dead-end jobs when held by older women. (Marsh, 1986, p. 140)

Both these points have to be borne in mind, especially when allotting class location on the basis of occupation to those who are unemployed. Further, it is necessary to recognise that such class categories have been largely devised in relation to male occupations and are insensitive to major differences within what are traditionally female occupations. For example, nurses tend to be placed in the same class category whether they are trained auxiliaries or Senior Nursing Officers (Abbott & Sapsford, 1987).

The amount of *income or wealth* that individuals possess is sometimes used as a way of distinguishing between classes. Weber, along with Marx, attributed crucial importance to private property in class formation. 'Property or productive wealth heaps many benefits and prerogatives upon its possessors, while those who must rely on selling their labour are severely handicapped in the struggle for resources' (Parkin, 1982, p. 91). While an examination of wealth and income may have little to tell us about the process of class formation (Mackenzie, 1982, p. 65), it does provide us with the same picture of inequality as the comparisons via occupation. Until the late 1970s there had been a long-term trend towards a marginal redistribution of wealth in the United Kingdom. Unfortunately, as Bryne (1987) comments, this trend was from the very rich to the rich, rather than from the rich to the poor. The clear effect of Thatcherite policy was to buttress existing extremes of wealth. For example, in 1984:

- over half (52 per cent) of all personal marketable wealth was owned by the richest 10 per cent;
- more than a fifth (21 per cent) of personal marketable wealth was concentrated in the hands of the richest one per cent;
- in stark contrast, the bottom 50 per cent of the population controlled just seven per cent of marketable wealth (Byrne, 1987, p. 35).

Although income was more evenly distributed than wealth, Conservative governments have instituted a major redistribution of income in favour of the well-off. Between 1979 and 1986 the real level of earnings of men in the top tenth of the earnings league increased at more than five times the rate of those in the bottom tenth. Between 1979 and 1985 the poorest families with children suffered a drop in the real value of their incomes of between 15·7 and 27·2 per cent (according to the number of children) (Walker, 1987, p. 131).

Since 1979 the gap between the high paid and the low paid has widened into a huge gulf. So much so that the poorest workers are now markedly more worse off compared to higher earners than they were 100 years ago . . . Around 8·8 million workers earn less, excluding overtime, than the Council of Europe level ['the minimum decency threshold']. (Bryne, 1987, p. 29)

The position was further exacerbated by tax and benefit changes in 1988. The Low Pay Unit estimated that these changes would bring about social security savings in excess of £1·1 billion and that the higher rate tax cuts alone would cost £2·2 billion (1988, p. 11).

When such figures are linked with occupations, then it quickly becomes apparent that particular groups of workers are consistently poorly paid – for example, clerical workers and the semi- and unskilled (Department of Employment, 1988a). Further, when one comes to examine the conditions, security and fringe benefits attached to certain occupations then a clear divide appears between the manual and non-manual categories. Adding such disparities to income differentials reveals that the scale of disadvantage is massive. In recent years this has been further magnified by the continuance and strengthening of a dual or stratified employment market (Jeffs and Smith, 1988, pp. 51–3). On the one hand there is a primary sector of jobs which are essential to the functioning of particular industries; on the other hand there is a secondary sector of less secure, worse paid and often temporary and part-time jobs. One of the key defining features of the contemporary employment situation is the substantial growth in the latter. For example, between 1983 and 1986, the number of temporary workers in Britain rose by nearly 70 000. This was entirely owing to an increase in part-time temporary employment. In 1987 there were 1·3 million temporary workers, 0·8 million of whom were female. 75 per cent of the latter worked part-time (CSO, 1988a, p. 74). At the same time some 5·47 million people (22·5 per cent of the labour force) were in part-time employment. As many as 86 per cent of these were female (Department of Employment, 1988d, p. 607). Young people have been particularly affected by this phenomenon. In 1979, four per cent of male and eight per cent of female employed teenagers worked part-time. By 1985 the proportions were 19 per cent and 30 per cent respectively (Lewis and Lunn, 1987, p. 3).

What is clear from the evidence provided by surveys of income and wealth distribution, when placed in the context of New Right thinking, is that the growth of inequality and poverty is no accident. It is not the unintended outcome from some broader social or economic vision or a short-term sacrifice:

> Rather, it is the intended and inevitable outcome of the government's policies. In fact, the immiseration of a growing section of the population may be seen as an episode in the long-standing struggle to maintain the status and privileges of the rich. (Loney, 1987, p. 9)

Inequality is seen as an engine of social change, and a punishment for those who fail to push at the ever-open door of enterprise. Less sanguine and, perhaps, better informed minds may see it as the penalty for choosing to be born in the wrong class and social group, in the wrong place, and at the wrong time.

Young people and class inequality

It is in this context that we must consider the experience of young people. In this section we will examine the position in respect of a number of key dimensions of their experience: in the labour market, the housing market, education and leisure. Similar patterns of difference and disadvantage exist in relation to health, crime and the delivery of welfare, but space only permits a general overview here.

Income, employment and the labour market

Roll (1988) has brought together data regarding young people's experiences in employment and the labour market. In the period from 1975 to 1987 there was a fall from 60 per cent to 17 per cent in the number of 16-year-olds in employment and a fall from 71 per cent to 44 per cent in the case of 17-year-olds (Roll, 1988, p. 7; see Figure 7.2). The numbers of young people continuing in education increased

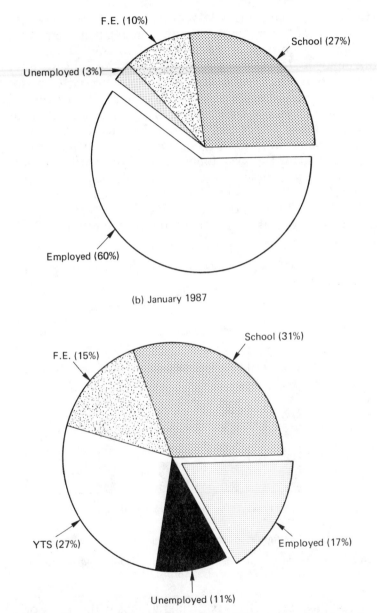

(a) January 1975

F.E. (10%)

School (27%)

Unemployed (3%)

Employed (60%)

(b) January 1987

School (31%)

F.E. (15%)

YTS (27%)

Employed (17%)

Unemployed (11%)

Source: Based on figures given by Roll, 1988, p. 6 and derived from *Employment Gazette*, September 1987, p. 460.

Figure 7.2 *Education and labour market status of 16-year-olds, 1975–87* (from 37 to 46 per cent of 16-year-olds); by 1987, 27 per cent of 16-year-olds were on the Youth Training Scheme (YTS); and there were rises in the number of 16- and 17-year-olds unemployed, from three and four per cent respectively, to 11 and 14 per cent. Within this there are, of course, major variations according to sex. In 1987, some 50 per cent of 16-year-old young women were in full-time education as compared with 41 per cent of the males. Just 23 per cent of young women were on YTS compared with 31 per cent of the young men. Roll also found major differences occurring in relation to ethnicity. 38 per cent of those identifying themselves as 'White' were in full-time education, compared with 68 per cent of those identifying themselves as 'Asian' and 53 per cent of those identifying themselves as 'Black, African or Caribbean' (see Figure 7.3).

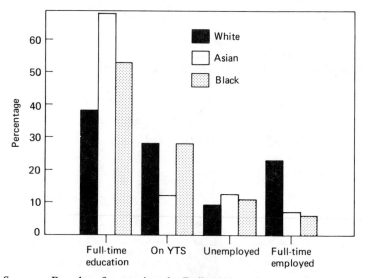

Source: Based on figures given by Roll, 1988, p. 7.

Figure 7.3   *Ethnicity and the education and labour market status of 16-year-olds, Spring 1986*

Unemployment affects particular groups within the work-force. The unemployment rate among 16–19-year-old males is higher than that for any other age group (irrespective of

sex), standing at 20 per cent as compared to 11 per cent for
25–34-year-old males and eight per cent for those aged 35 to
49 in 1985 (OPCS, 1987b, p. 21) (see Figure 7.4). From
Figure 7.4 it will also be apparent that there are significant
differences in relation to gender. Although deeply affected
by prevailing social attitudes, contrasting patterns occur
when non-married women are compared with men. Unemployment is unarguably linked to class. For example, in 1985
employers and managers accounted for six per cent of the
male unemployed, yet were 19 per cent of the male labour
force. In contrast, unskilled manual workers accounted for
14 per cent of male unemployment, yet are only five per cent
of total male labour force (OPCS, 1987a, p. 79). We must
also recognise that there are major spatial differences with
the rate of unemployment among inner-city residents being
more than 50 per cent greater than the national average in
1981 and more than 66 per cent greater than the rate in
towns and rural areas (Hasluck, 1987, p. 9). Also well

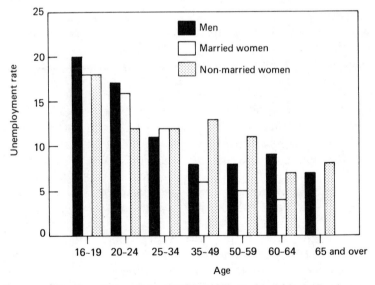

Source: Based on figures from OPCS, 1987b, p. 21, table 4.17.

Figure 7.4   *Economically active people aged 16 and over, by age, sex and
(for women) marital status, and unemployment rates, Great Britain, Spring
1985*

known is the scale of regional difference. As Massey comments: 'The old spatial division of labour based on sector, on contrasts between industries, has gone into accelerated decline and in its place has arisen to dominance a spatial division of labour in which a more important component is the interregional spatial structuring of production within individual industries' (1984, p. 297).

The relative material position of young people worsened in the 1980s. For example, following the introduction of the Youth Opportunities Programme (YOP) in 1978, the real value of the training allowances paid to young people dropped consistently. In 1987 the first year allowance stood at 70 per cent of what was paid nine years earlier in real terms. There came into effect in 1988 further legislation which withdrew the right to benefit from unemployed 16- and 17-year-olds apart from those in specific categories such as single parents and those who have disabilities. Simultaneously the relative position of the youth wage has declined. Data show that between 1979 and 1987 the average earnings of teenagers remained fairly stable in real terms, while the earnings of those aged over 21 has increased significantly (Lewis and Lunn, 1987, p. 4). As Allbeson comments, in that period a low priority was attached to protecting the incomes of young people; there was a delay in recognition of adult independence for the unemployed by the state, and a transfer of support for those on benefit from the state to the family (1985, p. 81), the latter being implemented with little acknowledgement of the financial burden that results. When all this is placed in the setting of ever-widening differentials in income and wealth, it can be seen that, generally, working-class households with young people have been substantially disadvantaged in the 1980s. There was an attack on the incomes of, and opportunities for, working-class young people. This led writers such as Willis *et al.* to suggest that in many ways the young unemployed have been thrust into a 'new social condition' of 'suspended animation between school and work' (1985, p. 218).

Government policies have been directed towards producing a generation of working-class young people who possess 'transferable' skills and an unquenchable appetite for work. Given the relative shortage of opportunities to indulge this appetite it has been important that they learn how to sustain these qualities through any periods of unemployment they experience. This has required that:

> suitably differentiated at school, and taught to know their place, these new model workers are to be instructed, through their training and work experience, and through the discipline of unemployment, to transcend the narrow trade practices and occupational loyalties of a now unwanted division of labour. (Finn, 1987, p. 190)

Although the titles, emphasis and duration of policies and practices may have altered, there remain powerful continuities. YTS provision exhibits considerable occupational sex-segregation: a widespread tendency for young women to conform to feminine job stereotypes, while young men follow their expected path (Cockburn, 1987). Similarly, Pollert argues that all evidence suggests that YTS, 'is not only entrenching but may be widening racial inequality, and information on the Community Programme suggests the same may be happening there' (1986, p. 195). Baqi (1987) found that racial stereotypes were a major barrier for Asian youngsters in gaining access to the 'better' elements of YTS.

In this focus on the 'transition from school to work', it is important to recognise that young women also experience particular pressure in the sexual market-place. Griffin notes that 'apart from moving from school into the full-time labour market, young working-class women also managing social and economic pressures to get a man' (1985, p. 187). This she understands in terms of their simultaneous positions in the sexual, marriage and labour markets. Such 'managing' also colours their experience of leisure, as well as affecting their actions in the workplace and within training and education. Certain occupations might be valued as being 'good for a girl' because they offer working-class young women access to eligible men in white-collar occupations (ibid., p. 189). There is a sense in which they are torn between the demands of these market-places. Young unemployed women are expected to contribute to housework and the general well-being of the household, whereas young men are not similarly expected to do so (Wallace, 1987, p. 143). Pressures to get a man and a job operate at the same time, but they are not directly interchangeable. Young women do not generally see marriage or motherhood as a substitute for full-time employment (Griffin, 1985, p. 189).

Again the situation facing young people from minority ethnic groups in the 'transition from school to work' is well documented. The 1985 Labour Force Survey showed that, while 18 per cent of white males between the ages of 16 and 24 were unemployed, the figure for ethnic minorities rose to 32 per cent (OPCS, 1987b, p. 23). For young women the comparable figures were 15 and 34 per cent. As Cross (1987) comments, such figures are misleading. A significantly higher proportion of ethnic minorities are 'sheltering' from unemployment outside the labour market, in schools and YTS. In addition, many more members of ethnic minority communities than whites are concentrated in the south of England, where overall unemployment rates are lower. Thus the national figure considerably understates the shortcomings of their position in comparison with whites in that labour market. Undoubtedly discrimination is a major factor in the marginal position of ethnic minorities in the labour force, but the differential in employment chances between non-white and white in inner-city areas is narrower than elsewhere in major urban areas. The chances for employment in these areas are poor for all people, regardless of their ethnic group. In this sense overcoming racialism in these local labour markets would mean that 'ethnic minorities would simply have an equally bad chance of employment with whites, just as they would have an equally bad chance of decent housing, adequate schools or a pleasant environment' (Cross, 1987, p. 125).

Housing

A further, crucial, dimension of young peoples' experience concerns housing. Since the turn of the century there has been a continuous improvement in housing conditions as measured in terms of the usually adopted criteria such as room occupancy, bathrooms, indoor toilets and the like. This lifting of standards continues, yet at the same time there remains a housing crisis in Britain, expressed in terms of disrepair, overcrowding and homelessness. Not surprisingly, youth unemployment, the diminished earnings of young people and a demographic change (see Chapter 2) mean that they are more likely to encounter housing difficulties than most other sections of the community. In relation to unemployment, the dilemma they face is often particularly stark, with cheap housing and surplus stock that can be made available being located in areas denuded of employment, while the jobs are found in those areas of greatest housing shortage. This mismatch has placed the government in a quandary. On the one hand they hope young people will 'get on their bikes' and seek out work, albeit, in the main, low paid, in the areas where it is to be found. While on the other hand, they desperately seek to stem the flow of young people from areas such as the North-East and Scotland who swell the numbers of homeless in the South. Hence the introduction of discriminatory restrictions upon allowances and transfers to those aged under 25 in order to keep all but the best qualified and fortunate trapped where they grew up. All this is tied in with discriminatory income support designed deliberately to keep young people within the family home up to the age of 25, and a Social Fund which is structured to prevent unemployed young people and single parents establishing themselves as independent householders (Lister, 1989).

A further key element has been the decline in the availability of private rented accommodation. Prior to 1914, approaching 90 per cent of the housing stock was in the hands of private landlords (Daunton, 1987, p. 13). By the 1980s this figure had dropped to seven per cent. As Brynin has observed, what is important here is that both young and single people are primarily dependent on this sector for their independent accommodation (1987, p. 25). He quotes a GLC survey in 1983/4 which showed that single adults occupied 55 per cent of the private rented sector in London. Some 40 per cent of furnished rented accommodation was

taken up by young people under 25. Thus the decline of this
sector has major ramifications for young people.

The determination of governments to encourage home
ownership, which was to be partially achieved by 'ruthlessly
cutting back the supply of council housing by reducing new
building and promoting the right to buy' (Malpass, 1986, p.
229) has had implications for young people. Firstly, the
designation of local authority housing as the sector of last
resort has meant that only young people possessing certain
characteristics, such as a dependent child, are able to gain
the chance of access to it. Secondly, young people growing
up and living in local authority accommodation, are finding
themselves more than ever before stigmatised by association. This affects their jobs and credit-worthiness and is
reflected in the attitudes of teachers, DHSS officials and so
on. Thirdly, the government, in order to undermine the
local authority sector and pave the way for private landlords
and landladies, has pushed up rents. Low-paid and unemployed young people decreasingly see rented property as an
attractive or feasible housing option, even in those areas
where it might be available to them. Rises in rents linked to
diminished investment in repairs, and the ageing nature of
the stock all combine to further stigmatise it in the eyes of
the consumer and of the wider populace. Fourthly, the 1988
Housing Act severs the rights of inheritance for young
people: they can no longer inherit the tenancy of local
authority property from parents who have died or moved
on.

Even a cursory glance at the data indicates considerable
success on the part of successive governments in their
endeavour to create home ownership as the primary tenure.
However success has been uneven, for wider economic
policies 'have made entry to home ownership prohibitively
expensive for an increasing proportion of young people'
(Malpass, 1986, p. 229). The operation of the labour market
and housing subsidies mean that middle-class young people
still remain relatively advantaged in securing entry into this
sector, but regional variations in house prices, linked to
rapid price inflation, is making entry in many areas difficult
even for those young people who have secured the best of

paid employment. Taking 1980 as the base (100), by 1986 housing prices nationally had risen to an index point of 164, with Greater London rising to 190 and the North to 140 (CSO, 1988b, p. 63). By mid-1988, the Halifax Building Society reported a difference of £89 000 in the price of an average semi-detached house between the two regions (*Guardian*, 10 September 1988). Growing home-ownership for young people has another significance. Linked to the declining size of the family it has created a stratum of young people who, although in the short term are disadvantaged by the high cost of entry, nevertheless will be the long-term beneficiaries either through inheritance or the use of parental property and wealth to secure financial liquidity. Nothing could be better designed to heighten and solidify social stratification and inequality among young people than the forces surrounding housing.

Housing policy is increasingly ghettoising young people along the lines of class. Until the entry to the labour market and now, increasingly, beyond that point, what determines young people's housing experience is almost exclusively the income and wealth of their parent(s).

Education

The educational system and, in particular, the school, has long been seen as having a key role in the socialisation of young people and in channelling them into distinctive roles and occupations. Yet debates about education contain many paradoxes, for, as Silver has suggested, education has been seen: 'both as a means of selecting and perpetuating elites and as a means of promoting social justice and undermining elites. It is discussed in terms of class domination and social control, but also of social liberation and progress' (1980, p. 19). Underpinning this is the desire both to train and to socialise. Given the class nature of society and the need to provide people disposed to, and fitted for, the evolving division of labour, it is necessary that schooling, and education generally, offer different opportunities to different groups. Debates about this process have centred on the inequities involved and the extent to which the socialisaton and training offered actually make people ready for the social and economic roles they are encouraged to play. The ways in which schools treat girls differently from boys, those with learning difficulties and physical impairments differently from those without them, and the stereotyping and racism that takes place in respect to ethnic minorities is documented elsewhere in this book. Here we will briefly survey the class experience of education. To do this we can focus on inequalities and inequities with regard to access, process and outcome.

We must begin by recognising that access to key forms of education are dependent upon wealth. The most obvious example here is the way in which it is possible to buy forms of schooling which provide advantage to the participants in terms of entry to higher education and elite jobs. As many as 62 per cent of top civil servants, 83 per cent of ambassadors, 80 per cent of the top judiciary and 86 per cent of top army officers came from public school backgrounds in the early 1970s (Scott, 1985, p. 48). Yet even after a period of growth, just seven per cent of all pupils in Great Britain are in independent schools. Thus the independent school sector exists to enable the privileged and wealthy to purchase for their offspring advantages in the race to qualification and employment, advantages which supplement those which already flow from their origins. The young people in this sector have little or no contact with those from other social groups; pursue a separate curriculum (as their schools are not obliged to follow the National Curriculum); and are led by the 'old school tie' to the 'right' universities, regiments, clubs, marriages and jobs.

Wealth is important in other respects in terms of access. For example, changes in the income support system in 1988 made it more difficult for those in low-income families to enter sixth forms and further education. Previously it had been possible for young people to claim unemployment benefit and study for up to two A levels. Young people from professional and managerial backgrounds are far more likely to stay on past the minimum leaving age than are those from manual ones. This is so even if they have the same academic ability. The figures for entry to university by British candidates are particularly startling, with 22 per cent of acceptances coming from social class I (Professionals), 48 per cent from social class II (Intermediate/Managerial) and just over one per cent from social class V (unskilled) (UCCA, 1984, quoted in Abercrombie *et al.*, 1988, p. 355). Given that the sizes of social class I and V are roughly equal, the scale of disadvantage is immense.

As might be expected from the pattern of access, outcomes of the formal educational process show distinctive class patterning. While examination results provide only a narrow insight into the situation, they are of obvious importance in relation to access to higher education and certain jobs. Here our understanding is hampered by the relative absence of large-scale and substantial research in England and Wales. However, figures from Scotland provide a graphic illustration of class difference (see Figure 7.5). In crude terms, what McPherson and Willms (1987; 1988) found was that children from skilled and partly manual backgrounds gained on average around one or two O-grades, compared to two

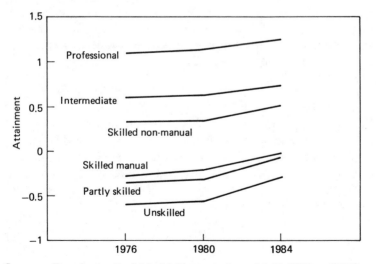

Source: Based on material in McPherson, A. and J. D. Willms (1988) p. 39.

Figure 7.5 *Average examination attainment by social class in Scotland, 1976, 1980, 1984*

Highers for the intermediate grouping (social class II) and four Highers for the professional grouping. What the figures also show is a general rise in attainment across all the social classes and that the gap between those from middle- and working-class backgrounds narrowed (by about one percentage point per annum over the period) (McPherson and Willms, 1988, p. 39). These results can be interpreted as lending some support to the argument that comprehensive schooling can both increase standards and reduce social class inequalities of attainment (Simon, 1988, pp. 36–41).

By sorting young people into different levels and specialisms and by providing the associated credentials, schools and colleges perform a selective function. They are a central element in the process by which a differentiated labour force is reproduced and in the sort of experience people can expect within the labour market. For example, in 1985 the unemployment rate for males with higher educational qualifications was three per cent (five per cent for women), while it was 17 per cent for those with no educational qualifications (13 per cent for women) (OPCS, 1987b, p. 23). Yet credentials are not the only means by which young people are differentiated by the experience of schooling. There is also the so-called 'hidden curriculum'. Arguably, 'the social relationships of education – the relationships between administrators and teachers, teachers and students, students and students, and students and their work – replicate the hierarchical division of labour' (Bowles and Gintis, 1976, p. 131). In this way, people are prepared to be willing and compliant workers, accepting their place in the order of production.

There remain considerable debates as to why working-class young people apparently 'under-achieve' within the educational system. One clear factor is poverty and relative material disadvantage, but how to judge the impact of this, as compared with other factors, is difficult. Earlier studies such as that of Bernstein (1971) placed an emphasis on the varying linguistic capacities of children from different social classes. There is further material which focuses on the cultural capital which middle-class parents possess. For example, it can be argued that there are more likely to be familiar with the educational system and its subject matter than are working-class parents. Other writers have suggested that the frame of reference that working-class young people take on from their parent and neighbourhood cultures allows them to interpret the experience of schooling in particular ways (Brown, 1987). Consequently they are disposed towards the attainment of certain types of work. Willis has argued that the development of a counter-school culture is less a function than a cause of educational failure (1977). Thus the school is evaluated in terms of what it might offer young people engaging in the process of becoming working-class adults.

Other explanations of differences in educational attainment have focused on the school and teachers. The latter, it is suggested, tend to have varying expectations of pupils from different social classes. Given the class background of teachers and the relative familiarity of formal educational forms to middle-class young people, it can be argued that teachers tend to reward this group (Reynolds & Sullivan, 1987). Other approaches have examined the structure and organisation of schooling. Thus the operation of the eleven plus system, the growth of independent schooling and practices such as streaming are singled out for special attention (for a discussion of these see Macdonald and Ridge, 1988). Halsey *et al.* (1980) explored the impact of schooling upon the long-term destination of its recipients. Their findings appear to suggest that cultural background was of particular significance in relation to explaining the experience of primary schooling and entry into the secondary sector (particularly where selection existed). On the other hand, material circumstances were seen to be of especial importance in decisions concerning qualifications and the age of leaving school. They also demonstrated that the nature and organisation of the school was a significant feature, a conclusion also shared by Rutter *et al.* (1979) (see also Reynolds & Sullivan, 1987). Working-class young people are materially disadvantaged within the educational system. Halsey, utilising data from the Oxford mobility study found that: 'the amount spent on the education of children of different origin, far from equalizing chances, helped to maintain class inequality ... those born into professional and managerial families had three times as much spent on them as those born into the families of agricultural labourers' (1986, p. 136). As he comments, the rewards for success and survival within that system are high.

Leisure

Distinctive patterns of leisure usage are associated with different social classes. The exact nature of these differ-ences, and the manner in which they can be interpreted, remain matters of considerable dispute (see Hendry, 1983; Roberts, 1983). Further, there are practical and conceptual difficulties with the very notion of leisure, particularly in relation to the experiences of women and girls (Hargreaves, 1982). Many of the activities that are necessary to the household economy, such as sewing, are frequently de-scribed as leisure activities, yet may not be experienced as such. It is important to recognise that debates about leisure are grounded in complex social forces. 'Patterns of employ-ment, domestic work (and the accompanying consumer technology), and free time intersect with the "normal" roles attributed to men and women' (Clarke & Critcher, 1985, p. 11).

Any discussion of leisure has to address the major changes that have taken place, particularly in relation to the develop-ment of mass leisure industries. As Clarke and Critcher (1985) have argued, such changes express a continuing segregation of leisure – spatially and temporally. There has also been a growing specialisation, with highly differentiated and uniquely packaged forms of leisure being marketed. This can be seen in the growth of theme pubs, the range of sporting clubs and facilities, and the massive expansion in various forms of home-based entertainment. Lastly, there has been institutionalisation. That is to say, new leisure forms have been progressively innovated, or at least ex-ploited, by large-scale business (ibid., p. 78). What has been particularly significant in this respect is that young people became special targets for commercial leisure, although that position is altering (see Chapter 2). In turn, the apparent 'adultness' of such leisure forms and, indeed, the quality of experience when compared to much municipal and voluntary provision, have made commercial leisure opportunities highly attractive to young people.

The way in which young people view and use leisure is deeply influenced by their experience within the household. This may be a matter of simple economics. For example, adults in semi-skilled and unskilled occupations are almost three times more likely not to have a holiday than those in managerial and professional occupations (CSO, 1988a, p. 164), an outcome largely of income level rather than of taste. At the same time, and often not unconnected with questions of disposable income, strong cultural factors are at work in shaping young peoples' disposition to various leisure forms. These are deeply embedded within the household and the neighbourhood and can reflect such dimensions as expectations about the kind of work experience people can anticipate; their role within the household; and their relationships with friends, relatives and neighbours. Parent cultures can be seen at work within working-class youth cultures (Hall and Jefferson, 1976; Cohen, 1972; Mungham and Pearson, 1976; McRobbie, 1978) and middle-class youth cultures (Willis, 1978; Aggleton, 1987). These may be expressed through tastes in music, dress, entertainment and so on. Again the masculine bias of such work and its general failure to attend adequately to the experiences of the mass of young people is a matter of concern (McRobbie, 1980). In some respects gender and ethnicity are more powerful influences regarding leisure than is class (Clarke and Critcher, 1985, pp. 145–79). Yet major class differences remain and here all we need to do is briefly report on some of the key dimensions in relation to young people.

Firstly, there are significant differentials with respect to watching television. Murdock and Phelps (1973) found that forty per cent of younger teenagers from lower-working-class households said that they watched four or more hours of television on an average weekday evening. The corresponding figures for upper-working-class pupils was 35 per cent, and for middle-class pupils 25 per cent. While television ownership is near universal, the same cannot be said of video machines, with, for example, in 1985, well over 40 per cent of managers' and employers' households possessing one, compared with 18 per cent of the unskilled manual. The figure for professional and skilled manual households was roughly equivalent at around 37 per cent (CSO, 1988a, p. 160).

Secondly, distinctive patterns emerge in respect of social habits such as smoking and drinking. For example, unskilled male manual workers are more than three times more likely to be heavy drinkers than are professionals (OPCS, 1984, p. 216), the factor in respect of females being of only a slightly smaller magnitude. Figures for cigarette smoking show that unskilled male manual workers are two-and-a-half times more likely to be smokers than are professionals (OPCS, 1984, p. 196). Comparative figures for females show that 41 per cent of the unskilled manual smoked, as against 21 per cent of professionals.

Thirdly, in terms of participation in different broad forms of leisure provision, there appears to be a declining degree of difference by class for adults, at least in terms of the manual/non-manual split (Gershuny and Jones, 1987, p. 19). Evidence that working-class young people, like adults, 'do less' has been challenged (Roberts, 1983, pp. 116–30). Nevertheless there are highly class-specific activities. For example, traditionally, football, rugby league, the combat sports and, more recently, the martial arts have been relatively popular with young men from working-class households, while activities which are more expensive to undertake are less popular (Sports Council, 1982). A bias towards the middle class emerges in respect of theatre attendance, the use of museums, and eating out. Given that middle-class households are more likely to own a car, possess a range of leisure goods and items such as books and have at their disposal larger amounts of money for use in leisure, such trends are hardly surprising. Expenditure on leisure within households with a gross weekly income of under £100 was £8·64 or 12·3 per cent in 1985, compared to £52·70 or 18·1 per cent households with an income over £300 (CSO, 1988a, p. 166). There is a substantial absolute difference in spending power and one which is inevitably to the advantage of young people in higher-income households. In the past it could have been argued that, with a larger proportion of working-class young people entering paid employment, they had relatively high levels of disposable income which could be spent on leisure. With major changes in the labour market and a relative devaluing of the youth wage, this position is difficult to sustain in the late 1980s.

Fourthly, middle-class young people are more likely to take advantage of school-based recreational activities (see Figure 7.6). As Roberts comments, this can be especially so in respect of those activities that involve staying on after going-home time to play badminton or squash, or to take part in drama, orchestras or whatever else might be provided. Further, 'those who proceed to college have privileged access to a splendid array of sporting and cultural facilities' (1983, p. 110). There is evidence that academically successful pupils often fuse school-life with leisure, while educational 'failures', largely working-class, compartmentalise these spheres (ibid.). Overall, as Hendry comments:

Leisure provision tends to be structured in a manner that assumes political users of facilities to have the characteristics of affluence, mobility and an ability to make rational selections

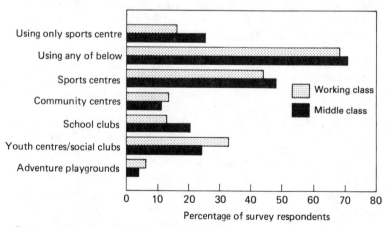

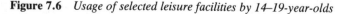
Source: Based on data from DES (1983b).

Figure 7.6 *Usage of selected leisure facilities by 14–19-year-olds*

among the leisure alternatives offered to them. There also appears to be an assumption on the part of leisure planners that social integration into the middle classes is the ultimate goal to which the working classes aspire. (1983, p. 109)

Major class differences in the use of leisure are apparent. This relates not just to individual engagement, but also to the whole pattern of activities. Class may less affect the 'choice' of specific leisure activities than the interrelationship between a set of leisure projects (Clarke and Critcher, 1985, p. 149). Particular leisure cultures can emerge in neighbourhoods and are liable to have a class quality. This is hardly surprising given that housing is frequently divided along class lines. Networks of leisure activities evolve which express and sustain particular assumptions and interests.

A discontinuity of experience?

It is argued that a discontinuity in the experience of working-class young people, when compared with their parents, has arisen. The latter moved with relative ease from school to employment, and were able to establish adult status and independence as wage earners with homes and families of their own. Coffield *et al.* comment in their study of young adults in the North-East:

> Getting married and/or raising a family on Social Security is a very different matter both psychologically and financially. Our evidence suggests that the customary roles of young women as domestic labourers have become intensified, while the traditional means of progressing from childhood to adulthood have been broken down for hundreds of thousands of working-class young men . . . The almost endless adolescence which for decades has become the lot of middle-class youth, is now the daily experience of their working-class contemporaries with one critical distinction: for the latter there will be no elite jobs to compensate for the long denial of status. (Coffield *et al.*, 1986, p. 205)

While there are clear fractures in the process of social and cultural reproduction, old ideas die hard. Wallace, in her study of young people on the Isle of Sheppey, found that: 'the ideology of full male employment and the ideology of the privatized nuclear family persisted even when these were not realizable in reality. Indeed, it could be argued that, at the symbolic and fantasy levels, they were reinforced' (Wallace, 1987, p. 225).

Such strong currents of continuity must temper claims that young people have been thrust into a 'new social condition' (Willis, 1985, p. 218). In the late 1970s and the 1980s economic change, coupled with the political direction of government policies, exacerbated and emphasised social divisions. The position of, and prospects for, the bulk of young people, particularly the working-class young, worsened. Changes in the industrial base, the decline of traditional manufacturing and the rise of new technologies had repercussions upon the class structure. As noted earlier, some young people are the undoubted beneficiaries of these, while others are the victims. Overall, the last two decades have tended to see a relative worsening in the expectations, life chances, and incomes of working-class young people. Certainly a majority of young people, according to what limited research we have, perceive this to be the case (DES, 1983b, p. 25); this has also been a common assumption within much of the literature (Willis, 1985; Davies, 1986; Brown, 1987). It may be the case that demographic and economic changes will lead to a reversal of this relative decline (see Chapter 2). Between 1985 and 1996, the number of 15–19-year-olds will go down by over one million. However, while this may alter the market position of more qualified young people (particularly in the southern half of Great Britain), the situation facing those who leave school or college with few qualifications still appears highly problematical. The position throughout this century has been one of rising living standards of which young people, until recently, more than many other sections, have tended to be the beneficiaries. Although it may have been halted, the evidence does not indicate that this trend has been reversed. We should not be enticed into the simplistic assumption that rising living standards can be equated with the decline of the salience of class as a dynamic feature or determining factor within the lives of young people. From this survey it is clear that young people have significant and often profoundly different experiences in employment, housing, education and leisure on the basis of their class position. Given the nature and scale of such class-based inequality, and the extent to which this is recognised in debates about welfare, it is extraordinary that class does not play a central role in practice and policy debates within youth work. Extraordinary, but hardly surprising, as we will now see.

The class structure of youth work

Youth provision is often portrayed as having middle-class management, lower-middle-class workers and a working-class membership. This formulation may have an attractive circularity, but it cannot be universally applied, as will be understood from the following examination of the various groupings within youth organisations.

The users

DES-sponsored research accompanying the Youth Service Review (DES, 1983b) found that the scouts and guides had a clear ABC1 bias. That is to say, some 50 per cent of those sampled with middle-class and white collar backgrounds had belonged to such organisations, compared with 33 per cent of those with skilled, semi-skilled and unskilled backgrounds (C2DEs) (1983b, p. 42). These findings are in line with earlier research (Dearnaley and Fletcher, 1968; Bone and Ross, 1972; Thomas & Perry, 1974).

    The same research provides corresponding data which demonstrate that use of youth clubs was determined by age, sex, race and class to a considerable degree. Significantly more C2DEs (67 per cent) had ever attended a youth club than ABC1s (57 per cent) and this was reflected in the current usage pattern (34 per cent C2DEs versus 23 per cent ABC1s). Of the 14–16-year-olds nearly two in five (38 per cent) were currently going to a youth club compared with less than one in five (19 per cent) of the over-16s. Around

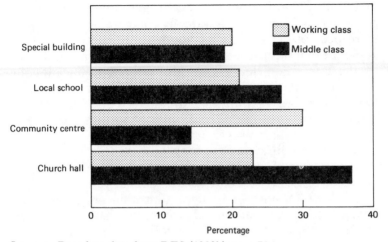

Source: Based on data from DES (1983b) page 78.

Figure 7.7 *Youth club attendance – location of provision*

one-third (32 per cent) of the boys attended a youth club
compared with just over one-quarter (26 per cent) of the
girls (1983b, p. 36). There is also a clear class difference in
the setting where the youth club takes place, as can be seen
from *Figure 7.7*. Middle-class young people are more likely
to attend a club in a school or church hall, whereas working-
class young people are more likely to attend a club in a
community centre.

In terms of class, this research does appear at first glance
to indicate a shift from earlier work. Bone and Ross (1972)
found that 85 per cent of the children of professional
households were attached to some sort of youth provision as
opposed to 56 per cent of those from unskilled households.
The figure for intermediate/managerial was 73 per cent,
skilled non-manual 71 per cent, skilled manual 64 per cent
and semi-skilled 55 per cent. However the way in which
these figures were constructed differs significantly, in that
they include a whole range of clubs and activities not usually
associated with the Youth Service. When they are broken
down the largest single group of attached young people in
the Bone and Ross research went to sports groups (42 per
cent). Next in popularity were youth clubs (36 per cent)

followed by social clubs (22 per cent) and cultural groups (18 per cent) (1972, p. 52). No directly comparable figures exist in respect of class usage of youth clubs, although it was apparent that interest-centred organisations were used most by the late school leavers, as also were the educationally linked organisations. Early leavers more often frequented less differentiated groups like youth clubs and social clubs. These figures may be taken as indicating that the change may not be as sharp as was first thought.

Class-based differences in usage also appear in respect of the frequency of attendance. Working-class young people are more likely to be frequent attenders at youth clubs (see Figure 7.8). A number of important points regarding the differential use of, and attendance at, youth clubs arise out of these figures. Firstly, they reinforce what has already been stressed – the importance of the culture of the household and neighbourhood. Such figures are much as might be surmised from accounts of adult affiliation and use of clubs and societies. Secondly, the figures underpin the importance of the material position of young people and their households. Cheaper and more geographically accessible provi-

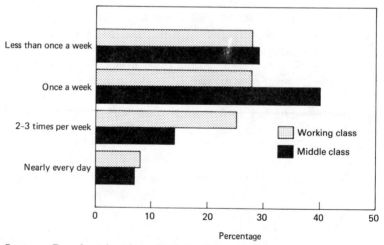

Source: Based on data from DES (1983b) page 78.

Figure 7.8   *Youth club attendance – frequency*

sion such as youth clubs are more likely to be attended by working-class young people. Similarly, given the relatively restricted availability of leisure facilities within lower-income homes and their relative overcrowding, it is hardly surprising that working-class young people are more likely to be regular attenders at youth clubs. Other factors are also at work here. It may well be that middle-class organised youth activities, such as a significant number of church-based youth clubs, may open at less frequent intervals, reflecting class-specific ideas as to what is an appropriate frequency of attendance (see Ellis, 1989).

The managers

We only have limited material on the background of managers and workers. Such research as we possess would suggest that management committees are dominated by people with professional, managerial and skilled non-manual occupations. For example, Lowe found that 80 per cent of the membership of the management committees she surveyed were from these groupings (1973, p. 4). Manual workers provided six per cent, housewives five per cent and the retired a further five per cent of the membership. Lowe concluded that the management committees in her survey were considerably more middle-class than the areas in which their clubs were situated. Historically, there has been a correlation between voluntary activity and class, to such an extent that those areas with a relatively small middle-class presence have tended to have low levels of voluntary organisation activity (Thane, 1982, p. 21). Poster (1977) makes a similar point in respect of the presence of teachers within a locality as a significant feature in the determination of the existence of youth provision.

Within the literature there is plenty of reference to the ethos and class nature of management committees; however, again this is not reflected in hard data. The significant outcome may be less concerned with the exact nature of the membership of management committees and more with the distribution of resources to youth provision. The ability of the middle class to secure influence and resources skews the distribution of youth provision. A parallel skewing can also be found in other forms of welfare provision, such as in the siting of health centres. Thus, whilst centres and units are rarely built in expensive neighbourhoods, they will often appear in adjoining ones so as to contain young people within their local area. In this way many small towns with a middle-class profile will possess relatively good youth facilities, while some urban areas, that are overwhelmingly working-class, do not.

The labour force

If we turn to the structure of the labour force a contrasting position emerges. From the outset it has to be recognised that 65 per cent of the work-force in youth clubs and projects are unpaid part-time workers and a further 32 per cent are paid part-timers (Harper, 1985, p. 6). In other words, even when allowance is made for the hours worked by full-timers, it can be seen that the vast bulk of youth work is undertaken by part-timers. Again we have only limited information concerning the class background of these. For example, Kendra, when analysing the occupational backgrounds of those part-timers presenting themselves for training in one region for which he had information (which was 41 per cent of all students), found that the main occupational group was that of 'housewife' (see Table 7.1). He also found that only

Table 7·1　*Occupational distribution of people undertaking part-time youth work training in one region ('known' occupations)*

	Percentage
Housewife	29·2
Teaching/education	17·2
Clerical secretarial	10·2
Engineering/technical	8·4
Skilled manual	6·1
Caring services/medical	6·1
Unemployed/projects	5·3
Commercial	5·1
Unskilled	4·6

Source:　Kendra, 1985, p. 9.

1·3 per cent of those recruited were in managerial posts, 0·2 per cent were accountants and there were no doctors, dentists or solicitors. Women made up just over 50 per cent of the students recruited. This is broadly in line with Butters and Newell's somewhat impressionistic findings (1978, p. 23). It does conflict, however, with Lowe's (1975) study of London youth workers. When she compared the previous occupations of full-time workers with the daytime occupations of part-time and voluntary workers she found that both groups recruited most heavily from

> the skilled non-manual occupations (clerical worker, secretary etc.) – 37 per cent of full-timers and 39 per cent of part-timers. A higher proportion of full-time youth workers than part-time workers tend to come from skilled manual or related trades (22 per cent as opposed to 10 per cent). On the other hand, one in three part-timers have professional or managerial daytime jobs, (compared with fewer than one in five full-timers). (1975, pp. 4–5)

The background of those entering full-time youth work does appear to have altered since Lowe undertook her research. According to Kuper (1985), of the staff in post in 1983, 27 per cent had received specialist training, 43 per cent were qualified teachers, 17 per cent trained through alternative routes or received individual recognition and 13 per cent were unqualified. Holmes (1988) has suggested that the position has changed and, while using figures which are not strictly comparable, he argues that teachers comprise 36 per cent of the labour force and specialist trained personnel 37 per cent. Similarly, much of the labour force research was undertaken prior to the onset of large-scale unemployment. It also took place before the sustained attempts by central government to control and cut back local authority spending and to disband ILEA (which operated the largest and best resourced youth service in the United Kingdom). In the mid- to late 1980s it became apparent that in many authorities part-time workers were being substituted for full-timers, particularly in youth clubs and centres. Further, there appears to have been a trend towards the consolidation of

216   *Young People, Class Inequality and Youth Work*

part-time sessions into the equivalent of half-time jobs (or more) both in order to accommodate this process and in an attempt by workers to expand their paid employment. For many part-time youth workers, their income from this activity is their only source of wages. Not only does this mean that a significant number of workers experience poverty, but it also means that skilled workers are caught in the very dual labour market we discussed earlier.

At the beginning of this section we painted a somewhat stereotypical picture of the class structure of youth work. We have seen that such a profile does accord with certain forms of provision, most notably the open youth club. With largely working-class members and middle-class management, the workers appear to be caught between the two. Eggleston describes workers, particularly those 'in charge' of units, as exercising a focal and 'absorbing' role between the demands of the organisation and the demands of the members: 'He stands at the personal frontiers of both sides in a characteristically exposed and vulnerable "man in the middle" position much like that of the foreman in industry or the receptionist at the airline desk' (1976, p. 134). Even allowing for the somewhat dramatic, heroic and masculine representation, there is an important sense in which workers in this position are engaged in attempting to reconcile and pacify competing class interests on a day-to-day basis. They may not recognise them as such. These interests appear in the guise of personal preferences and problems. None the less practitioners are frequently obliged to attempt to strike bargains between conflicting class positions.

Youth work and class interests

Elsewhere we have offered an account of the operation of the state, the class interests it represents, and how this feeds through into the practice of youth work (Jeffs and Smith, 1988). In the same work we explored the relationship of youth work practice to deeper workings of the economy and the way in which key values within the capitalist system found concrete expression in the operation of youth work units. In addition, the role of ideology and its manifestation in different traditions of work has been examined (Jeffs and Smith, 1987; 1988; Smith, 1988). What we have sought to show are the ways in which bourgeois frames of thinking and practice achieve a dominant position within welfare generally and youth work in particular. Here we just need to underline the way these frames have had to be reworked in order to secure the allegiance of young people.

Much of the early rhetoric of youth work concerned the condition and behaviour of working-class young people. However the reality of actual provision was somewhat different. The early work was predominantly directed at young people in the same class groupings as the provider. For example, very few young people with fathers in unskilled and semi-skilled jobs joined the uniformed movements (Springhall, 1977, pp. 25, 127). The institutions which became closely identified with youth work were largely controlled by members of the middle class. They carried with them specific themes (particularly an attack on working-class cultures); developed forms which are recognisable in present-day practice; and sought to engage the services of particular 'types' of adult (Smith, 1988, p. 19). Nevertheless these institutions and practices were not just the providers' making. Where working-class young people were attracted to provision there was often considerable resistance to what was offered. In order to pacify and solicit these customers, appealing activities had to be offered. These, in turn, were often reinterpreted and refashioned by the young people. A parallel process occurred within those organisations which had a more middle-class membership. Here the cultural distance between members and leaders may have been less pronounced, but middle-class young people still had to be attracted to provision. Out of these processes what might be called 'bourgeois youth work' was formed. It can be characterised as seeking to aid the maintenance and development of the social and economic order as conceived by key members of the middle class. It adopted distinctively bourgeois forms and values. Public schools and the military service provided models, as did the paradigms of middle-class leisure. The 'club', ideas of service and leadership, organised games and *esprit de corps*, and preconceptions regarding the correct behaviour for 'ladies', are examples of this. Indeed adolescence itself can be seen to be largely a bourgeois construction. Lastly, 'bourgeois youth work' acted to salve middle-class consciences by enabling philanthropists to feel they were doing something about the worst excesses of capitalism. The very fact that *they* were providing help, and others were defined as not, also allowed them to justify their pre-eminent position (Smith, 1988, p. 23).

Then, as now, youth workers had to compete with long-established traditions of popularly organised entertainment and commercial provision. If they were to attract young people on any scale they would have to reach some sort of accommodation with these cultural forms. Dancing, mixed provision, free-and-easy atmospheres, and the relative freedom from adult interference appeared to be what was valued by many young people. For large numbers of those middle-class adults involved in early youth work this situation was fraught with difficulties, as it was often these very things which they sought to counteract. However, with the development of mass socialising institutions such as schooling and the media, and the continuing need to contain the excesses of the young, a shift occurred in the character of youth work during the 1930s and 1940s, changes aided by the emergence of more organic forms of youth provision based in neighbourhood organisations and the development of state-sponsored work (particularly during the Second World War).

Overall, there was a general move from improvement to containing enjoyment; a major increase in the number of youth clubs; a substantial rise in attendance, particularly among working-class young people; and changes in the background of youth workers, with the representation of the early 'care-taking' elite declining (Jeffs, 1979, pp. 19–30; Smith, 1988, pp. 29–47). As a result it is possible to talk of the development of 'popular youth work', a youth work which specifically appealed to popular cultural forms, and which aimed to attract young people generally. Much of this provision was made under the auspices of middle class-dominated institutions. However it is also possible to discern specifically working-class forms of youth work provision. Whereas bourgeois provision simply used, and reached an accommodation with, the popular in order to attract young people, such working-class examples of youth work actually gained their identity in significant part from popular cultural forms.

There remains a deep concern in many policy pronouncements and in commentaries upon youth work concerning working-class young people and, in particular, working-class young men. This is perhaps best seen in the observations upon young people in the *Albemarle Report* (HMSO, 1960, pp. 13–34). Subsequently, this has been overlaid with panics regarding the perceived behaviour of black young men (DES, 1967; HMSO, 1982; DES, 1987a) and more general liberal disquiet about the needs of girls and young women (HMSO, 1982; DES, 1988a), those with disabilities (NACYS, 1989), the unemployed (DES, 1988b) and those living in rural areas (NACYS, 1988a). However the broadly social democratic sentiments expressed in such policy and discussion documents was hardly likely to appeal to New Right thinking (Davies, 1986, pp. 109–14). Also, while the standpoint may have been generally liberal, it remained paternal and dominated by bourgeois concerns. Thus, not only did such thinking not appeal to the Right, it also has become subject to criticism from black activists (John, 1981; Williams, 1988) and feminists (see Chapter 3). Even some of the more 'progressive' forms of working which have sometimes been labelled as 'issue-based' can be interpreted as forms of cultural imperialism (see Jeffs & Smith, 1989b).

The class nature of youth work programmes

As well as recognising the class structure of youth work provision, it is also important to explore the class nature of the experiences generated. The stated aims and direction of many programmes are, frankly, imperialistic and nationalistic – as an examination of the content of some elements of scouting or the Duke of Edinburgh's Award Scheme demonstrates. The capitalist system is brought into these relationships in a very direct manner, for example, through the use of sponsorships and promotion within national youth organisations. At a more insidious level it can be seen that many of the activities and behaviours valued by youth workers and sponsors correspond to what might be described as bourgeois norms. In part, this is an obvious outcome of youth work's predominantly middle-class leadership, a position further heightened by the presence of many aspiring lower middle-class workers and helpers. However we must also recognise the power of traditions of thinking and viewing the world that have been handed down by preceding generations of workers and sponsors. Certain ideas, values and behaviours have achieved special status. As Hanmer has noted, there seems to be a tendency to think in mutually exclusive categories:

> Terms such as active and passive use of leisure, being with or without interests, being clubbable and unclubbable are dichotomies. Each has its opposite, or opposing concept. A system of values is implied by the approval and non-approval given to these categories. One is considered good, the other is considered bad. (1964, p. 17)

Not only can this system of values be seen to act to the disadvantage of girls and young women (ILEA, 1984), it can also be seen to endorse the world of the middle-class male. 'Being without interests' may be translated as 'not appreciating what we like'. Once this is understood, we can see a similar phenomenon is occurring in much of the work sponsored by bourgeois white organisations and directed at young people of different cultures. When such thinking is placed in the existing relations of subordination and exploitation, then the direction of much youth work becomes clear. 'Playing the game' can become dangerously close to 'don't rock the boat' and 'respect your elders and betters'.

To attract young people to places of improvement it has been necessary to reach some accommodation with popular, and apparently more 'dangerous', cultural forms such as dancing and the informality of the cafe and pub. Often these have been offered in exchange for participation in other,

more 'purposeful' activities, rather than approached as valid
and vibrant sites for dialogue and exploration. To do this,
however, it is essential to gain an active appreciation of the
way in which young people experience youth provision and
the frames of reference they use. Approached from this
angle, we can begin to see that, for example, many working-
class young people use youth provision instrumentally.
Some may want to advance in terms of bourgeois paradigms.
Many others will have little identity with the aims and values
of the organisation, but are happy to use its services for as
long as there is some benefit to them. They take opportunities and facilities and reinterpret them to their own ends.
Yet we should not fall into the trap of thinking that the
assumption of an instrumental orientation leaves them un-
touched by their experience of youth provision. Their encounter with middle-class attitudes and forms can simultaneously confirm them in their separateness and sustain a
belief in their political and economic inferiority. In other
words, the fact that they are consumers, rather than in-
itiators and organisers of provision, places them in a specific
social relationship, one which will have been familiar in
school, in the shopping mall, in training and further education and at work. At the same time, the sense of middle-class
cultural forms being different and somehow 'not them' can
be strengthened. This consuming relationship within much
youth provision has to be contrasted with the emphasis on
self-organisation within the more middle-class student
sphere.

Such a view of youth work does have to be tempered by a
recognition that there are forms of provision where the
workers have a more organic relationship with those they
work with, where, say, working-class Afro-Caribbean young
people feel at home with their organisation (although this is
not always the case – see Williams, 1989). However one sure
test of the political and social direction of provision is to ask
to what extent workers address the questions and divisions
outlined in earlier sections of this chapter. Do they, for
example, seek to encourage working-class young people to
reflect critically on their experiences in the labour market?
Or do they simply seek to ameliorate the situation?

The underclass

Before leaving this discussion of working-class young people and youth work it is important to note one further dimension of policy and practitioner thinking. Running through a number of commentaries and statements is the notion of an underclass; a 'class' distinct from the working class; a grouping of the 'socially inefficient' and the 'rough'. Inevitably this group is represented as being a particular social problem, possessing multiple deprivations and social disadvantages. In addition, its members are portrayed as being alienated from mainstream mores and resistant to welfare interventions and to the normal operation of the market. A further dimension of this view is that this deprivation and disadvantage is passed on from generation to generation. Perhaps the best known British enunciation of this was Sir Keith Joseph's series of speeches on the 'cycle of deprivation' (1972–4, quoted by MacNicol, 1987). Within youth work the idea appears most graphically in the rescuing traditions of practice (see, for example, Stowe, 1987; Wilson, 1985), but it has also found its way into official statements and reports in a modified form via such manifestations as 'indigenous workers', 'the inner city' and the 'problem estate' (see, for example, DES, 1987a).

A common approach is to identify particular behavioural traits as anti-social, while ignoring other dimensions that do not fit the picture: 'As part of this exercise, it is necessary for proponents of the underclass concept to lump together a wide range of diverse human conditions (in order to make the problem appear significant), yet attribute them to a single cause (so that it appears a problem amenable to solution)' (MacNicol, 1987, p. 315). Many of the racier accounts of youth work have made sustained use of the idea and there is a kind of machismo associated with the efforts of those who work at 'The Razor's Edge' (Blandy, 1967), with 'Gutter Feelings' (Wilson, 1985) or tackle 'heavy end' IT. Within such rescuing traditions (Smith, 1988, pp. 56–7) young people are seen as in need of saving. They have to be 'rescued' by the worker from the situation they are in. Such judgements are usually based upon an ideology drawn from a particular social movement, often religious in nature, where certain behaviours and situations are labelled as evil or sinful, or as putting people in danger. The problems faced are seen, not so much as structural, but as personal and often moral. The central deficit is often portrayed as emotional: 'emotional deprivation is caused by a loss of adequate relationships while factors such as bad environment, education, and housing add to the problem but are not causes in themselves. It is often the lack of close family relationships that are [sic] at the root of violent behaviour' (Wilson, 1985, p. 92). However, when it comes to finding a solution, what is frequently offered is 'love'. Youth workers have to love those they work with. Through that love, young people may be 'kept alive', their capability to feel, nurtured (ibid., p. 88). Alongside this giving, there is a strong current of sacrifice by the worker.

> Often I'm told to give up the kids 'because they're too bad'. And humanly speaking there does seem little chance for the established criminal . . . but I know that Jesus died for the world, and that He never gives up on anyone. To feel battered, to go into the club time after time and have to face up to conflict cannot be explained, only experienced. (ibid., p. 116)

It is easy to dismiss such sentiments as arising from particular religious dispositions or self-images. Yet the smell of burning martyrs is not confined to this quarter. Similar heroic encounters with the underclass can be found in the literature of girls and detached work, and in the vogue for work with the 'heavy end' in IT, the bourgeois in workers often being offended by the supposed brutality, emotional poverty and material deprivations of young peoples' lives in the underclass. Such feelings have been consistently expressed within youth work. Apart from providing a justification for intervention, the more horrific the story, the more likely the donation of funds for such endeavours. The givers may be worried by the deprivations described, guilty about doing little directly about it, and thankful that others are. As we have commented elsewhere, such approaches often display a contempt for the cultures encountered, a self-confident belief in the rightness of intervention, and the desire to impose bourgeois behaviours and values.

The idea of an inter-generational underclass has figured in debates about social policy for a century or more. Yet, while being subjected to sustained empirical research, it remains an unsubstantiated concept. MacNicol suggests that five elements are usually associated with it (1987, pp. 315–16). Firstly, it is essentially an administrative device used to define certain types of contact with state institutions. Thus it may be simply that those dependent upon state benefits are so labelled. Secondly, there is a tendency to add the completely separate question of inter-generational transmission in order to give the idea a spurious scientific legitimacy. Thirdly, there is the identification of particular behaviours as anti-social and the ignoring of others. Fourthly, the underclass 'problem' usually relates to debates and concerns regarding resource allocation, particularly at moments of economic recession. Lastly, the idea tends to be supported by those who wish to constrain the redistributive potential of welfare. In this way it can be seen as part of a broader conservative view.

Within debates and discussion about youth work, the idea of an underclass has an extraordinary ability to survive. It may become reworked in such notions as marginalisation, and take on more liberal or left concerns (see, for example, Chapman and Cook, 1988; Cross, 1987), but it retains considerable power. The tendency to hive off the experiences of particular groups of working-class young people into a separate category which is somehow below or beyond class or at the margins of society may be seen as one more mechanism by which class considerations become hidden.

Conclusion

As an active organising idea, class has been largely absent from the forefront of practitioner and policy thinking within youth work. Yet underpinning the endeavours of many youth workers there is a basic acceptance of the class structure and of the capitalist system which sets the vast bulk of young people at such a disadvantage. There has been a correct emphasis by a number of practitioners on work which seeks to combat sexism and racism. There has even been some work on disability and sexuality. However these endeavours have generally been able to be conducted within a broadly liberal framework, one that is basically accepting of the prevailing economic and political system. Within that liberal position it has been just about possible to talk of, and even promote, in a limited way, autonomous black organisation, self-advocacy and feminist critiques. For the most part, and partially as a consequence, only half an adequate analysis is present. By approaching each discretely, it is possible to overlook the basic structural and material circumstances which underpin and sustain inequality and injustice. Here attention to class relationships and dynamics becomes crucial to any adequate understanding and action.

Yet all is not pessimism. Within youth work, socialist and radical traditions of practice have survived and developed (see Taylor, 1987; Smith, 1988, pp. 48–64). What they have demonstrated is that to approach class in any sustained manner is to begin to question many of the basic premises upon which youth work has been predicated. When this is linked with constructing an analysis of the relations of subordination and exploitation generally, then the possibilities for a liberating practice become clearer. At its core is the development of critical thought and action.

> There is no freedom in simply following what has been determined theoretically beforehand, even if one ascribes to the particular theory being implemented. Emancipation lies in the possibility of taking action autonomously. That action must be *informed* by certain theoretical insights, but it is not *prescribed* by them. (Grundy, 1987, p. 113, emphasis as in original)

Moving beyond literal interpretations and fragmented modes of reasoning requires social relationships which allow people to challenge, engage and question the form and substance of the learning process (Giroux, 1983, p. 202). Youth workers have to work at situations in order that young people may make and take the opportunity 'to speak with their own voices, to authenticate their own experiences' (ibid., p. 203).

> Manipulated by the ruling classes' myths, the dominated classes reflect a consciousness that is not properly their own. Hence, their reformist tendency. Permeated by the ruling class ideology, their aspirations, to a large degree, do not correspond to their authentic being. These aspirations are superimposed by the most diversified means of social manipulation. (Freire, 1985, p. 159)

In the contributions to this book we have seen a desire to sustain and develop practice which unmasks these forms of manipulation, to clear away the various mechanisms that the dominant classes employ to prevent the dominated from seeing themselves as such. A central, perhaps *the* central, problem which youth workers must address is the ideological process by which one type of oppression is played off against another. As a consequence people 'are led to focus on their own specific form of oppression rather than understanding how one form links with another to constitute a structure of oppression' (Allman, 1988, p. 93). This process has certainly happened within youth work. Practitioners, who already occupy a contradictory position in the class structure, are under various pressures to recast or label their work in more acceptably liberal guises, most notably in terms of 'issues'. But the danger is that they leave out class and other dimensions and, by so doing, allow their practice to become disconnected and limited. More than this, concentration on one dimension to the exclusion of others plays into the hands of those who wish to 'divide and rule'. Yet this process is not inevitable. It can be combated. As contributors to this book have demonstrated, the elements of practice are there. Furthermore the nature of youth work organisation and practice allows a certain space to act. Even where there is constraint, it is often possible for workers to use this in order to enable others to recognise something of the structure of oppression that limit their actions (Smith, M., 1984). This is why we remain optimistic. While youth workers have to 'swim in a sea of capitalism' (Lacey, 1988, p. 91), they need not be consumed by it.

Notes on the Contributors

Don Blackburn is a lecturer at Humberside College of Higher Education, Hull.

Annie Franklin works for the Save the Children Fund (UK Department).

Bob Franklin works at the Centre for Television Research, University of Leeds.

Tony Jeffs is a lecturer in the Department of Social Work and Social Policy, Newcastle-upon-Tyne Polytechnic.

Peter Kent-Baguley is a lecturer at Crewe and Alsager College.

Keith Popple is a lecturer in the Department of Social Work, Health and Community Studies, Plymouth Polytechnic.

Mark Smith is a tutor at the Centre for Professional Studies in Informal Education, YMCA National College, London.

Jean Spence is a lecturer in the Department of Social Science, Sunderland Polytechnic.

Bibliography

Abbott, P. and R. Sapsford (1987) *Women and Social Class*, London: Tavistock.

Abercrombie, N., A. Warde, *et al.* (1988) *Contemporary British Society*, Cambridge: Polity Press.

Abrams, M. (1959) *Teenager Consumer Spending*, London: Exchange Press.

Abrams, M. and J. O'Brien (1981) *Political Attitudes and Aging in Britain*, London: Age Concern.

Abrams, P. (1971) 'Age and generation' in P. Barker (ed.), *A Sociological Portrait*, Harmondsworth: Penguin.

Abrams, P. (1978) *Work, Urbanism and the United Kingdom Today*, London: Weidenfeld & Nicolson.

ACE (1980) 'Disruptive Units', *Where*, No. 158.

Adams, G. (1982) *Falls Memories*, Dingle, Co. Kerry: Brandon.

Adams, G. (1986) *The Politics of Irish Freedom*, Dingle, Co. Kerry: Brandon.

Aggleton, P. (1987) *Rebels Without a Cause: Middle-class youth and the transition from school to work*, Lewes: Falmer Press.

Agnello, T. J. (1973) 'Aging and the sense of political powerlessness' *Political Opinion Quarterly*, vol. 37, pp. 251–9.

Akehurst, M. (1983) *Groundwork, Young people and the Youth Service in the countryside*, Leicester: National Association of Youth Clubs.

Allbeson, J. (1985) 'Seen but not heard: young people', in S. Ward, (ed.), *DHSS in Crisis*, London: Child Poverty Action Group.

Allen, S. and A. Waton (1986) 'The effects of unemployment: experience and response' in S. Allen, A. Waton, K. Prucell and S. Wood (eds), *The Experience of Unemployment*, London: Macmillan.

Allman, P. (1988) 'Gramsci, Freire and Illich. Their contributions to education for socialism', in T. Lovett, (ed.), *Radical Approaches to Adult Education*, London: Croom Helm.

ALTARF (1984) *Challenging Racism*, London: ALTARF.

Altman, D. (1986) *AIDs and the New Puritanism*, London: Pluto Press.

Apple, M. (1979) *Ideology and Curriculum*, London: Routledge & Kegan Paul.

Ariès, P. (1962) *Centuries of Childhood*, London: Jonathan Cape.

Aronoff, C. (1974) 'Old age in prime time', *Journal of Communication*, vol. 24, pp. 86–7.

Artley, A. (1988) 'How Age Can Wither the Authority of a Woman', *Independent*, 9 March.

Ashton, D. and M. Maguire (1987) *Young Adults In the Labour Market*, Research Paper 65, London: Department of Employment.

Bahro, R. (1982) *Socialism and Survival*, London: Heretic Books.

Bains, H. S. (1988) 'Southall Youth: An old-fashioned story' in P. Cohen and H. S. Bains (eds), *Multi-Racist Britain*, London: Macmillan.

Baker, J. (1986) 'Comparing National Priorities: Family and Population Policy in Britain and France', *Journal of Social Policy*, 15 (4).

Baldwin, S. (1985) *The Cost of Caring*, London: Routledge & Kegan Paul.

Baldwin, S. *et al.* (1981) 'The disabled person and cash benefits', in D. Guthrie (ed.), *Disability, Legislation and Practice*, London: Macmillan.

Ball, R. (1988) 'Student Vacation Workers and the Labour Market', *Youth and Policy*, no. 24, pp. 30–5.

Banton, M. (1985) *Promoting Racial Harmony*, Cambridge: Cambridge University Press.

Baqi, L. (1987) *Too little, too late. Asian young people and the Youth Training Scheme*, London: London YTS Asian Monitoring Group.

Barker, D. and S. Allen (eds), (1976) *Dependence and Exploitation in Work and Marriage*, London: Longman.

Barwick, S. (1988) 'Sleepy Castleisand Enjoys Home Comforts in the Global Office', *Independent*, 30 August.

Bates, I., J. Clarke, P. Cohen, D. Finn, R. Moore and P. Willis (1984) *Schooling for the Dole? The new vocationalism*, London: Macmillan.

de Beauvoir, S. (1985) *Old Age*, Harmondsworth: Penguin.

Belfield, R. and S. Carroll (1985) 'Out of School Activities', *New Statesman*, 1 February, pp. 8–9.

Benwell CDP (1978) *The Making of a Ruling Class. Final Report No. 6*, Newcastle: Benwell CDP.

Bernstein, B. (1971) *Class Codes and Control*, vol. 1, London: Routledge & Kegan Paul.

Birke, L. (1986) *Women, Feminimism and Biology*, Brighton: Wheatsheaf.

Birmingham Community Relations Council (1980) *Annual Report 1979/80*, Birmingham: Birmingham Community Relations Council.

Black, D. (1986) *All Our Tomorrows: Growing old in Britain*, London: BMA.

Blagg, P. (1987) 'Corporate Strategies and Social Space', Lancaster: University of Lancaster, unpublished paper.

Blanch, M. (1979) 'Imperialism, nationalism and organised youth', in J. Clarke *et al.* (eds), *Working Class Culture*, London: Hutchinson.

Blandy, M. (1967) *Razor Edge: The story of a youth club*, London: Gollancz.

230   Bibliography

Blythe, R. (1979) *The View in Winter. Reflections on old age*, London: Allen Lane.

Bohning, W. R. (1981) 'The self-feeding process of economic migration from low wage to post-industrial countries with a liberal capitalist structure', in P. Braham *et al.* (eds), *Discrimination and Disadvantage: the experience of black workers*, London: Harper & Row.

Bone, M. and E. Ross (1972) *The Youth Service and Similar Provision for Young People*, London: HMSO.

Bornat, J., C. Phillipson and S. Ward (1985) *A Manifesto for Old Age*, London: Pluto Press.

Bosche, S. (1983) *Jenny Lives with Eric and Martin*, London: Gay Men's Press.

Bourgeois-Pichat, J. (1987) 'The unprecedented shortage of births in Europe', in K. Davies *et al.* (eds), *Below Replacement Fertility in Industrial Societies*, Cambridge: Cambridge University Press.

Bowles, S. and H. Gintis (1976) *Schooling in Capitalist America*, London: Routledge & Kegan Paul.

Bowman, I. (1981) 'Maladjustment. A history of the category', in W. Swann (ed.), *The Practice of Special Education*, Oxford: Blackwell.

Bradshaw, J., D. Lawton and K. Cooke (1987) 'Income and Expenditure of Teenagers and their Families', *Youth and Policy*, no. 19, pp. 15–19.

Braverman, H. (1974) *Labor and Monopoly Capital*, New York: Monthly Review Press.

Britton, M. (1986) 'Recent Population Changes in Perspective', *Population Trends*, 45, pp. 33–41.

Brown, F. and D. Green (1986) 'Housing in the Cities: The End of Consensus?', in P. Lawless and C. Raban (eds), *The Contemporary British City*, London: Harper & Row.

Brown, J. (1988) *Child Benefit: Investing in the future*, London: CPAG.

Brown, P. (1987) *Schooling Ordinary Kids. Inequality, unemployment and the new vocationalism*, London: Tavistock.

Brown, S. (1987) *Critical Theory and Practice in a Black Youth Club*, Newcastle: Youth and Policy.

Bryan, B., S. Dadzie and S. Scafe (1985) *The Heart of the Race. Black Women's Lives in Britain*, London: Virago.

Bryne, D. (1987) 'A Disposable Workforce – the Youth Labour Market After the 1986 Wages Act', *Youth and Policy*, 20, pp. 15–18.

Brynin, M. (1987) 'Young homeless: pressure groups, politics and the press', *Youth and Policy*, 20, pp. 23–33.

Burston, J. R. (1975) 'Granny bashing', *British Medical Journal*, vol. 3, p. 592.

Burt, C. (1952) *The Causes and Treatment of Backwardness*, London: University of London Press.

Butler, R. N. (1969) 'Age-ism. Another form of bigotry', *The Gerontologist*, vol. 9, no. 4, pp. 243–6.

Butters, S. with S. Newell (1978) *Realities of Training*, Leicester: National Youth Bureau.

Byrne, D. (1987) 'Rich and poor: the growing divide', in A. and

C. Walker (eds), *The Growing Divide. A social audit, 1979–87*, London: Child Poverty Action Group.

Byrne, E. (1978) *Women and Education*, London: Tavistock.

Cameron, D. (1985) *Feminism and Linguistic Theory*, London: Macmillan.

Campbell, M. and D. Jones (1982) *Asian Youths in the Labour Market. A study of Bradford*, Bradford: EEC/DES Transition to Work Project, Bradford College.

Carey, S. and A. Shukur (1986) 'A profile of the Bangladeshi community in East London', *New Community*, vol. xii, no. 3.

Carpenter, V. (1985) 'Racism and the Boundaries of Work with Girls', *Working with Girls*, no. 28.

Carpenter, V. and L. Rowley (1985) 'AGM Revisited', *Working with Girls Newsletter*, no. 25.

Carpenter, V. and K. Young (1986) *Coming in from the Margins. Youth work with girls and young women*, Leicester: National Association of Youth Clubs.

Carpenter, V., L. Hart and G. Salvat (1982) 'Working with Girls', in A. Curno *et al.* (eds), *Woman in Collective Action*, London: Association of Community Workers.

Cashmore, E. E. (1983) *Rastaman: The Rastafarian Movement in England*, London: Unwin.

Cashmore, E. E. (1984a) *No Future*, London: Heinemann.

Cashmore, E. E. (1984b) *Dictionary of Race and Ethnic Relations*, London: Routledge & Kegan Paul.

Castles, S. and G. Kosack (1981) 'The function of labour immigration in western Europe capitalism', in P. Braham *et al.*(eds), *Discrimination and Disadvantage in Employment: the experience of black workers*, London: Harper & Row.

Castles, S. *et al.* (1984) *Here for Good: Western Europe's New Ethnic Minorities*, London: Pluto Press.

Central Statistical Office (1986) *Annual Abstract of Statistics*, London: HMSO.

Central Statistical Office (1988a) *Social Trends 18*, London: HMSO.

Central Statistical Office (1988b) *Regional Trends*, London: HMSO.

Chamberlain, N. and J. Jones (1986) 'Knowing the risk', *Lesbian and Gay Socialist Journal*, Autumn 1986.

Champion, T. and A. Green (1988) *Local Prosperity and the North-South Divide*, Coventry: University of Warwick Institute for Employment Research.

Chapman, T. and J. Cook (1988) 'Marginality, youth and government policy in the 1980s', *Critical Social Policy*.

Cheetham, J. *et al.* (1981) *Social and Community Work in a Multi-Racial Society*, London: Harper & Row.

Cheseldine, D. E. and D. M. Jeffree (1981) 'Mentally Handicapped Adolescents. Their use of leisure', *Journal of Mental Defficiency*, vol. 25.

Children's Society (1987) *Young People Under Pressure: Somewhere to Live*, London: Children's Society.

Churchill, D. (1988) 'Britain's Youth Market Grows Up', *Financial Times*, 11 May.

Clarke, J. and C. Critcher (1985) *The Devil Makes Work. Leisure in Capitalist Britain*, London: Macmillan.

Coard, B. (1971) *How the West Indian Child is Made Educationally Subnormal in the British School System*, London: New Beacon Books.

Coates, D. (1984) *The Context of British Politics*, London: Hutchinson.

Cochran, R. and M. Billig (1983) 'Youth and Politics', *Youth and Policy*, 2(1) pp. 31–4.

Cockburn, C. (1987) *Two Track Training. Sex Inequalities and the YTS*, London: Macmillan.

Coffield, F., C. Borrill and S. Marshall (1986) *Growing Up at the Margins: Young Adults in the North East*, Milton Keynes: Open University Press.

Cohen, P. (1972) 'Sub-cultural conflict and working-class community', *Working Papers in Contemporary Cultural Studies*, no. 2, Birmingham: Centre for Contemporary Cultural Studies.

Cohen, P. (1988) 'The perversions of inheritance: studies in the making of multi-racist Britain', in P. Cohen and H. S. Bains (eds), *Multi-Racist Britain*, London: Macmillan.

Cohen, S. (1972) *Folk Devils and Moral Panics. The creation of the mods and rockers*, London: McGibbon & Key.

Coleman, J. S. and T. Husen (1985) *Becoming Adult in a Changing Society*, Paris: OECD.

Coles, B. (1986) 'School Leaver, Job Seeker, Dole Reaper: Young and Unemployed in Rural England', in S. Allen, A. Waton, K. Purcell and S. Wood (eds), *The Experience of Unemployment*, London: Macmillan.

Comfort, A. (1976) 'Age prejudice in America', *Social Policy*, vol. 7, no. 3, pp. 3–8.

Comfort, A. (1977) *A Good Age*, London: Mitchell Beazley.

Commission for Racial Equality (1980) *The Fire Next Time. Youth in a Multi-racial society*, London: CRE.

Commission for Racial Equality (1981) 'Black Self Help', in Cheetham *et al.* (eds), *Social and Community Work in a Multi-Racial Society*, London: Harper & Row.

Commission for Racial Equality (1982) *Young People and the Jobs Market*, London: CRE.

Community Relations Commission (1977) *Seen but not served. Black youth and the Youth Service*, London: CRC.

Cooke, K. (1986) 'Problems of Income Support for Young People', *Youth and Policy*, no. 15, pp. 5–8.

Coombe, V. (1978) 'Racial discrimination and the coloured elderly. Britain's other elderly', *New Age*, vol. 3, p. 10.

Cornell, C. and R. J. Gelles (1982) 'Elder abuse. The status of current knowledge', *Family Relations*, vol. 31, pp. 457–65.

Corrigan, P. (1979) *Schooling the Smash Street Kids*, London: Macmillan.

Craig, J. (1986) 'The Most Densely Populated Areas of England and Wales', *Population Trends*, pp. 34–41.

Crane, P. (1982) *Gays and the Law*, London: Pluto Press.

Crewe, I. (1983) 'How Labour was routed', *Guardian*, 14 June 1983.

Crewe, I. (1987) 'A new class of politics', *Guardian*, 15 June 1987.

Cross, C. (1977) 'Youth Clubs and Coloured Youths', *New Community*.

Cross, M. (1987) 'Generation jobless: The need for a new agenda in ethnic relations policy', *New Community*, xiv: 1/2, pp. 123–7.

Cross, M. J. *et al.* (1982) *Special Problems and Special Measures: Ethnic Minorities & YOP*, Birmingham: Research Unit on Ethnic Relations, University of Aston.

Cunningham, J. (1985) 'The Outnumbered Generation', *Guardian*, 29 May.

CVS (1982) *Race in Britain: an information pack*, London: Council for Voluntary Service.

Daunton, M. J. (1987) *A Property-Owning Democracy? Housing in Britain*, London: Faber & Faber.

Davies, B. (1986) *Threatening Youth: Towards a National Youth Policy*, Milton Keynes: Open University Press.

Davies, K. *et al.* (eds) (1987) *Below Replacement Fertility in Industrial Societies*, Cambridge: Cambridge University Press.

Dearnaley, E. J. and M. H. Fletcher (1968) 'Cubs and Brownies – social class, intelligence and interests', *Educational Research*, 10, pp. 149–51, 281–2.

Deem, R. (1978) *Women and Schooling*, London: Routledge & Kegan Paul.

Demeny, P. (1987) 'Pro-natalist policies in low fertility countries', in K. Davies *et al.* (eds) *Below Replacement Fertility in Industrial Societies*, Cambridge: Cambridge University Press.

Dennis, J. (1982) '"How dare you assume I made a mistake?" Young Black women with Children', *Working with Girls Newsletter*, no. 9.

Department of Employment (1985) *New Earnings Survey*, London: HMSO.

Department of Employment (1986a) *Employment Gazette*, March/April.

Department of Employment (1986b) *Employment Gazette*, October.

Department of Employment (1987) 'Ethnic origins and economic status', *Employment Gazette*, January, pp. 18–29.

Department of Employment (1988a) *Training for Employment*, Cmnd 316, London: HMSO.

Department of Employment (1988b) *Employment Gazette*, April.

Department of Employment (1988c) *Employment Gazette*, October.

Department of Employment (1988d) *Employment Gazette*, November.

Department of Environment (1981) *Single and Homeless*, London: HMSO.

DES (1967) *Immigrants and the Youth Service* ('The Hunt Report') London: HMSO.

DES (1969) *Youth and Community Work in the 70's* (The Fairbairn-Milson Report) London: HMSO.

DES (1971) *Last to Come In*, London: HMSO.

DES (1978) *Behavioural Units. A survey of special units for pupils with behaviour problems*, London: HMSO.

DES (1983a) *Three Lambeth Youth Clubs, ILEA. Report by HM Inspectors*, London: DES.

DES (1983b) *Young People in the 80's. A Survey*, London: HMSO.

DES (1987a) *Youth work in Eight Inner City Areas*, London: DES.

DES (1987b) *Higher Education: Meeting the Challenge*, Cmnd 114, London: HMSO.

DES (1988a) *Report by HM Inspectors on Youth Service Responses to the Needs of Young Women in Selected LEAs*, London: DES.

DES (1988b) *Report by HM Inspectors on Youth Work Responses to Unemployment*, London: DES.

DHSS (1985) *Social Security Statistics*, London: HMSO.

Dickinson, P. (1982) 'Facts and Figures. Some Myths', in J. Tierney (ed.), *Race, Migration and Schooling*, Eastbourne: Rinehart and Winston.

Dilnot, A. W., J. A. Kay and C. N. Morris (1984) *The Reform of Social Security*, Oxford: Clarendon Press.

Dixon, M. (1988) 'High-fliers On the Move', *Financial Times*, 29 June.

Dorn, A. and P. Hibbert (1987) 'A comedy of errors: Section 11 funding and education', in B. Troyna (ed.), *Racial Inequality in Education*, London: Tavistock.

Dorn, N. and N. South (1983) *Of Males and Markets: a critical review of 'youth culture' theory*, Research Paper 1, London: Centre for Occupational and Community Research, Middlesex Polytechnic.

Dowd, J. J. (1975) 'Ageing as exchange. A preface to theory', *Journal of Gerontology*, vol. 30, pp. 584–94.

Driver, G. (1977) 'Cultural competence, social power, and school achievement: West Indian pupils in the West Midlands', *New Community*, vol. 5, no. 4.

Driver, G. (1981) 'Classroom stress and school achievement', in A. James and R. Jeffcoate (eds), *The School in the Multi-cultural Society*, London: Harper & Row.

Driver, G. and R. Ballard (1979) 'Comparing performance in multi-racial schools: South Asians at 16 plus', *New Community*, vol. 7, no. 2.

Dugdale, R. L. (1877) 'The Jukes. A study in crime, pauperism, disease and heredity', in *Proceedings* (Saratoga).

Duncan, S. S. (1977) 'The housing question and the structure of the housing market', *Journal of Social Policy*, vol. 6, no. 4.

Dunnell, K. (1979) *Family Formation*, London: HMSO.

Dyhouse, C. (1981) *Girls Growing Up in Late Victorian and Edwardian England*, London: Routledge & Kegan Paul.

Easterlin, R. (1980) *Birth & Fortune: The Impact of Numbers on Personal Welfare*, London: Grant McIntyre.

EEC (1986) *Economic and Social Consultative Assembly. Demographic Situation in the Community*, Brussels: EEC.

Eggleston, J. (1976) *Adolescence and Community. The Youth Service in Britain*, London: Edward Arnold.

Ehrenreich, B. and J. Ehrenreich (1971) 'Professional–Managerial Class', *Radical America*, vol. 11, no. 2.

Elcock, H. (1983) 'Young Voters 1988: will they break the mould?', *Youth & Policy*, 2(2), pp. 30–4.

Elder, G. (1977) The Alienated. Growing old today. London: Writers and Readers.

Ellis, J. (1989) 'Informal education in churches', in T. Jeffs and M. Smith (eds), *Using Informal Education*, Milton Keynes: Open University Press.

Emmett, I. (1977) *Draft Report to the Sports Council on Decline in Sports Participation After Leaving School*, London: Sports Council.

Employment Gazette (1988) 'New Entrants to the Labour Market in the 1990s', May, pp. 267–74.

Engels, F. (1969) *The Condition of the Working Class in England*, London: Panther.

Engles, F. (1973) in K. Marx and F. Engels, *Selected Works*, London: Lawrence & Wishart.

Ermisch, J. F. (1983) *The Political Economy of Demographic Change*, London: Heinemann.

Evans, K. (1987) 'Participation of Young Adults in Youth Organisations in the United Kingdom: a Review', *International Journal of Adolescence and Youth*, 1 (1) pp. 7–31.

Evans, W. (1965) *Young People in Society*, Oxford: Blackwell.

Family Policy Studies Centre (1987) *One-Parent Families Fact Sheet*, London: FPSC.

Fennell, G., C. Phillipson and H. Evers (1988) *The Sociology of Old Age*, Milton Keynes: Open University Press.

Finn, D. (1984) 'Leaving School and Growing Up: Work Experience in the Juvenile Labour Market', in I. Bates, J. Clarke, P. Cohen, D. Finn, R. Moore and P. Willis (eds), *Schooling for the Dole?*, London: Macmillan.

Finn, D. (1987) *Training Without Jobs. New deals and broken promises*, London: Macmillan.

Fisher, G. and M. Day (1983) *Towards a Black Perspective. An Experimental Afro-Caribbean Training Project*, London: Commission for Racial Equality.

Fitzpatrick, K. and J. Logan (1985) 'The Aging of the Suburbs, 1960–1980', *American Sociological Review*, 50, pp. 106–17.

Fitzpatrick, M. and D. Milligan (1987) *The Truth Behind the AIDs Panic*, London: Junius.

Flynn, P. and D. Miller (1984) 'Trade Union Education and Racism Awareness Training. A report from the North East of England', Unpublished paper.

Fopp, R. (1987) 'Youth Housing: Prerequisites For Planning', *The Bulletin of the National Clearinghouse for Youth Studies* (Australia) 6(1), pp. 12–19.

Ford, J. et al. (1982) *Special Education and Social Control. Invisible Disasters*, London: Routledge & Kegan Paul.

Franklin, B. (1986) 'Children's Political Rights', in B. Franklin (ed.), *The Rights of Children*, Oxford: Blackwell.

Freire, P. (1985) *The Politics of Education*, London: Macmillan.

Fryer, P. (1984) *Staying Power. The History of Black People in Britain*, London: Pluto Press.

Fuller, M. (1981) 'Black Girls in a London Comprehensive', in A. James and R. Jeffcoate (eds), *The School in the Multi-cultural Society*, London: Harper & Row.

Fuller, M. (1982) 'Young, Female and Black', in E. Cashmore and B. Troyna (eds), *Black Youth in Crisis*, London: George Allen & Unwin.

Galloway, D. (1982) *Schools and Disruptive Pupils*, Harlow: Longman.

Gantz, W., H. Gartenburg and C. Rainbow (1980) 'Approaching invisibility. The portrayal of the elderly in magazine adverts', *Journal of Communication*, vol. 30, no. 1, pp. 56–60.

Gapper, J. (1988) 'Sweet Sixteen and Getting Sweeter', *Financial Times*, 6 May.

Garrett, B. (1986) *1000 Links. Youth activity in Croydon*, Croydon: Croydon Guild of Voluntary Organisations.

Gerbner, G., L. Gross, M. Eeley, M. Jackson Beecker, S. Jeffries-Fox and N. Signorelli (1977) 'Television violence profile No. 8. Two highlights', *Journal of Communication*, vol. 27, pp. 171–80.

Gerbner, G., L. Gross, N. Signorelli and M. Marga (1980) 'Ageing with television. Images of television drama and conceptions of social reality', *Journal of Communication*, vol. 30, no. 1, pp. 37–47.

Gerry, C. (1985) 'Small enterprises, the recession and the "Disappearing Working Class"', in G. Rees *et al.* (eds), *Political Action and Social Identity. Class, locality and ideology*, London: Macmillan.

Gershuny, J. and S. Jones (1987) 'The changing work/leisure balance in Britain: 1961–1984', in J. Horne *et al.* (eds), *Sport, Leisure and Social Relations*, London: Routledge & Kegan Paul.

Giddens, A. (1980) *The Class Structure of the Advanced Societies* (2nd edn), London: Hutchinson.

Giddens, A. (1987) *Social Theory and Modern Sociology*, Cambridge: Polity Press.

Giddens, A. and D. Held (eds), (1982), *Social Class and the Division of Labour*, Cambridge: Cambridge Univesity Press.

Gillis, J. R. (1974) *Youth and History. Tradition and Change in European Age Relations 1770–Present*, New York: Academic Press.

Gilroy, P. (1981) 'You can't fool the Youths', *Race and Class*, vol. 23.

Gilroy, P. (1987) *There Ain't No Black in the Union Jack. The cultural politics of race & nation*, London: Hutchinson.

Giroux, H. (1983) *Theory and Resistance in Education*, London: Heinemann.

Gittens, D. (1985) *The Family in Question*, London: Macmillan.

Gladstone, F. (1979) 'Vandalism Among Adolescent Schoolboys', in R. Clarke (ed.), *Tackling Vandalism. Home Office Research Study no. 47*, London: HMSO.

Glendinning, C. (1983) *Unshared Care*, London: Routledge & Kegan Paul.

Goddard, H. (1912) *The Kallikak Family. A study in the heredity of feeblemindedness*, New York: Macmillan.

Goldthorpe, J. H. (1982) 'On the service class', in A. Giddens and G. Mackenzie (eds), *Social Class and the Division of Labour*, Cambridge: Cambridge University Press.

Goldthorpe, J. H. *et al.* (1987) *The Affluent Worker in the Class Structure* (2nd edn), Cambridge: Cambridge University Press.

Gorz, A. (1982) *Farewell to the Working Class. An essay on post-industrial Socialism*, London: Pluto Press.

Grant, J. (1986) 'Struggling for equal opportunities for lesbians in local services', *Critical Social Policy*, no. 16.

Graydon, R. (1983) 'But it's more than a game. It's an institution', *Feminist Review*, no. 13.

Greater London Council (1985a) *Changing the World. A charter for gay and lesbian rights*, London: Greater London Council.

Greater London Council (1985b) *Policing London Now*, London: GLC Police Committee Support Unit.

Greater London Council (1986) *A Handbook of Lesbian Rights. (GLC Women's Committee)*, London: Greater London Council.

Green, P. (1981) *The Pursuit of Inequality*, Oxford: Martin Robertson.

Griffin, C. (1985) *Typical Girls. Young women from school to the job market*, London: Routledge & Kegan Paul.

Griffin, C. (1987) 'Youth Research: young women and the "gang of lads" model', in J. Hazekamp, W. Meeus and Y. te Poel (eds), *European Contributions to Youth Research*, Amsterdam: Free University Press.

Grinter, R. (1985) 'Bridging the gulf: the need for an antiracist multicultural education', *Multicultural Teaching*, vol. 3, no. 2, pp. 7–10.

Grundy, S. (1987) *Curriculum: Product or praxis*, Lewes: Falmer Press.

Guilmot, P. (1978) *The Demographic Background in* Council of Europe, *Population Decline in Europe*, London: Edward Arnold.

Gurnah, A. (1984) 'The politics of Race Awareness Training', *Critical Social Policy* (Autumn).

Guthrie, D. (1981) *Disability, Legislation and Practice*, London: Macmillan.

Hakim, C. (1987) 'Trends in the Flexible Workforce', *Employment Gazette*, November, pp. 549–60.

Hall, R. and P. Ogden (1985) *Europe's Population in the 1970s and 1980s*, Cambridge: Cambridge University Press.

Hall, S. and T. Jefferson (eds), (1976), *Resistance through Rituals. Youth subcultures in post-war Britain*, London: Hutchinson.

Halsey, A. H. (1978) *Change in British Society* (2nd edn), Oxford: Oxford University Press.

Halsey, A. H. (1986) *Change in British Society* (3rd edn), Oxford: Oxford University Press.

Halsey, A. H. and L. Gardner (1953) 'Selection for secondary education', *British Journal of Sociology*, vol. 47.

Halsey, A. H., A. F. Heath and J. M. Ridge (1980) *Origins and Destinations: family, class and education in modern Britain*, Oxford: Clarendon Press.

Hamilton, P. (1981) 'Violence at Work', *Working with Girls Newsletter*, no. 6.

Hamnett, C. and B. Randolph (1988) 'Ethnic minorities in the London

238   *Bibliography*

labour market. A longitudinal analysis 1971–81', *New Community*, xiv:3, pp. 333–46.

Hanmer, J. (1964) *Girls at Leisure*, London: London Union of Youth Clubs.

Hargreaves, Jennifer (ed.), (1982), *Sport, Culture and Ideology*. London: Routledge & Kegan Paul.

Harper, B. (1985) *People Who Count. Youth work resources in local authorities*, Leicester: National Youth Bureau.

Harrison, J. (1983) 'Women and aging. Experience and implications', *Ageing and Society*, vol. 3, pp. 209–37.

Haskey, J. (1984) 'Social Class and Socio-Economic Differentials in Divorce in England and Wales', *Population Studies*, 38, pp. 419–38.

Haskey, J. (1986a) 'One-parent Families in Great Britain', *Population Trends* (45), pp. 5–13.

Haskey, J. (1986b) 'Recent Trends in Divorce in England and Wales: the Effects of Legislative Changes', *Population Trends* (44), pp. 9–16.

Haskey, J. and D. Coleman (1986) 'Cohabitation before marriage: a comparison of information from marriage registration and the General Household Survey', *Population Trends* (43), Spring.

Hasluck, C. (1987) *Urban Unemployment. Local labour markets and employment initiatives*, Harlow: Longman.

Hatcher, J. (1977) *Plague, Population and the English Economy 1348–1530*, London: Macmillan.

Heath, A. and S.-K. McDonald (1987) 'Social change and the future of the left', *Political Quarterly*, 58:4, pp. 364–77.

Hemmings, S. (ed.), (1982), *Girls are Powerful. Young women's writings from Spare Rib*, London: Sheba.

Hemmings, S. and K. Ellis (1976) 'How fair is television's image of older Americans?', *Retirement Living*, April.

Hendricks, J. and C. D. Hendrichs (1977) *Ageing in Mass Society. Myths and Realities*, Massachusetts: Winthrop Inc.

Hendry, L. B. (1983) *Growing Up and Going Out. Adolescents and leisure*, Aberdeen: Aberdeen University Press.

Hesse-Biber, S. and J. Williamson (1984) 'Resource theory and power in families', *Family Process*, vol. 23, pp. 261–98.

Hindess, B. (1987) *Freedom, Equality and the Market*, London: Tavistock.

HMSO (1938) *Report of the Consultative Committee on Secondary Education with Special Reference to Grammar Schools and Technical High Schools* ('The Spens Report') London: HMSO.

HMSO (1943) *Report of the Secondary Schools Examination Council on Curricula and Examinations in Secondary Schools* ('The Norwood Report') London: HMSO.

HMSO (1944) *Education Act*, London: HMSO.

HMSO (1959) *15 to 18. Report of the Central Advisory Council (England)* ('The Crowther Report') vol. 1, London: HMSO.

HMSO (1960) *The Youth Service in England and Wales* ('The Albermarle Report') London: HMSO.

HMSO (1963) *Half our Future. Report of the Central Advisory Council (England)* ('The Newsom Report') London: HMSO.

HMSO (1967) *Children and their Primary Schools. Report of the Central Advisory Council (England)* ('The Plowden Report') London: HMSO.

HMSO (1974) *Report of the Committee on One-Parent Families* ('The Finer Report') Cmnd 5629, London: HMSO.

HMSO (1978) *Special Educational Needs. Report of the Committee of Enquiry into the Education of Handicapped Children and Young People*, London: HMSO.

HMSO (1981a) *Committee of Enquiry into the Education of Children from Ethnic Minority Groups: West Indian Children in our Schools, Interim Report* ('The Rampton Report') London: HMSO.

HMSO (1981b) *The Brixton Disorders 10–12 April 1981. Report of an Inquiry by the Rt. Hon. The Lord Scarman OBE*, London: HMSO.

HMSO (1982) *Experience and Participation. Review Group on the Youth Service in England* ('The Thompson Report') London: HMSO.

HMSO (1985) *Education for All. The Report of the Committee of Inquiry into the Education of Children from Ethnic Minority Groups* ('The Swann Report') London: HMSO.

HMSO (1988a) *Training For Employment*, Cmnd 316, London: HMSO.

HMSO (1988b) *Community Care: Agenda For Action* (Griffiths Report) London: HMSO.

Holmes, J. (1981) *Professionalisation – a misleading myth*, Leicester: National Youth Bureau.

Holmes, J. (1986) 'Women Students in youth & community work courses', *Youth and Policy*, no. 17.

Holmes, J. (1988) 'In defence of initial training', *Youth and Policy*, 23, pp. 1–4.

Home Office (1981) *Racial Attacks. Report of a Study*, London: HMSO.

House of Commons Home Affairs Select Committee (1981) *Racial Disadvantage 1980/81*, London: HMSO.

Hoyles, M. (1979) *Changing Childhood*, London: Writers and Readers.

Hubbuck, J. and S. Carter (1980) *Half a Chance: A report on job discrimination against young blacks in Nottingham*, London: Commission for Racial Equality.

Hudson, A. (1983) 'The welfare state and adolescent femininity', *Youth and Policy*, vol. 2, no. 1.

Huhner, M. (1924) *A Practical Treatise on Disorders of the Sexual Function in the Male and Female*, Philadelphia: F. A. Davies & Co.

Humphries, S. (1981) *Hooligans or Rebels? An Oral History of Working-class Childhood and Youth 1889–1939*, Oxford: Blackwell.

ILEA (1980) *Youth Service Provision for Girls. Report of the working party set up by the London Youth Committee*, London: Inner London Education Authority.

ILEA (1984) *The Youth Service. A Fair Deal for Girls?*, London: Inner London Education Authority.

ILEA (1986a) *Policy and Practice on Lesbian and Gay Issues*, London: Inner London Education Authority.

ILEA (1986b) *Positive Images. A resource guide to materials about homosexuality*, London: Inner London Education Authority.

Irving, D. and S. Whitmore (1987) 'We're Not All Rich in the South', *Youth Social Work*, 4, pp. 13–14.

Ives, R. (1986) 'Children's sexual rights', in B. Franklin (ed.), *The Rights of Children*, Oxford: Blackwell.

Jamdagni, L. (1980) *Hamari Rangily Zindagi. (Our Colourful Lives)*, Leicester: National Association of Youth Clubs.

Jeffs, T. (1979) *Young People and the Youth Service*, London: Routledge & Kegan Paul.

Jeffs, T. (1988) 'Preparing Children and Young People For Participatory Democracy', in B. Troyna and B. Carrington (eds), *Children and Controversial Issues*, Brighton: Falmer.

Jeffs, T. and M. Smith (eds), (1987) *Youth Work*, London: Macmillan.

Jeffs, T. and M. Smith (eds), (1988) *Welfare and Youth Work Practice*, London: Macmillan.

Jeffs, T. and M. Smith (eds), (1989a) *Using Informal Education*, Milton Keynes: Open University Press.

Jeffs, T. and M. Smith (1989b) 'Taking issue with issues', *Youth and Policy*, no. 26.

Jenkins, R. (1982) *Managers, Recruitment Procedures and Black Workers: Working Papers on Ethnic Relations*, no. 18, Birmingham: Research Unit on Ethnic Relations, University of Aston.

Jenkins, R. (1983a) *Lads, Citizens and Ordinary Kids*, London: RKP.

Jenkins, R. (1983b) *Hightown Rules*, Leicester: National Youth Bureau.

Jensen, G. D. and F. B. Oakley (1982) 'Ageism across cultures', *International Journal of Ageing and Human Development*, vol. 15, no. 1.

John, G. (1981) *In the Service of Black Youth. The political culture of youth and community work with Black people in English cities*, Leicester: National Association of Youth Clubs.

John, G. (1984) 'The Power of Racism', in *NYB, Working With Black Youth*, Leicester: National Youth Bureau.

Joint Council for Gay Teenagers (1980) *I Know What I Am. Gay Teenagers and the Law*, London: Joint Council for Gay Teenagers.

Joint Council for Gay Teenagers (1981) *Breaking the Silence*, London: Joint Council for Gay Teenagers.

Jolly, J., S. Creigh and A. Mingay (1980) *Age as a Factor in Employment. Research Paper No. 11*, London: Department of Employment.

Jones, G. (1987) 'Leaving the Parental Home: an Analysis of Early Housing Careers', *Journal of Social Policy*, 16(1), pp. 49–74

Jowell, R. and C. Airey (1984) *British Social Attitudes, the 1984 Report*, London: Gower.

Junankar, P. (1987) 'The Labour Market For Young People', in *From School to Unemployment?* (ed.) P. Junankar, London: Macmillan.

Junankar, P. and A. Neale (1987) 'Relative Wages & the Youth Labour Market', in *From School to Unemployment?* (ed.) P. Junankar, London: Macmillan

Kahn, V. S. (1982) 'The role of the culture of dominance in structuring the experience of ethnic minorities', in C. Husband (ed.), *Race in Britain. Continuity and change*, London: Hutchinson.

Katz, J. H. (1978) *White Awareness*, Oklahoma: University of Oklahoma.

Kendra, N. (1985) *Training Across the Region. Evaluation of the Yorks & Humberside training scheme*, Leicester: National Youth Bureau.

Kennedy, A. (1984) *Shadows of Adolescence*, Leicester: National Youth Bureau.

Kent-Baguley, P. (1984) 'The silence is broken', *Youth in Society*, no. 95.

Kent-Baguley, P. (1985) 'Is being gay Okay?', *Youth and Policy*, no. 14.

Kent-Baguley, P. (1986) 'Education – no go area for lesbians and gays', *Lesbian and Gay Socialist* (Spring).

Kent-Baguley, P. (1988) 'One too many', *Youth and Policy*, no. 24, pp. 1–7.

Kiernan, K. (1977) 'Characteristics of Young People Who Move Inter-regionally: a Longitudinal Study', in J. Hobcraft and P. Rees (eds), *Regional Demographic Developments*, Beckenham: Croom Helm.

Kiernan, K. (1985) *The Departure of Children. Centre For Population Studies Research Paper 85 (3)*, London University.

Klug, F. (1982) *Racist Attacks*, London: Runnymede Trust.

Kuhn, M. (1978) 'The Gray Panther rides again', *New Age*, vol. 5, pp. 7–9.

Kuper, B. (1985) 'The Supply of Training', *Youth and Policy*, no. 13.

Lacey, C. (1988) 'The idea of a socialist education', in H. Lauder and P. Brown (eds), *Education: In search of a future*, Lewes: Falmer Press.

Lam, R. (1982) *Getting Together. A study of members of PHAB Clubs*, London: NFER-Nelson.

Larkin, P. (1974) 'The Old Fools', in *High Windows*, London: Methuen.

Laslett, P. (1965) *The World We Have Lost*, London: Methuen.

Lawrence, D. (1974) *Black Migrants – White Natives. A study of race relations in Nottingham*, London: Cambridge University Press.

Lawton, R. (1977) 'Regional Population Trends in England and Wales, 1750–1971', in J. Hobcraft and P. Rees (eds), *Regional Demographic Developments*, Beckenham: Croom Helm.

Layard, R., D. Pichaud and M. Stewart (1978) *The Causes of Poverty*, Royal Commission on the Distribution of Income and Wealth Report 5, Background Paper 5. London: HMSO.

Leaman, O. (1984) 'Sit on the Sidelines and Watch the Boys Play', *Sex differentiation in physical education*, Harlow: Longman.

Lee, G. and J. Wrench (1983) *Skill Seekers. Black youth apprenticeships and disadvantage*, Leicester: National Youth Bureau.

Lee-Sang, P. (1982) 'Black girls talking', *Working With Girls Newsletter*, no. 10.

Lees, S. (1986) 'A new approach to the study of girls', *Youth and Policy*, no. 16.

Leete, R. (1979) *Changing Patterns of Family Formation and Dissolution in England and Wales 1964–1976. OPCS Studies on Medical and Population Studies*, London: HMSO.

Leftwitch, A. (1983) *Redefining Politics. People, resources and power*, London: Methuen.

Leonard, D. (1980) *Sex and Generation. A study of courtship and weddings*, London: Tavistock.

Lesbian and Gay Youth Magazine (1983) no. 15.

Lesbians and Education Group (1986) *ILEA Policy and Practice on Lesbian and Gay Issues*, London: Lesbians in Education Group.

Lewis, I. and G. Vulliamy (1980) 'Warnock or Warlock? The sorcery of definitions', *Educational Review*, vol. 23, no. 1.

Lewis, P. and T. Lunn (1987) 'Youth unemployment: the changing response', *Youth and Policy*, 20.

Lister, R. (1989) 'Social workers and the social fund', in P. Carter *et al.* (eds), *Social Work and Social Welfare Yearbook*, no. 1, Milton Keynes: Open University Press.

Lloyd, T. (1985) *Work with Boys*, Leicester: National Youth Bureau.

Lockwood, B. (1978) 'Sex discrimination and the older women. A case of double discrimination', *New Age*, vol. 3, Summer, pp. 6–8.

London Gay Teenage Group (1982) *The Thompson Report – A response by the London Gay Teenage Group*, London: London Gay Teenage Group.

London Media Project (1986) *Are We Being Served? The representation of lesbians and gay men on television and radio*, London: London Media Project.

Loney, M. (1987) 'A war on poverty or on the poor?', in A. and C. Walker (eds), *The Growing Divide. A social audit 1979–1987*, London: Child Poverty Action Group.

Low Pay Unit (1988) *Low Pay Review*, no. 33, London: Low Pay Unit.

Lowe, J. (1973) *The Managers. A survey of youth club management*, London: Inner London Education Authority.

Lowe, J. (1975). *Youth Leadership. A survey of leaders, attitudes, training and work patterns*, London: Inner London Education Authority.

Maas, F. (1987) 'Unsupported Students – Still on the Outside', *The Bulletin of the National Clearinghouse for Youth Studies* (Australia) 6(2) pp. 12–15.

Macdonald, M. and J. Ridge (1988) 'Schools' in A. H. Halsey (ed.), *British Social Trends Since 1900* (2nd edn), London: Macmillan.

Macfarlane, A. and M. Mugford (1984) *Birth Counts*, London: HMSO.

MacInnes, J. (1988) *The North-South Divide: Regional employment change in Britain 1975–87*, Glasgow: University of Glasgow Centre for Urban and Regional Studies.

McIntosh, C. A. (1987) 'Recent pronatalist policies in Western Europe', in K. J. Davies *et al.* (eds), *Below Replacement Fertility in Industrial Societies*, Cambridge: Cambridge University Press.

Mackenzie, G. (1982) 'Class Boundaries & the Labour Process', in A. Giddens and G. Mackenzie (eds), *Social Class and the Division of Labour*, Cambridge: Cambridge University Press.

Maclean, M. and J. Eekelaar (1986) 'The Financial Consequences of

Divorce: the Wrong Debate', in *The Year Book of Social Policy in Britain 1985–86* (eds) M. Brenton and C. Ungerson, London: Routledge & Kegan Paul.

MacLennan, E. (1985) *Working Children*, London: Low Pay Unit.

McNabb, R., N. Woodward and J. Barry (1979) *Unemployment in West Cornwall. Research Paper 8*, London: Department of Employment.

MacNicol, J. (1987) 'In pursuit of the underclass', *Journal of Social Policy*, 16:3, pp. 293–318.

McPherson, A. and D. J. Willms (1987) 'Equalisation and improvement: some effects of comprehensive reorganisation in Scotland', *Sociology*, 21:4.

McPherson, A. and D. J. Willms (1988) 'Comprehensive schooling is better and fairer', *Forum*, 30:2.

McRobbie, A. (1978) 'Working-class girls and the culture of feminity', in Women's Studies Group CCCS (eds), *Women Take Issue. Aspects of women's subordination*, London: Hutchinson.

McRobbie, A. (1980) 'Settling accounts with subcultures', *Screen Education*.

McRobbie, A. and J. Garber (1976) 'Girls and subcultures: an exploration', in S. Hall and T. Jefferson (eds), *Resistance Through Rituals. Youth subcultures in post-war Britain*, London: Hutchinson.

Madray, G. *et al.* (1985) 'Racism awareness in training', *Working with Girls Newsletter*, no. 28.

Maillat, D. (1978) 'Economic Growth' in Council of Europe. *Population Decline in Europe*, London: Edward Arnold.

Malpass, P. (1985) 'Beyond the "Costa del Dole"', *Youth and Policy*, 15, pp. 12–15.

Malpass, P. (ed), (1986) *The Housing Crisis*, London: Croom Helm.

Mannheim, K. (1942) *Diagnosis of Our Time. Wartime Essays of a Sociologist*, London: Kegan Paul, Trench, Trubner & Co.

Mansfield, P. and J. Collard (1988) *The Beginning of the Rest of Your Life? A portrait of newly-wed marriage*, London: Macmillan.

Marsh, C. (1986). 'Social class and occupation', in R. G. Burgess (ed.), *Key Variables in Social Investigation*, London: Routledge & Kegan Paul.

Marshall, G., D. Rose, H. Newby and C. Volger (1988) *Social Class in Modern Britain*, London: Hutchinson.

Marshall, S. and C. Borrill (1984) 'Understanding the invisibility of young women', *Youth and Policy*, no. 9.

Marx, K. (1974) *Capital*, vol. 3, London: Lawrence & Wishart.

Marx, K. and F. Engels (1969) *The Communist Manifesto*, Harmondsworth: Penguin.

Marx, K. and F. Engels (1973) *Selected Works*, London: Lawrence and Wishart.

Massey, D. (1984) *Spatial Divisions of Labour. Social structures and the geography of production*, London: Macmillan.

Matthews, R. (1986) 'Out of House and Home? – the Board and Lodging

Regulations', *Poverty*, no. 62.

Matthews, V. (1988) 'Empty Nest Lined With Gold', *Guardian* 18 February.

Meadows, P. and R. Cox (1987) 'Employment of Graduates 1975 to 1990', *Employment Gazette*, April.

Meager, N. (1988) 'Job-sharing & Job-splitting: Employer Attitudes', *Employment Gazette*, pp. 383–8.

Meiksins, P. (1986) 'Beyond the boundary question', *New Left Review*, no. 157, pp. 101–21.

Midwinter, E. (1983) *Ten Million People*, London: Centre for Policy on Ageing.

Miliband, R. (1977) *Marxism and Politics*, Oxford: Oxford University Press.

Millar, J. (1987) 'Lone Mothers', in C. Glendinning and J. Millar (eds), *Women and Poverty in Britain*, Brighton: Wheatsheaf.

Milligan, D. (1973) *The Politics of Homosexuality*, London: Pluto Press.

Mintel (1988) *Youth Lifestyles*, London: Mintel.

Montagu, L. (1904) 'The Girl in the Background', in E. J. Urwick (ed.), *Studies in Boy Life in our Cities*, London: Dent.

Moorehead, C. (1987) *School Age Workers in Britain Today*, London: Anti-Slavery Society.

Morgan, P. (1986) 'Feminist attempts to sack father: a case of unfair dismissal?', in D. Anderson and G. Dawson (eds), *Family Portraits*, London: Social Affairs Unit.

Morse, M. (1965) *The Unattached*, Harmondsworth: Penguin.

Mukherjee, T. (1988) 'The journey back', in P. Cohen and H. S. Bains (eds), *Multi-Racist Britain*, London: Macmillan.

Mullard, C. (1984) *Anti-racist Education. The three O's*, London: National Association for Multi-cultural Education.

Mungham, G. and G. Pearson (eds), (1976) *Working-Class Youth Cultures*, London: Routledge & Kegan Paul.

Murdock, G. (1976) 'Youth in contemporary Britain. Misleading imagery and misapplied action', in D. Marsland and M. Day (eds), *Youth Service, Youth Work and the Future*, Leicester: National Youth Bureau.

Murdock, G. (1984) 'Reporting the riots. Images and impacts', in J. Benyon (ed.), *Scarman and After*, Oxford: Pergamon.

Murdock, G. and G. Phelps (1973) *Mass Media and the Secondary School*, London: Macmillan.

Musgrove, F. (1964) *Youth and the Social Order*, London: Routledge & Kegan Paul.

Myron Johnson, J. (1976) 'Is 65 old?', *Social Policy*, vol. 7, no. 3, pp. 9–12.

NACYS (1988a) *Youth Work in Rural Areas*, London: DES.

NACYS (1988b) *A Consultation Paper on Youth Work with Girls and Young Women*, London: DES.

NACYS (1989a) *Changing Attitudes. The Youth Service and young people with disabilities*, London: DES.

NACYS (1989b) *Youth Work with Girls and Young Women*, London: DES.

Nairn, I. (1981) *The Break-up of Britain* (2nd edn), London: Verso.

National Association of Asian Youth (1978) *Annual Report 1978*, London: National Association of Asian Youth.

National Economic Development Office and Training Commission (1988) *Young People and the Labour Market, a Challenge For the 1990s*, London: NEDC.

Nava, M. (1984) 'Youth Service Provision, Social Order and the Question of Girls', in A. McRobbie and M. Nava (eds), *Gender and Generation*, London: Macmillan.

NCVO (1982) *Race in Britain. An information pack*, London: National Council of Voluntary Organisations.

Newby, H., D. Rose, G. Marshall and C. Volger (1989) *Class. An introduction*, London: Hutchinson.

Nicholson, S. (1985) *Out of Town, Out of Mind? A Study of Rural Unemployment*, Leicester: Leicester Diocesan Board for Social Responsibility.

Nilsen, A. P. (1978) 'Old blondes just dye away', *Language Arts*, vol. 55, no. 2, pp. 175–9.

Noyer, P. du (1988) 'The New Nashville Cats', *Q Magazine*, pp. 40–8.

OPCS (1984) *General Household Survey 1982*, London: HMSO.

OPCS (1985) *Population Projections 1983–2023. Series PP2 No. 13*, London: HMSO.

OPCS (1986a) *General Household Survey 1984*, London: HMSO.

OPCS (1986b) 'The Changing Balance of the Sexes in England and Wales, 1851–2001', *Population Trends*, 46.

OPCS (1986c) *Population Projections. Series PP3 No. 6*, London: HMSO.

OPCS (1987a) *General Household Survey 1987*, London: HMSO.

OPCS (1987b) *Labour Force Survey 1985*, London: HMSO.

OPCS (1987c) *Population Projections 1985–2025*, London: HMSO.

Open University (1982) *Ethnic Minorities and Employment* (E 354, block 4, units 11 & 12), Milton Keynes: Open University.

Pahl, R. (1984) *Divisions of Labour*, Oxford: Blackwell.

Palmore, E. (1978) 'Are the aged a minority group?', *Journal of American Geriatric Society*, vol. 26, no. 5, pp. 214–17.

Parker, H. J. (1974) *View from the Boys*, Newton Abbott: David & Charles.

Parker, S. (1980) *Older Workers and Retirement*, London: HMSO.

Parkin, F. (1979) *Marxism and Class Theory. A Bourgois Critique*, London: Tavistock.

Parkin, F. (1982) *Weber*, London: Tavistock.

Parmar, P. (1982) 'Gender, Race and Class. Asian women in resistance', in *Centre for Contemporary Cultural Studies. The Empire Strikes Back: Race and Racism in 70's Britain*, London: Hutchinson.

Parmar, P. (1985) 'Taking the lid off . . . Racism and girls work', *GEN*, no. 6.

Parmar, P. (1988) 'Gender, race and power: the challenge to youth work practice', in P. Cohen and H. S. Bains (eds), *Multi-Racist Britain*, London: Macmillan.

Patterson, S. (1963) *Dark Strangers*, London: Tavistock.

Peach, C. (1968) *West Indian Migration to Britain*, London: Oxford University Press.

Peter, M. (1977) 'The Education Secretary replies', *Special Education – Forward Trends*, vol. 4, no. 3.

Phillipson, C. (1982) *Capitalism and the Construction of Old Age*, London: Macmillan.

Phizacklea, A. and R. Miles (1980) *Labour and Racism*, London: Routledge & Kegan Paul.

Pinto-Duschinsky, M. & S. (1987) *Voter Registration: Problems and Solutions*, London: Constitutional Reform Centre.

Plant, R. (1985) 'The very idea of a welfare state', in P. Bean *et al.* (eds), *In Defence of Welfare*, London: Tavistock.

Plumb, J. H. (1972) *In the Light of History*, Harmondsworth: Pengiun.

Policy Studies Institute (1984) *Black and White Britain. The third PSI Survey*, London: Policy Studies Institute.

Political and Economic Planning (1948) *Population Policy in Great Britain*, London: PEP.

Pollert, A. (1986) 'The MSC and the ethnic minorities', in C. Benn and J. Fairley (eds), *Challenging the MSC*, London: Pluto Press.

Popple, K. (1983) 'This Green and Pleasant Land', *Youth and Policy*, vol. 2, no. 3.

Popple, K. and S. Popple (1986) 'Black children's rights', in B. Franklin (ed.), *The Rights of Children*, Oxford: Blackwell.

Poster, C. (1977) 'Community Education & the Youth Service', *Youth in Society*, 25.

Postman, N. (1985) *The Disappearance of Childhood*, London: W H Allen.

Powell, L. A. and J. D. Williamson (1985) 'The mass media and the aged', *Social Policy*, vol. 16.

Pritchard, D. G. (1963) *Education of the Handicapped*, London: Routledge & Kegan Paul.

Pryce, K. (1979) *Endless Pressure*, Harmondsworth: Penguin.

Ramdin, R. (1987) *The Making of the Black Working Class in Britain*, Aldershot: Wildwood House.

Reddaway, W. (1977) 'The Economic Consequences of Zero Population Growth', *Lloyds Bank Review* (124), pp. 14–30.

Reed, C. (1987) 'Greying at the Temple', *Guardian*, 23 April.

Reid, I. (1981) *Social Class Differences in Britain* (2nd edn), London: Grant McIntyre.

Rex, J. (1986) *Race and Ethnicity*, Milton Keynes: Open University Press.

Rex, J. and R. Moore (1967) *Race, Conflict and Community. A study of Sparkbrook*, London: Oxford University Press.

Reynolds, D. and M. Sullivan (1987) *The Comprehensive Experiment*, Brighton: Falmer.

Riley, D. and M. Shaw (1985) *Parental Supervision & Juvenile Delinquency, Home Office Research Study No. 83*, London: HMSO.
Ritchie, N. and M. Marken (1984) *Anti-Racist Youth Work. A practical guide to recognising racism and taking steps to combat it through youth work*, Leicester: National Youth Bureau.
Roberts, K. (1983) *Youth and Leisure*, London: George Allen & Unwin.
Roberts, K. (1984) *School Leavers and their Prospects. Youth and the labour market in the 1980s*, Milton Keynes: Open University Press.
Roberts, K. (1987) 'ESRC's New 16–19 Initiative', *Youth and Policy* (22), pp. 15–24.
Roll, J. (1988) *Young People at the Crossroads: Education, jobs, social security and training*, London: Family Policy Studies Centre.
Rose, R. and I. MacAlister (1986) *Voters Begin to Choose. From closed doors to open elections*, London: Sage.
Rousseau, J.-J. (1963) 'A discourse on the origin of inequality', in G. D. H. Cole (trans) *Rousseau. The Social Contract and Discourses*, London: Dent.
Rowntree, B. S. (1901) *Poverty. A Study of Town Life*, London: Macmillan.
Rubin, A. M. (1982) 'Directions in television and ageing research', *Journal of Broadcasting*, vol. 26, pp. 537–53.
Runnymede Trust/Radical Statistics Race Group (1980) *Britain's Black Population*, London: Heinemann.
Russell, B. (1983) *Power. A new analysis*, London: George Allen & Unwin.
Rutter, M., B. Maughan, P. Mortimore and J. Ouston (1979) *Fifteen Thousand Hours: secondary schools and their effects on children*, London: Open Books.
Sawbridge, M. and J. Spence (1988) *Women Workers in the North East*, Durham: Durham University/Sunderland Polytechnic.
Scott, D. (1982) *Youth and Community Work in a Multi-Racial Society* (E 354, Unit 16), Milton Keynes: Open University.
Scott, J. (1985) 'The British upper class', in D. Coates *et al.* (eds), *A Socialist Anatomy of Britain*, Cambridge: Polity.
Scout Association (1985), details given in letter to author.
Seabrook, J. (1980) *The Way We Are. Old people talk about themselves. Conversations with Jeremy Seabrook*, London: Age Concern.
Seabrook, J. (1982) *Unemployment*, London: Paladin/Granada.
Search Project (undated) *Against Ageism*, Newcastle upon Tyne: Search Project.
Self, D. (1987) 'Pluggers', *Times Educational Supplement*, 10 April.
Sharron, H. (1985) 'The child poverty trap', *Times Educational Supplement*, 10 May.
Shaw, C. (1988) 'Components of Growth in the Ethnic Minority Population', *Population Trends* (52), pp. 26–30.
Shearer, A. (1972) *Our Lives*, London: Campaign for Mental Health.
Silver, H. (1980) *Education and the Social Condition*, London: Methuen.

Simon, B. (1971) *Intelligence, Psychology and Education*, London: Lawrence & Wishart.

Simon, B. (1988) *Bending the Rules. The Baker 'Reform' of Education*, London: Lawrence & Wishart.

Simon, J. (1983) 'The Present Value of Population Growth in the Western World', *Population Studies*, 37(1) pp. 5–21.

Simpson, A. (1981) *Stacking the Decks. A study of race, inequality and council housing in Nottingham*. Nottingham: Nottingham & District Community Relations Council.

Sivanandan, A. (1985) *'Preface' to Institute of Race Relations. How Racism came to Britain*, London: Institute of Race Relations.

Smith, C. (1968) *Adolescence*, London: Longman.

Smith, D. (1984) 'The problems of youth and problems in the sociology of youth', *Youth and Policy*, vol. 2, no. 4, pp. 41–6.

Smith, M. (1984) *Questions for Survival*, Leicester: NAYC Publications.

Smith, M. (1987) *Political Education. Approaches in the community*, Occ. Paper 4, Newcastle: Youth and Policy.

Smith, M. (1988) *Developing Youth Work. Informal education, mutual aid and popular practice*, Milton Keynes: Open University Press.

Smith, N. (1984) *Youth Service Provision for Girls and Young Women*, Leicester: National Association of Youth Clubs.

Social Security Advisory Committee (1988) *Sixth Annual Report*, London: HMSO.

Spender, D. (1980) *Man Made Language*, London: Routledge & Kegan Paul.

Spender, D. (1982) *Invisible Women*, London: Readers & Writers Publishing Co-op.

Sports Council (1982) *Sport in the Community. The next ten years*, London: Sports Council.

Springhall, J. (1977) *Youth, Empire and Society. British Youth Movements 1883–1940*, London: Croom Helm.

Springhall, J. (1986) *Coming of Age: Adolescence in Britain 1860–1960*, Dublin: Gill and Macmillan.

Springhall, J., B. Fraser and M. Hoare (1983) *Sure and Steadfast. A history of the Boys Brigade 1883 to 1983*, London: Collins.

Stanworth, M. (1984) 'Women and class analysis. A reply to John Goldthorpe', *Sociology*, 18:2.

Stark, D. (1982) 'Class struggle and the transformation of the labour process', in A. Giddens and D. Held, *Classes, Power and Conflict*, London: Macmillan.

Steffenmeier, D., C. Streifel and M. Harper (1987) 'Relative Cohort Size and Youth Crime in the United States 1953–1984', *American Sociological Review* 52(5), pp. 702–10.

Stone, M. (1981) *The Education of the Black Child. The myth of multicultural education*, London: Fontana.

Stowe, P. (1987) *Youth in the Inner City*, London: Hodder & Stoughton.

Stuart, F. (1982) *Leisure for Mentally Handicapped People*, London: Mencap.

Sutherland, G. (1977) 'The magic of measurement. Mental testing and

English education 1900–1940', *Transactions of the Royal Historical Society*, vol. 27.

Sutherland, G. (1984) *Ability, Merit & Measurement: Mental testing and English education 1880–1940*, Oxford: Oxford University Press.

Swann, W. (1981) *The Practice of Special Education*, Oxford: Blackwell.

Sweet, R. (1988) 'The Youth Labour Market: a Twenty Year Perspective', *The Bulletin of the National Clearinghouse for Youth Studies* (Australia) 7(3), pp. 31–6.

Tatchell, P. (1986) *AIDs. A guide to survival*, London: Gay Men's Press.

Taylor, B. (1984) 'The view from the white highlands', *Youth in Society*, no. 97.

Taylor, R. and G. Ford (1983) 'Inequalities in old age. An examination of age, sex, class differences in a sample of community elderly', *Ageing and Society*, vol. 3, no. 2, pp. 183–205.

Taylor, T. (1984) 'Anti-sexist work with young males', *Youth and Policy*, no. 9.

Taylor, T. (1987) 'Youth workers as character builders. Constructing a socialist alternative', in T. Jeffs and M. Smith (eds), *Youth Work*, London: Macmillan.

Taylor-Gooby, P. (1985) *Public Opinion. Ideology and State Welfare*, London: Routledge & Kegan Paul.

Thane, P. (1982) *The Foundations of the Welfare State*, Harlow: Longman.

Thomas, M. and J. Perry (1975) *National Voluntary Youth Organisations*, London: Political and Economic Planning.

Thompson, J. (1987) 'Ageing of the Population: Contemporary Trends and Issues', *Population Trends*, 50, pp. 18–22.

Thomson, D. (1986) 'The overpaid elderly', *New Society*, 7 March.

Thornes, B. and J. Collard (1979) *Who Divorces?*, London: Routledge & Kegan Paul.

Times Educational Supplement (1988) 'Firms Face Contest For Teenagers' 6 May.

Tomlinson, S. (1981) *Educational Subnormality. A study in decision making*, London: Routledge & Kegan Paul.

Tomlinson, S. (1982) *A Sociology of Special Education*, London: Routledge & Kegan Paul.

Townsend, P. (1979) *Poverty in the United Kingdom*, Harmondsworth: Penguin.

Townsend, P. (1981) 'The structural dependency of the elderly. A creation of social policy in the twentieth century', *Ageing and Society*, vol. 1, pp. 5–28.

Trenchard, L. and H. Warren (1984) *Something to Tell You. The experiences and needs of young lesbians and gay men in London*, London: London Gay Teenage Group.

Trenchard, L. and H. Warren (1985) *Talking about Youth Work*, London: London Gay Teenage Group.

Troyna, B. (1981) *Public Awareness and the Media*, London: Commission for Racial Equality.

Troyna, B. (1984) 'Fact or artefact? The "educational under-achievement" of black pupils', *British Journal of Sociology of Education*, vol. 5, no. 2, pp. 153–66.

Troyna, B. (1987) 'A conceptual overview of strategies to combat racial inequality in education: introductory essay', in B. Troyna (ed.), *Racial Inequality in Education*, London: Tavistock.

Turnbull, C. (1976) *The Forest People*, London: Picador.

Turner, B. S. (1986) *Equality*, London: Tavistock.

Tutt, N. (1987) 'The Future of IT in Scotland – the Seminar Review', *IT News* 57, pp. 5–6.

Usdan, M. (1984) 'New Trends in Urban Geography', *Education and Urban Society*, 16(4), pp. 399–414.

Van Dyke, R. (1984a) 'Femininism and PE. Some ideas and questions', *GEN*, no. 4.

Van Dyke, R. (1984b) 'Girls, women and sport', *GEN*, no. 4.

Wadsworth, M. (1979) *Roots of Delinquency*, London: Martin Robertson.

Walker, A. (1982) *Unqualified and Underemployed*, London: Macmillan.

Walker, A. (1987) 'Conclusion – a divided Britain', in A. and C. Walker (eds), *The Growing Divide. A social audit 1979–87*, London: Child Poverty Action Group.

Wallace, C. (1987) *For Richer, For Poorer. Growing up in and out of work*, London: Tavistock.

Walmsley, R. and Karen White (1979) *Sexual Offences, Consent and Sentencing. Home Office Research Study 14*, London: HMSO.

Walvin, J. (1982) *A Child's World*, Harmondsworth: Penguin.

Watts, M. W. and J. Zinnecker (1987) 'Youth Culture and Politics Among German Youth: Effects of youth centrism', in J. Hazekamp, W. Meeus and Y. te Poel (eds), *European Contributions to Youth Research*, Amsterdam: Free University Press.

Wear Working with Girls Development Group (1984) *Policy Statement*, Durham: Wear Working with Girls Development Group.

Werner, B. (1988a) 'Fertility Trends in the UK and in Thirteen Other Developed Countries, 1966–1986', *Population Trends*, 50 pp. 18–24.

Werner, B. (1988b) 'Birth Intervals: Results From the OPCS Longitudinal Study 1972–1984', *Population Trends*, 51.

West, D. (1982) *Delinquency: its roots, careers and prospects*, London: Heinemann.

Westergaard, J. and H. Resler (1976) *Class in a Capitalist Society. A Study of Contemporary Britain*, Harmondsworth: Penguin.

Wilkie, P. and D. Wilkie (1975) 'Demography and Social Policy', in K. Jones (ed.), *The Yearbook of Social Policy in Britain 1974*, London: Routledge & Kegan Paul.

Williams, L. (1988) *Partial Surrender: Black youth and the Youth Service*, Lewes: Falmer Press.

Williams, L. (1989) 'The role of black youth clubs and black workers', in P. Carter *et al.* (eds), *Social Work and Social Welfare Yearbook No. 19*, Milton Keynes: Open University Press.

Williams, P. and B. Schoultz (1982) *We Can Speak for Ourselves. Self*

Advocacy by Mentally Handicapped People, London: Souvenir Press.
Williams, W. (1985) *When Was Wales?*, Harmondsworth: Penguin.
Willis, P. (1977) *Learning to Labour*, Farnborough: Saxon House.
Willis, P. (1978) *Profane Culture*, London: Routledge & Kegan Paul.
Willis, P. (1984a) 'Youth Unemployment: Thinking the Unthinkable', *Youth and Policy*, 2(4), pp. 17–24.
Willis, P. (1984b) 'A new social state', *New Society*, 29 March.
Willis, P. (1984c) 'Ways of living', *New Society*, 5 April.
Willis, P. *et al.* (1985) *The Social Condition of Young People in Wolverhampton in 1984*, Wolverhampton: Wolverhampton Borough Council.
Wilson, P. (1985) *Gutter Feelings. Youth work in the inner-city*, Basingstoke: Marshalls.
Winyard, S. (1987) 'Divided Britain' in A. and C. Walker (eds), *The Growing Divide*, London: Child Poverty Action Group.
Working with Girls Newsletter 12 (1982) 'Activities', Leicester: NAYC.
Working with Girls Newsletter (1987) 'Campaign Issue', Sheffield: CYWU Women's Caucus, for Girls Work Unit Campaign.
Wright, C. (1987) 'Black students, white teachers', in B. Troyna (ed.), *Racial Equality in Education*, London: Tavistock.
Wright, E. O. (1982) 'Class boundaries and contradictory locations' in D. Held and A. Giddens (eds), *Classes, Power and Conflict*, London: Macmillan.
Wright, E. O. (1985) *Classes*, London: Verso.
Youthaid (1985) Youthaid Bulletin No. 23. London: Youthaid.
Youth Service Information Centre (1972) *Youth Service Provision for Young Immigrants*, Leicester: Youth Service Information Centre.

Name Index

Subject Index

260 *Subject Index*